HISTORY OF THE POSSESSIONS OF THE HONORABLE EAST INDIA COMPANY

F. Sargent — Alfred Adlard

CALCUTTA

HISTORY
OF
THE POSSESSIONS
OF THE HONORABLE
EAST INDIA COMPANY

BY

R. MONTGOMERY MARTIN, F.S.S.

SEAL OF THE HON. EAST INDIA COMPANY

VOL. I.

GYAN

Published by

GYAN

Gyan Publishing House
5, Ansari Road
Daryaganj, New Delhi-110002
Phone: 011-47034999, 9811692060
E-mail: books@gyanbooks.com

Distribution Network
gyanbooks.com
India, USA, Canada, UK, Australia, France

ISBN : 978-81-212-3547-1 (PB)
First Published, London, 1838

2nd Impression 2020

Printed at: Gyan Press, Delhi.

History of The Possessions of the Honorable East India Company
Author: R. Montgomery Martin

CONTENTS.

BOOK I.

CHAPTER I.

Rise and Progress of the British power in Asia—Conquest and Formation of the Territories under the Presidency of Bengal . . . . p. 1

CHAPTER II.

WESTERN INDIA, OR UPPER BENGAL CONQUEST.

Wars with Scindiah, Holkar, &c.—Burmese conquests, &c. . . . . p. 23

CHAPTER III.

Madras Presidency—Wars with Hyder and Tippoo p. 40

CHAPTER IV.

Bombay Presidency—The Mahratta Confederacy, &c. p. 54

CHAPTER V.

Stipendiary Princes—Subsidiary and Protected States —And Feudatory and Tributary Chieftains of British India—Examination of our Subsidiary Policy p. 61

CHAPTER VI.

State of India—Consequences resulting from the British Conquest of Hindostan . . . . p. 75

CHAPTER VII.

Physical Aspect of British India—Area and Geography of each Province—Mountains—Rivers and Lakes—Principal Cities—Towns, &c. . . . . p. 91

CHAPTER VIII.

Geology, Soil, and Climate of British India . . p. 177

CHAPTER IX.

Vegetable and Animal Kingdoms—Variety of Timber —Grain and Fruits, &c.—Mineral Kingdom—Coal, Iron, Copper, &c. . . . . . . p. 216

CHAPTER X.

Population of Bengal, Madras, and Bombay by Districts—Houses, Villages, &c.—Great Varieties of Character and Distinguishing Features of the People . . . . p. 250

CHAPTER XI.

Varieties of Language, their Filiation, &c.—Appearance and Stature of the Hindoos—Phrenological Indications—Personal Prowess, &c. . . . . p. 283

APPENDIX. Population Returns . . . . . p. 345

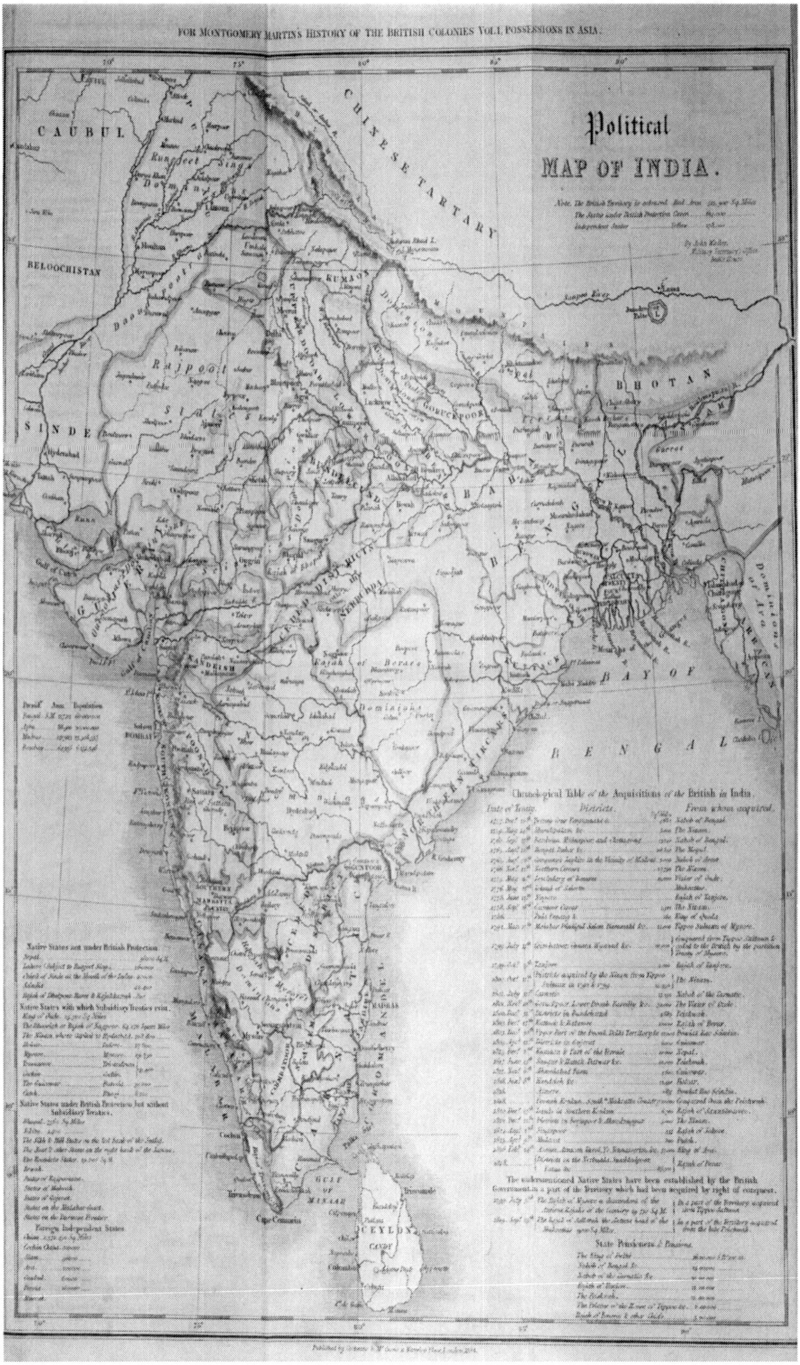

FOR MONTGOMERY MARTIN'S HISTORY OF THE BRITISH COLONIES VOL.I. POSSESSIONS IN ASIA.
Political
MAP OF INDIA.
CAUBUL
CHINESE TARTARY
BELOOCHISTAN
SINDE
BHOTAN
BAY OF
BENGAL
CEYLON
BOMBAY
MADRAS
Chronological Table of the Acquisitions of the British in India.
Native States not under British Protection
Native States with which Subsidiary Treaties exist.
Foreign Independent States
State Pensioners & Pensions.

EAST INDIES.

BOOK I.

BENGAL, MADRAS, AND BOMBAY.

CHAPTER I.

RISE AND PROGRESS OF THE BRITISH POWER IN ASIA—CONQUEST AND FORMATION OF THE TERRITORIES UNDER THE PRESIDENCY OF BENGAL.

The British empire on the continent of Asia is without a parallel in the history of the world: a generation has scarcely passed away [1] since a few English merchants skirted the coasts of the far famed peninsula of Hindostan, as humble suppliants to establish mercantile residencies on its fertile and wealthy shores, amidst myriads of brave and comparatively civilized men: while within the brief space of half a century, an active and intelligent population of 100,000,000 souls,* and a dominion of upwards of one million

[1] The dewany or stewardship of Bengal and Bahar was finally ceded to the East India Company in 1765.

square miles [1] of the richest portion of the earth, has been restored from unheard of anarchy and bloodshed, to comparative order, peace and prosperity.

The earliest authentic European account of Hindostan is derived from Alexander's army which the Macedonian chief pushed across the different rivers of the Punjaub without however reaching the Ganges. At this period a considerable portion of India was subject to the Persian monarchy. Subsequently the Hindoos became tributaries to the all-pervading sway of the disciples of Mahomet, and finally subjects of the victorious Moslems, who, headed by Timur or Tamerlane, extended their conquests from the Irtish and Volga to the Persian Gulf, and from the Ganges to the Archipelago. A century after the death of Tamerlane, the Portuguese appeared on the coast of India, having effected a passage to the eastward by doubling the Cape of Good Hope, and thus completely changed the European route of commerce with the eastern hemisphere, which had previously been carried on by the Red Sea and Egypt, or by the Black Sea and Constantinople. The example of the Portuguese was followed by the Dutch, French, and English. Within less than a century after the death of Timur, or Tamerlane, the Portuguese under Vasco De Gama arrived in India, and found the west coast of Coromandel divided between

[1] The total British territory under the immediate government of the East India Company, is 514,190 square miles (i. e. *ten times* the size of England !) and the extent in square miles of British territory in India, and of territories protected by Great Britain, is 1,128,800¾.—[*Parliamentary Returns*, 1831.]

two great sovereigns—the king of Cambay and the Zamorin; by aiding the petty princes who were dependent on the latter, the Portuguese soon acquired a paramount influence on the Malabar shore, and at the commencement of the sixteenth century secured themselves in, and fortified Goa, which they made the capital of their settlements and commerce in the eastern seas, extending over the east coast of Africa, the coasts of Arabia and Persia, the two peninsulas of India, Ceylon, the Mollucas—their trade even stretching to China and Japan. At this period they levied tribute on 150 native princes, and claimed and exercised a power to sweep from the Indian seas every European vessel that sailed without their permission. Of this mighty dominion scarcely a vestige now exists. The annexation of Portugal to the crown of Spain, and the war waged against the Hollanders, led to the Dutch, who had heretofore been content with the carrying trade between Lisbon and the north of Europe, proceeding to India; and at the commencement of the seventeenth century they became formidable rivals of the Portuguese, stripping them first of Malacca and Ceylon, then driving them from various settlements on the Malabar coast, and finally usurping their place on the shores of Coromandel. The enterprizing spirit of the English was not long behind in establishing a trade in the eastern hemisphere, and they were followed by the French, who became the most powerful rivals of the former after the dominion and trade of the Portuguese and Dutch had declined.

Although it is not within the province of this

work to enter into details of the conquests of the colonial possessions of Britain, it is impossible to avoid bestowing a few pages in explanation of the mode by which our acquisitions on the continent of Asia were obtained; and for the better understanding of the subject, it will be necessary to consider the presidencies of Bengal, Madras, and Bombay separately, (Agra presidency is only a lieutenancy of Bengal) as regards their subjugation to the prowess of England, making brevity, as far as it is consistent with perspicuity, the leading feature of a work in which *utility* may well be deemed of more consequence than ornateness of style or elaborateness of diction. The first charter for the incorporation of the East India Company, was granted by Queen Elizabeth on the last day of the sixteenth century, and was one of exclusive trade in the Indian seas for fifteen years with promise of renewal. In 1635, Charles I. being in want of money, granted a license to Sir William Courten and others, to trade where the existing East India Company had no settlements, but such collision ensued, that a compromise was effected the year preceding the Commonwealth. In 1653 the East India trade was thrown open by Cromwell for four years, and history informs us it was found expedient to reinstate the Company in their entire privileges in 1657, Cromwell and his council being convinced of the national advantages resulting from the incorporation of the East India Company. The subscribed capital of the Company then amounted to 739,782*l.* Charles II. granted a new Charter with ample privileges in 1661. In 1665 the Company commenced a trade with China, and among the orders to their factor at Bantam in 1667, was "100 *lb. weight of the best tay he could gett.*" As the territorial conquests and acquisitions of the East India Company had now commenced, it will be necessary to detail briefly the history of passing events, merely premising that the East India Company's Charter was confirmed by Charles II. in 1677, again in 1683, and subsequently by James II. In 1686 a new Company was formed by dint of shameful bribery and corruption; the Duke of Leeds was impeached, and the project fell to the ground. Government being in want of 2,000,000*l.*, the avaricious ministers established a rival joint stock company in 1698; the rivalship was productive of serious injury to both companies and to the nation at large, and under Lord Godolphin's arbitration an union took place in 1702, since which period, as will be seen by the following history, the principal conquests in India have been made.

BENGAL PRESIDENCY—ITS CONQUEST AND FORMATION.—The British territories under the presidency of Bengal are divided into the *Lower*, or permanently settled, and the *Upper*, or western provinces. Lower Bengal is situate towards the eastern part of Hindostan between the 21° and 27° north latitude, being three hundred and fifty miles long, with an average breadth of three hundred miles: the distinct language and peculiar written character of its people is the chief test of its boundaries and antiquity. Hamilton says, that at the time of the war of the Mahabarat, Bengal formed part of the Magadha or Bahar, and that it was dismembered before the Mahomedan invasion of Hindostan. In 1203 A.D. Cuttub ud Dheen, then on the Mahomedan throne of Delhi, sent an army and conquered Bengal, and until 1340 this granary of Hindostan was ruled by viceroys or soubahs, with power delegated from Delhi; but in this year Fakher ud Dheen revolted and erected Bengal into an independent kingdom, governed by Mussulman kings. Thus it continued, and in a terrible state of anarchy, until re-conquered by the Emperor Acbar's army in 1576, and re-erected into a soubah or viceroyalty of Delhi. From 1576 to 1632, seventeen viceroys held sway in Bengal, collecting the revenues of the country, administering justice, and remitting to the imperial treasury the balance of the taxes left after defraying the expenses of the government. When the power of the Mahomedan princes at Delhi was on the wane, the English appeared in Bengal as traders, subsequently as Soubah, or, as it was termed, Dewan (steward) of Bengal for the Mogul Emperor, and finally as rulers not merely of Bengal, but of Delhi itself and the whole peninsula of Hindostan! The mode in which the British acquired territorial supremacy was as follows:—The Moslems had held sway in Lower Bengal for four centuries, when in 1632, A.D. the Mogul Emperor, Shah Jehan, granted permission to the English to trade and establish a factory at Piply [1], a sea-port in Orissa, the principal

[1] District of Midnapoor, twenty-eight miles east-north-east from Balasore, latitude 21° 42′ north, longitude 87° 20′ east. Now almost washed away, and scarcely to be discovered.

resort of European merchants, there being no other port to which they were then admitted.

In 1656, owing to the skill of an English doctor (Boughton) the East India Company received the Mogul's or emperor of Delhi's sanction to locate themselves on the right bank of the river Hooghly (one of the branches of the Ganges, latitude 22° 54′ north, longitude 88° 28′ east), along the banks of which river the Portuguese, Dutch, French, and Danes had previously erected factories within ten miles of each other, viz. at Hooghly, Chinsurah, Chandernagore, and Serampore. The East India Company subsequently formed factories at Cossimbuzar on the same river (latitude 24° 10′ north, longitude 88° 15′ east), and at Patna on the Ganges (latitude 25° 37′ north, longitude 85° 15′ east). In 1681 the Bengal factories, still merely trading concerns, were formed into a separate government from those of Madras, under the control of which latter named factory they had previously been. The exactions of the Mahomedan officers from Delhi continued to be so great and uncontrollable, that in 1686 the English chief at Hooghly came to a rupture with the Moslem commander at the same place; a battle followed between the British factory and the Nabob's troops, in which the latter were defeated with considerable loss, a Moslem battery destroyed, and eleven guns spiked. Although Captain Nicholson, with an armed fleet of ten merchant vessels, opportunely arrived, the Company's factors quitted Hooghly on the 20th December, 1686, as they considered it indefensible, and feared meeting the same fate as their European predecessors had done[1]. The factors fixed their residence at Chuttanutty village (now Calcutta), on the left bank of the Hooghly, twenty-six miles nearer to the sea, from which it is distant 100 miles. Here the East India Company carried on their trade until 1696, when the rebellion of Soubah Sing against the Mogul at Delhi took place; and the Dutch, French, and English at Chinsurah, Chandanagore, and Chuttanutty (Calcutta), requested and received permission to erect defences around their factories; being the first time that the Mahomedans in Bengal had permitted Europeans to fortify their residencies.

In 1700 Azim Ushaun, viceroy of Bengal, and grandson of Aurungzebe, being in want of treasure to dispute the succession to the Mogul throne, accepted from the East India Company a large sum of money for the township on which their factory at Chuttanutty stood, together with the adjacent lands of Calcutta and Govindpoor. in the whole stock of the Company in Bengal was removed to Calcutta or Fort William (so called out of compliment to the king), the garrison of which consisted of

[1] The Portuguese and Moguls having quarrelled, the latter invested Hooghly with a large army, besieged it for nearly four months, and then carried the town by assault. Thousands were put to the sword, notwithstanding their previous offer of submission; one vessel containing 2000 Portuguese was blown up by the commander, lest it should fall into the hands of their foes, and out of sixty-four large ships, fifty-seven grabs and 200 sloops which were anchored off Hooghly, only one grab and two sloops were saved from the wrath of the Moslems.

129 soldiers (only sixty-six of whom were Europeans), and a gunner and his crew of about twenty-five men; and in 1707 Fort William was dignified with the title of a presidency, forming the foundation of that wonderful empire which ere long was destined to spread its authority from the Ganges to the Indus—from Cape Comorin to the Himalaya[1].

For nearly half a century the British at Calcutta pursued a peaceful and profitable commerce, until in 1756 the ferocious moslem Surajee ud Dowlah in-

[1] It has before been remarked how the English were indebted in 1655 to the skill of an English doctor for permission to settle at Piply; in 1713 our country was again indebted to its medical skill for further privileges; Mr. Hamilton, a surgeon in the East India Company's service, having accompanied an embassy to Delhi soliciting certain privileges, a powerful opposition was met in the mogul court, and the embassy were on the point of returning unsuccessful, when it so happened that the emperor (Ferokshere) was seized with a dangerous illness which baffled the skill of the native physicians. Mr. Hamilton's advice was solicited, given and successful; on being desired to name his reward, he nobly cast aside private advantages, and implored a grant of the objects of the mission, which were gratefully conceded. Hamilton's remains rest without a stone to mark their interment in the burial ground at Calcutta, his patriotism and his services unremembered; and although the natives of India have been more linked to England in ties of personal affection by means of the skill of our surgeons and physicians than by any other class of the East India Company's servants, they are the worst paid and most ill-requited officers in the east: their lives are spent in doing good, and old age brings with it little to solace but the remembrance of the past: it is to be hoped that a profession combining in its exercise science, extensive knowledge and christian charity will soon meet its deserts.

vested and captured the East India Company's factory of Fort William, placed Mr. Holwel and his 146 companions in a dungeon (the "*black hole*") only eighteen feet square; and in less than twenty-four hours not more than twenty-four Englishmen (and prisoners) remained of the British presidency in Bengal:—an inauspicious prelude to the future.

But one of those epochs which mark the decline or advance of a nation had now spread its influence over Britain, who found it necessary to combat for existence, as well as pre-eminence, in Europe and in Asia with her Gallic neighbour, who so often has disputed the palm of superiority with her insular compeer; and fortunately for the latter, as regarded the progress of England in the east, there then started into busy life one of those extraordinary personages who, overcoming all impediment, seem destined to succeed in whatever undertaking they commence. And here let the author be permitted to observe, that it does not fall within his province in a work like the present to analyze motives or criticise the means by which the British possessions have been acquired in any part of the globe. Unfortunately the annals of man from the earliest ages shew that when the desire and the power to seize on the property or rights of others are combined, occasions are soon found for the purpose; yet it may afford some consolation to think that Britain more than any other great nation has been less guilty of wars of aggression;—her acquisitions in India as well as other places originating principally in the all imperious necessity of self-preservation.

It may be said 'the English were now forcibly expelled from Bengal by the *natives*, and they had no right to return,'—such in fact has been the argument used from the days of Burke to the present period; but the assertion is neither just, nor founded on the right of nations, which is merely in a more extended sense the principles by which an individual of the social compact is governed. Granting for argument sake that the English had been driven from Bengal by the "*natives*," in the first place, the former were entitled to compensation for the loss of their factory which they had been legally permitted to purchase, and unless restitution were made, the sufferers had a moral right to obtain it by force, as also to punish the murderers of their countrymen, who had committed no offence and offered every possible submission.

In the second place the British and French nations were at war in Europe, and from the small and insulated position of the former, the power and dominion which France was rapidly and zealously obtaining in Hindostan would, if permitted to progress, be ere long fatal to the independence of the British isles; hence the absolute and unavoidable necessity of establishing a power in India at least equal to that of France, or, if possible, superior: indeed, the different maritime kingdoms of Europe sought a preponderating balance of power by the acquisition of dominion in Asia; and if England had refused to play for the extraordinary stake which would recompense her for the loss of her American provinces, and place her at the head of the potentates of the earth, the commanding influence of her opinions and councils, whether for good or ill, would have expired with the last century; not only, however, was there an imperious necessity to prevent by every possible means the dominion of French authority in India or in Egypt, but there arose also the peculiar rights of security and *vicinage*, the enforcement of which became a matter not merely of expediency or prudence, but of absolute requirement; this point will be the more readily granted as proven, when it is demonstrated that in the third place—it was *not the natives* who expelled in so barbarous a manner the British from their peaceful pursuits on the banks of the Ganges, but their Moslem conquerors, who, to the number of some thousands, kept millions of one of the most timid and passive races of men in abject subjection by means of murder, torture, and confiscation, to an extent never witnessed in the western world, and which (being continued for centuries) would, under a less genial clime, or with a less enduring people, have been terminated by total depopulation. The destruction of the Moslem sway in Bengal by Britain, must indeed be considered as a blessing rather than an evil by any person who has perused the records of that ill-fated but beautiful land, whose historic scroll had for ages been bedewed with human gore, either for internal insurrections, or from the attempts of fresh locusts who sought to share in the spoils of their more fortunate brethren.

To return from this digression.—In August, 1756, the alarming state of the East India Company's affairs at Calcutta reached Madras; and Lieutenant-

Colonel Clive[1], who had just returned from Europe as deputy-governor of Fort St. David, threw his prompt and energetic councils into the Madras government, for the purpose of re-establishing the East India Company's factory at Calcutta, and avenging the sanguinary deed of Surajee ud Dowlah. After considerable deliberation, the advice of Clive for the resumption of British power in Bengal was followed; and he was nominated to command the force destined for the perilous purpose. The armament consisting of 900 Europeans and 1500 Sepoy troops, and a naval squadron, comprising the *Kent* of sixty-four guns, *Cumberland* of seventy, *Tiger* of sixty, *Salisbury* of fifty, and the *Bridgewater* of twenty, under the command of rear admirals Watson and Pocock, sailed from Madras, 16th October, 1756, and with the exception of the *Cumberland* of seventy guns, (with the flag of admiral Pocock) which grounded on the

[1] This extraordinary individual who influenced so powerfully the fate of the British empire in the east, was the son of a country gentleman of ancient family, but of small estate, at Styche, in Shropshire, and born on the 29th September, 1725; his father practised the profession of the law at Market Drayton, which young Robert Clive was at first destined to follow, had not his daring disposition induced his father to accept for him the offer of a writership in India, from the duties of which he was soon roused by the French bombardment of Madras in September, 1746; after serving with wonderful intrepidity as a volunteer in several actions, Clive solicited and obtained the appointment of ensign in 1747, and lieutenant in 1749. How Clive escaped unhurt from all the perilous achievements in which he was engaged, is indeed a matter of astonishment. Lord Clive died in his 50th year.

sand heads off Saugur, and subsequently bore up for Vizigapatam; anchored in the river Hooghly, off Fulta, twenty miles south-south-west from Calcutta, 15th November, where the remnant of the British factory was found. The fort of Mayapore was taken 28th April; the Governor of Calcutta (Moneek Chund) attempted to make a stand near the fort of Budge Budge, ten miles south-south-west of Calcutta, with 2000 foot, and 1500 horse, but, after a short contest, he fled utterly routed to Calcutta.—Budge Budge fortress was besieged and breached by Admiral Watson, 29th December, 1756, and evacuated by the enemy during the night, on the firing and summons of a drunken sailor, who was thought by the Hindoos to be followed by the whole English army[1].

The furious onslaught of the British had so alarmed the governor of Calcutta, that he fled on the approach of Colonel Clive, leaving but 500 of the Nabob's troops for its protection, who only stood a few broadsides from our ships, (after losing about twenty men), when Calcutta factory became once more the property of the East India Company. The town of Hooghly was next taken possession of by assault, after a slight resistance; but on the 2nd of February, 1757, the Nabob Surajee Dowlah arrived before Cal-

[1] The sailor was named Strachan; and on being brought on board his ship and flogged for going on shore, his characteristic reply, was, that he'd be d——d if ever he'd take another fort for them! The remains of the fort choked up with ruins still exist, but the greater part of its materials were recently employed in the more useful structure of an English inn.

cutta with a large army and artillery, rejecting any armistice or negotiation. He was immediately attacked by Clive, with a force consisting of 650 troops of the line, 100 artillery men, with six field pieces, 800 sepoys, and 600 seamen. After a severe contest, in which the dogged valour of British troops struck terror into the enemy[1]; the former returned to Calcutta, and a peace was concluded with Surajee, and the East India Company were authorized to reassume their possessions in tranquillity, to fortify strongly Calcutta and carry on trade as before.

Intelligence of war being declared between Great Britain and France having reached India, and it being seen that Surajee was only temporizing, until he saw a more favourable opportunity for the expulsion of the English, Colonel Clive formed the project of deposing the Soubah or Nabob, (the supreme power at Delhi was now little more than nominal) and placing Meer Jaffier, one of the highest military characters in Bengal on the Musnud, or government seat; it being the opinion of Clive, that Meer Jaffier owing his seat to the Company, would be less disposed to molest them. A treaty was therefore entered into with Meer Jaffier by Colonel Clive, Admiral Watson, and the court and council of Calcutta, that, in the event of his being raised to the Nabob or viceroyship, the French nation were to be entirely

[1] The British loss in *killed*, was, Europeans of the line 27; seamen 12; sepoys 18: in *wounded*, Europeans 70; seamen 12; sepoys 35. The Nabob lost 22 officers of distinction, 600 men, 500 horses, 4 elephants, several camels, and a great many bullocks.

excluded from Bengal; a territory around Calcutta was to be secured to the Company, with an indemnity of ten millions of rupees for the injuries inflicted by Surajee; 5,000,000 rupees to the British inhabitants; 2,700,000 rupees to the natives and Armenians who were living at the time under the protection of the Company; 2,500,000 rupees were to be allotted to the army, and a like sum to the navy.

This project was commenced by Colonel Clive marching to attack the French settlement and fort of Chandernagore [1], sixteen miles above Calcutta, on the Hooghly; of which he began the siege, 14th March, 1757, instantly driving in the outposts and investing the fort. The land forces were seconded by Admirals Watson and Pocock, with two line of battle ships. The French were unable to withstand the combined attack, and after a brave defence, in which numbers fell on both sides, Chandernagore surrendered on the 22nd March, and a part of the garrison escaped to the army of Surajee Dowlah, whom Colonel Clive marched towards to Cossimbuzar to attack on the 13th of June following, with a force of 2000

[1] The French have now a settlement of two or three miles in extent at Chandernagore, and our government ought to take steps for its cession to Great Britain, as also of the contiguous settlement of the Danes at Serampore; their maintenance is of no use to those powers, and they are an eyesore and detriment to the heart of our dominions. The necessity of abolishing all the petty settlements of European powers on the Peninsula of Hindostan, was most forcibly pointed out by the Marquess Wellesley while Governor-general of India. See his Lordship's Despatches, vols. ii. and iii.

sepoys, 900 Europeans, 100 topasses, eight six-pounders and two howitzers. On the 16th June, Clive reduced Pattee, a fortified post on the Cossimbuzar river, as also the town and castle of Cutwah, twelve miles higher up the river; and on the 22nd of the same month, the little British army arriving opposite Cossimbuzar island, came in sight of Surajee's army of 50,000 foot, 8000 horse, a body of French officers, and a strong train of artillery consisting of fifty pieces, encamped on the celebrated plain of Plassey [1].

The result of this celebrated battle is well known: Clive stood on the defensive from day-light till 2 p.m., his small band being covered by a grove and high bank, when taking advantage of the confusion and slaughter, which his artillery caused in the dense ranks of the enemy, and the death of their principal general, he became the assailant; Meer Jaffier's corps separated from Surajee's army, a total rout followed, the Nabob fled on his swiftest elephant, escorted by 2000 chosen cavalry, and astonishing to say, Clive remained master of the battle field and its tents, artillery, camp equipage, provisions, &c., with only a loss in killed, of Europeans eight, and Sepoys sixteen, and in wounded, of Europeans twelve, and Sepoys thirty-six.

Meer Jaffier was saluted by Clive Nabob of Bengal, Bahar and Orissa; Surajee in his flight, disguised, fell into the hands of a poor peasant whom he had

[1] A town in Nuddea, thirty miles from Moorshedabad, latitude 23° 45′ north, longitude 88° 15′ east.

formerly in his tyranny caused to be deprived of his ears[1], and the soldiers of Clive, engaged in his pursuit, made the deposed Nabob prisoner, who soon fell a victim to the dagger of the son of Meer Jaffier. The new Nabob paid down of his stipulations to the British 800,000*l.* out of 22,000,000 rupees, or 2,750,000*l.* sterling, and engaged to furnish the remainder by instalments. From this extraordinary battle may be dated the commencement of the British empire in Bengal, for the power of investing the Soubahs, or Nabobs, with authority in Bengal, was now assumed by the East India Company's government; the sway of the Mahomedans, at Delhi, being merely nominal when unsupported by the Mahrattas, or other states.

At this period a formidable attack, made by the Dutch against the English in Bengal, with 700 Europeans, 800 Malay troops, and a squadron of seven ships, was defeated and destroyed by Colonel Forde, under the orders of Clive.

At the close of 1758, the eldest son of the Mogul emperor Allumgeer II., thinking to recover the government of Bengal by force of arms, marched to attack it, but Meer Jaffier being joined by the Company's forces under Clive, concluded an important but bloodless campaign, 24th May, 1758, during which the Mogul's son retired, for want of support from his allies, and to the Company were ceded some

[1] An interesting eastern romance has been founded on this incident; the Hindoos delight in pointing to such instances of the retributive justice of heaven.

districts in Bahar, along the bank of the river Ganges, yielding saltpetre in great abundance.

Shah Allum, eldest son of the late Mogul emperor, who had been put to death by the Mahrattas, having now ascended the nominal Mogul throne, made another effort for the recovery of the ancient supremacy of his family over Bengal, on the 22nd of February, 1760, aided by the Nabob, or vizier of Oude[1], but he was defeated, at Patna, by the Company's forces, and Meer Jaffier; the latter, however, proving an indolent, tyrannical ruler, and the country rapidly deteriorating under his sway, was deposed, and his son-in-law Meer Cossim elevated in his stead.

The Mogul emperor was finally routed by Major Carnac, and the remnant of his French auxiliaries, under M. Law, captured. Meer Cossim was soon found as unsuited for his station as his father-in-law, and a series of depositions, intrigues, and contests took place; to end which the East India Company, in 1765, sent out Colonel (now Lord) Clive; whom they considered the founder of their fortunes in the

[1] Oude, like Bengal, was one of the Viceroy, or Soubahships under the government of Delhi, and is situate along the banks of the Ganges, (which bound it to the W.) between the 26th and 28. N. lat. being in length 250 miles, and in breadth 100. It was early subdued after the Mahomedan invasion of India, and remained attached to the throne of Delhi until the dissolution of the Mogul empire on the death of Aurungzebe; the descendants of the Mahomedan Soubahs continue to govern Oude as tributary to Great Britain, with the title and style of king, but, its disturbed and ill-governed condition render its contemplated final annexation to the British dominions a matter of necessity.

east, inasmuch, as he had been the means of obtaining a re-footing in the country, of establishing an extensive commercial intercourse, and of directing the foreign influence of the native government, in whose hands still remained the administration of civil and criminal justice, the collection of the revenue, and the general powers of internal superintendance.

That the desire of the East India Company, even at this period, was peace, and not conquest, is evident from the language of their numerous despatches, and if the home orders could have been followed, we should now have possessed little beyond the townships of Calcutta, Madras, and Bombay. So early as 1768, the Court of Directors, in one of their despatches, remark, "if we once pass these bounds we shall be led from one acquisition to another, till we shall find no security but in the subjection of the whole, which, by dividing your force, would lose us the whole, and end in our extirpation from Hindostan." "We utterly disapprove and condemn offensive wars," say the Court, in another dispatch. Clavering, Monson, and Francis, in their discussions with Warren Hastings, ably and strenuously advocated the same principles; and it was truly remarked at the time, that it was not ambition that first tempted the East India Company to embark in those wars,—*necessity* led the way, and conquest had now brought them to the choice of dominion or expulsion. Self-preservation first awakened them from commerce victory gained the great advantages enjoyed; and force now could only preserve them: the East India Company had, therefore, no alternative but to be all or nothing.

Lord Clive arrived at Calcutta in May, 1765, when he learned the death of the late Nabob Meer Jaffier, the minority of his natural son, the war with, and deposition of Jaffier's son-in-law Meer Cossim, the junction of Sujah Dowlah (the Nabob Vizier of Oude) with Shah Allum (the reigning Mogul Emperor), the repeated defeat of their united forces by General Carnac, Sir Robert Fletcher, Hector Munro, and other distinguished Bengal officers, the subsequent separation of the Mogul from Sujah Dowlah, Vizier of Oude, and his junction with the English, and the Mahratta troops under his command, and, finally, that Sujah Dowlah had voluntarily surrendered himself to the British at Allahabad.

Thither his Lordship immediately proceeded, his prophetic mind foreseeing the necessity of the East India Company assuming the sovereignty of Bengal, Bahar, and Orissa, if they would attend to self-preservation; negotiations were instantly commenced, and, after a brief period, the Mogul Emperor resigned all sovereign claims over Bengal, and part of Bahar [1], and Orissa [2], to the East India Company, receiving in return an annual stipend of 325,000*l.* sterling; the fertile districts of Corah and Allahabad were secured to his Majesty (the revenue of which was estimated at 250,000*l.*), and his quiet occupation of the Delhi throne; to Sujah Dowlah, the Nabob, or Vizier of

[1] Situate between 22° and 27° north latitude, and comprising an area of 26,000 square miles, north and south of the Ganges.

[2] Between 18° and 23° north latitude, bounded by the Bay of Bengal on the east.

Oude, Lord Clive restored the whole of his territories, with the condition of paying a subsidy to the East India Company for the keeping up of a military force to protect Oude from foreign aggression, while Nujeem Ul Dowlah, a minor and natural son of Meer Jaffier, the former Nabob or Soubahdar of the Bengal provinces, was allowed to retain his father's title, with a pension of 662,000*l.* a-year; thus, by the force of uncontrollable circumstances, the East India Company were in less than ten years elevated from refugees of an insignificant mud fort at Calcutta to sovereigns over one of the richest kingdoms in the world, extending over 150,000 square miles, and with an active, ingenious, and peaceful population of upwards of 30,000,000 souls, and estimated to produce a yearly revenue of 25,000,000 of rupees! Such was the Dewany of Bengal, now known under the name of the lower, or *permanently settled provinces.*

In 1775, Asoph-ud-Dowlah, Vizier of Oude, ceded the rich province of Benares to the East India Company, in return for their aid during the preceding year, by which the vizier reduced to subjection the tributary Rohilla chiefs, a warlike and gallant tribe in the north-west. The fine territory, thus acquired, contained 12,000 square miles, between 24° and 26° north latitude, of which 10,000 comprised a fertile alluvial flat on either side of the Ganges.

It may be useful to give here the dates of the principal Governors-general of Bengal, from the time of Colonel Clive to the present period.

GOVERNORS.

Col. R. Clive	from June	1758	to	Jan.	1760.
J. L. Holwell	.. Jan.	1760	..	July	1760.
H. Vansittart	.. July	1760	..	Nov.	1764.
J. Spencer	.. Dec.	1764	..	May	1765.
Lord Clive	.. May	1765	..	Jan.	1767.
Harry Verelst	.. Jan.	1767	..	Dec.	1769.
J. Cartier	.. Dec.	1769	..	Apr.	1772.
Warren Hastings	.. Apr.	1772	..	Feb.	1785.
Sir J. Macpherson	.. Feb.	1785	..	Sept.	1786.
Marquess Cornwallis	.. Sept.	1786	..	Oct.	1793.
Sir J. Shore	.. Oct.	1793	..	Mar.	1798.
Marquess Wellesley	.. May	1798	..	July	1805.
Marquess Cornwallis	.. July	1805	..	Oct.	1805.
Sir G. Barlow	.. Oct.	1805	..	July	1807.
Earl Minto	.. July	1807	..	Oct.	1813.
Marquess of Hastings	.. Oct.	1813	..	Jan.	1823.
Lord Amherst	.. Aug.	1823	..	Apr.	1828.
Lord W. Bentinck	.. June	1828	..		1834.
Lord Auckland	..	1835			

CHAPTER II.

WESTERN INDIA, OR UPPER BENGAL CONQUEST[1].

WARS WITH SCINDIAH, HOLKAR, &c.—BURMESE CONQUESTS, &c.

It is as much in the course of nature for mind to prevail over matter, as strength over weakness. The

[1] A large portion of the territory under this section embraces the new lieutenancy of Agra, or the fourth Indian Presidency;

continued progress of a power so civilized as England, over a country so harassed by internal dissensions, and depressed, degraded, and enfeebled by many centuries of unrelenting Moslem despotism, was naturally to be expected. We accordingly find that the East India Company were next necessitated to contend not only for dominion in the west of India, but for their actual maintenance in Bengal, with the powerful confederacy, headed by the wily chieftain Sindia, whose territories verged on the fragments of the Mogul Emperor's dominion, and who found himself placed (independent of auxiliaries) at the head of an army of 200,000 cavalry, ten formidable brigades of infantry, and 500 guns, disciplined and commanded by the ablest French and German officers.

The avowed object of the fierce and sanguinary Mahrattas was the complete expulsion of the English from India. This they had for some time been endeavouring to accomplish on the western side of Hindostan; and Sindia, after conquering Bundlecund, and subduing other provinces in the north-west to his interests, at length induced the Mogul Emperor, Shah Allum, to resign his amity with the English, and to make the Mahratta chiefs and French officers masters of Agra, Delhi, and other strong places in the north-west provinces, by which step the aged monarch forfeited the treaty concluded with Lord Clive.

The original country of the daring and subtle Mah-

I am induced, however, to adopt this division in order to simplify the history of our acquisitions to those persons who are not very familiar with Indian affairs.

rattas comprehended, according to Hamilton, Candeish, Baglana, and part of Berar, extending towards the north-west as far as Gujerat and the Nerbudda river: to the west they possessed the narrow but strong tract of country which borders on the Concan, and stretches parallel with the sea from Surat to Canara, the whole territory of great natural strength, interspersed with mountains, defiles, and fortresses, and admirably calculated for defensive warfare. The Mahrattas seem to have been under the government of feudal chieftains until their strength was concentrated under a bold leader named Sevajee, who, at his death, in 1680, had extended his empire along the Malabar coast from Surat (latitude 21° 11′ north) to near Goa (latitude 15° 30′ north), and as far as the range of hills that terminate the table land forming the eastern boundary of the Concan. The territories which the Mahrattas conquered were considered as predatory acquisitions, to be held only by the sword, for to the subtle and aspiring Brahmin, war and plunder were the two great sources of revenue; hence the quartering of a Mahratta army in a province was more destructive than myriads of locusts or years of drought and pestilence, while of their rulers it has been aptly observed, that their musnuds were their horsecloths, their sceptres their swords, and their dominions the wide line of their desolating marches. At the festival which annually took place on proceeding to collect *chout* (tribute), the chiefs cut each a handful of corn with his sword to denote the predatory object of the undertaking, and the war-horses had a sheep sacrificed to each, and were sprinkled with the blood. This extraordinary people, who contested for the supremacy of India with England, on the fall of the Mogul dynasty, are in general diminutive in stature, of unparalled cunning, brave, vindictive, and possessing more talent and independent principles than any other class of the Hindoos, save the Rajpoots.

Warren Hastings in 1780, endeavoured to check the progress of the Mahrattas on the Bombay side of India, by detaching small bodies of troops from Bengal to make incursions into the enemies' territories, a supreme controlling power being now vested in the Governor-general and council of Bengal; but on the accession of the Marquess Wellesley to the supreme government in 1798, that nobleman soon perceived that England must either acquire general influence, or be engaged in a constant series of hostilities, from which wide spreading ruin would result[1].

In 1801, his Lordship obtained from the Nabob or Vizier of Oude (in commutation for the military subsidy which he had promised, by treaty with Lord

[1] The view which I took in the first and second edition of this work relative to the policy of the Marquess Wellesley, has been most fully confirmed; the noble Marquess unreservedly placed before me the whole of his vast mass of dispatches, minutes and correspondence, leaving to my judgment a selection of such of these state papers, as would fully illustrate the momentous events of his Lordship's splendid, and no less useful administration. Four volumes of those dispatches are now before the public; their amplitude and authority, saves me the trouble of expanding this work by details of the means by which we acquired so great an accession of territory, or of the motives which led to the acquisition. To the noble Marquess they are—*Monumentum exegi perennius.*

Clive, to pay to the East India Company), the extensive provinces in the north-west of India,—of Bareilly (6,900 square miles), Moradabad (5,800 square miles), Shahjehanpoor (1,420 square miles), &c. in Rohilcund; of the lower Doâb and the districts of Furruckabad (1,850 square miles), Allahabad (2,650 square miles), Cawnpoor (2,650 square miles), Goruckpoor (9,250 square miles), Azimghur (2,240 square miles), &c. embracing territory to the extent of 32,000 square miles, and a population of about 15,000,000 souls.

In 1803, that portion of the British army which the Marquess Wellesley destined for the conquest of the Mahrattas in Upper Bengal, was placed under the command of General (afterwards Lord) Lake, with instructions to free the Mogul Emperor from the thraldom of Sindia, and to offer every reasonable inducement to the French officers to quit the Mahratta service. The Mahratta and French auxiliaries were defeated by General Lake at Coel in the Doâb (27° 54′ north 78° east), 29th of August, 1803; the strong fort of Alighur (53 miles north of Agra), of a square form with round bastions, a formidable ditch and glacis, and a single entrance protected by a strong ravelin, which formed the chief depôt of the enemy, was next captured after a desperate slaughter, and Lake marched with 4500 men to give battle to 20,000 Mahratta and French, encamped in a strong position under the fortifications of the imperial city of Delhi, the ancient capital of the Patan and Mogul empires (in latitude 28° 41′ north, longitude 77° 5′ east). General Lake on nearing the enemy pretended to fly, the Mahrattas quitted their trenches in eager pursuit of the supposed English fugitives, but the latter at a given signal instantly wheeled to the right, and by a single charge completely routed the enemy, who sustained a loss of 3000 men in killed and wounded, and their whole train of artillery, baggage, &c. The result of the battle was soon made apparent; the aged Mogul, once more released from bondage, and in a state of abject destitution, threw himself again on the humanity of the British, by whom he was once more established in his ancestral capital, with an annual stipend for the support of himself and family of 1,200,000 rupees (together with certain privileges), and Lake entered Delhi amidst the general rejoicings of its wretched inhabitants, who for years had been the prey of war and internal rapine and feuds. This distinguished officer next marched to attack the numerous Mahratta troops posted in and around the strong and ancient fortress of Agra, on the south-west side of the Jumna; which was reduced after a short but animated resistance, 17th October, 1803; persons and private property were respected, and 280,000*l*. public treasure was divided as prize-money among the victorious troops. While these proceedings were occurring in the Doâb, Major General Wellesley (now Duke of Wellington) was gaining a series of splendid victories over the combined forces of Sindia and the Rajah of Berar, on the Bombay frontier. The power of Sindia in Upper Bengal was now finally annihilated by the defeat of his best disciplined army, consisting of 9000 foot, 5000 cavalry, and a numerous train of well organized artillery, by General Lake, with a small British force, on the 1st November, 1803, after one of the most brilliant and daring contests ever witnessed. The consequences of these extraordinary achievements was a treaty with Sindia, 30th December, 1803, by which there was ceded to the British under the Bengal presidency, the Upper Doâb (a large territory between the river Ganges and Jumna), Delhi, Agra (3500 square miles), Hurriana, Saharaunpoor (5900 square miles), Meerut, Alighur (3400 square miles), Etawah (3450 square miles), Cuttack (9040 square miles), Balasore, Juggernath, &c. (8260 square miles): the power of the French and Mahrattas in the north-west was destroyed, and the decayed but still respected representative of a long line of monarchs was secured in peace and comfort on the titular musnud of Ackbar.

The tranquil possession of these fine provinces by the East India Company was for a time interrupted by the celebrated Holkar, who, after the downfal of Sindia, endeavoured to rally the remaining branches of the Mahratta confederacy for the purpose of "overwhelming the British by repeated attacks of his army, like the waves of the sea[1]." The standing army of Holkar, while professing peace, was 150,000 cavalry, 40,000 well disciplined foot, 200 pieces of artillery, and a numerous corps of auxiliaries, by which latter he was enabled to carry on a devastating and desultory war for some time. After attempting the recapture of Delhi, his army, subsequent to a series of desperate actions with Lord Lake, General Frazer, and

[1] Vide Holkar's letter to General Wellesley.

Colonels Ochterlony, Monson, and Burns, was finally routed, 17th November, 1804, by the gallant Lake, who, whether with cavalry or infantry, invariably gained the day by trusting to the nerve of a Briton at the sabre or bayonet point. A furious charge by the English cavalry cut to pieces 3000 of the Indian horse; the remaining troops of Holkar escaped by a rapid flight to their infantry at the fortress of Deeg[1], which Lake invested, breached after ten days' cannonading, and carried by storm with almost incredible intrepidity on the night of the 23rd of November. Holkar sought protection from the fortress of Bhurtpore[2], a vast mud fort, which, with the town, is nearly eight miles in circumference, flanked with numerous

[1] The fortress of Deeg is situate in latitude 27° 30′ north, longitude 77° 12′ east, fifty-seven miles north-west of Agra city. In 1760 it was strongly fortified by Sooraj Mull, the Jaut Rajah, but in 1776 captured after twelve months siege by Nudjiff Khan. It now belongs to the Rajah of Bhurtpore.

[2] BHURTPORE. Latitude 27° 17′ north, longitude 77° 23′ east, thirty-one miles west by north from Agra. When Lord Lake approached the fortress, a large expanse of water at the north-west side of the town instantly disappeared, and it was subsequently discovered that the whole lake had been admitted into the ditch that surrounds the town and fort. The carnage during the siege was enormous, considering the small force of the besiegers; the first storming party lost 456, the second 591, the third 894, the fourth 987, which together with 172 casualties, made a total of killed and wounded of 3100 of the flower of the small British army. A perusal of Lord Lake's private correspondence convinces me that our disaster was partly owing to the contempt in which his Lordship held Holkar and the Bhurtpore fort. (See vol. iii. of the Marquess Wellesley's Despatches).

bastions at short intervals, well defended with immense cannon, and surrounded by a very wide and deep fosse. The garrison was complete, amply provisioned, and confident in the impregnability of their ramparts. Lake and his little band of heroes sat down before this formidable place on the 3rd of January, 1805; the trenches were soon opened, but wherever a breach was made the defenders speedily filled it up or fortified it with stockades, and, in addition to the most galling and destructive artillery and musketry, showered on the besiegers logs of burning wood and hot ashes, lighted bales of cotton steeped in oil, earthen pots filled with fire and combustibles of every kind. Four times did the British troops attempt to storm the breach, and four times were they obliged to retire, staggering under the (to them) terrible loss of upwards of 3000 men of the flower of the army. And here let it be recorded, that his Majesty's 75th and 76th regiments (heretofore deemed, like Ney, "the bravest of the brave," and, like Murat, always foremost in the heady current of battle,) became panic-struck at the fury of their enemies, and refused to follow their officers, until, shamed by seeing the East India Company's 12th regiment of Bengal sepoys once more heroically plant their colours on the enemy's walls, and stung by the merited reproaches of their general, they loudly implored to be permitted to wash the stains from their honour in the fourth attack, which, notwithstanding their desperate valour, was still unsuccessful. The Rajah of Bhurtpore, foreseeing by the persevering gallantry of Lake that nothing would induce him to abandon his purpose, dispatched his son to the British camp with the keys of the fortress; a treaty was concluded, 17th April, Holkar compelled to quit the territories, and the Rajah was obliged to pay two million rupees towards defraying the expenses of the war; his son was given in hostage of his pacific intentions; and Holkar, after several gallant but fruitless efforts against Lord Lake in the field, was so reduced as to flee almost unattended for life.

The comprehensive and unavoidable policy of the Marquess of Wellesley, which has not been sufficiently done justice to by Indian historians or statesmen, was now laid aside by the Marquess Cornwallis, who resumed the supreme government in July, 1805, but died on proceeding to the Upper Provinces in the month of October in the same year. Lord Cornwallis tried in vain to introduce the principle of European treaties into Indian diplomacy, the failure of which was exemplified in the triple alliance between the British Government, the Nizam, and the Peishwa; while the system of defensive subsidiary alliances, from not being carried far enough, was equally unproductive of beneficial results[1]. Through the exertions of Lord

[1] The maurading war of 1817 demonstrated the lasting advantages of the comprehensive policy of the Marquess of Wellesley, the key-stones of whose political arch rested on Calcutta, Bombay, and Madras. N. B. Edmonstone, Esq., at present one of the Directors of the East India Company, and who most ably filled the high offices of Persian translator and secretary to Government under Lord Wellesley, informed me, that if the Marquess Wellesley had not arrived in India, in 1798, we should have been entirely expelled from India. The despatches of the noble Marquess amply attest the truth of the observation.

Lake, whose talents in the cabinet were as useful as his tactics and bravery in the field were remarkable, the fruits of the past were not entirely lost; and Holkar was admitted to peace on favourable terms.

The Ghoorkhas, a warlike but uncivilized tribe, who had possessed themselves of the beautiful valleys of Nepaul, began encroachments on the whole north frontier of the British territories, under a brave and skilful chief (Ameer Sing), in 1814; and without any previous intimation, attacked and massacred the people of two thannahs or stations in Goruckpoor and Sarun; upon which the Marquis of Hastings sent against the invaders a force of 30,000 men, who met with various successes against the Nepaulese and Ghoorkha hill forts, which were valiantly defended. The contest was brought to a successful issue by the activity, skill, and sagacity of Sir David Ochterlony and the brave General Gillespie, who fell at the head of a storming party when cheering on his men before the Fort of Kalunga[1]. The Nepaulese were glad to ratify a treaty on the 4th March, 1816, which they had evaded the preceding year; by which the East India Company obtained possession of the entire province of Kumaon (7000 square miles), a portion of Garhwal (3000 square miles), the valley of the Dheera

[1] Situated on the verge of a ridge of hills, two miles and a half north-east of the town of Deyrah, capital of the Valley or *Doon*, latitude 30° 20′ north, longitude 78° 5′ east, at an elevation above the sea of 2326 feet. The British forces under Gillespie and Manly, in 1814, lost more officers and men before this small stone fortress than they would have suffered in several pitched battles. The fortress is now razed.

Dhoon, with the adjacent mountainous districts of Jounsar and Bawar, together with Sabbathoo and other tracts on the skirts of the Himalaya, and in the delta of the rivers Jumna and Sutlej; and the territories of several hill chiefs were brought under British protection. The Company also obtained undisputed possession of a long line of forest and pasture land, extending along the base of the Himalaya Mountains, termed *Tarryani*, which defined the northern boundary of their dominions, and enabled them to open commercial communications with China and Tartary. But the misfortunes arising from the defensive policy of the amiable Lord Cornwallis were not yet terminated. The Pindaries, a predatory body of mounted robbers, who could collect under one of their chiefs thirty thousand cavalry! and who were secretly favoured by the yet unannihilated Mahratta confederacy, made several plundering incursions into the British territories, killing and wounding many hundred peaceable British subjects, and carrying off and destroying property to the amount of several hundred thousand pounds. These desperate freebooters originated in the province of Malwa, where they first occupied the country in the vicinity of Nemawur, Kantapoor, Goonas, Beresha, and part of the Bilsah and Bhopaul territories, but gradually extended themselves to the centre of this fine district. The Pindaries were principally composed of Mahomedans, but their leaders, although true Moslems, admitted into their bands all the discontented and restless spirits which the previous disbanding of the large armies of India left without occupation. They systematically carried on a war of plunder and devastation, and terrified the neighbouring princes into subsidizing them as a guarantee against invasion. As an instance of the Pindarie marauding, it may be mentioned, that a body of these bandits entered the British territory of Ganjam, in January, 1817, destroyed property to the amount of 250,000*l*., burnt 269 houses, and plundered 6203 mansions; and of the sufferers by the robbers 183 were killed, 505 were wounded, and 3603 subjected to torture. The scene of these depredations was not far distant from Madras or Calcutta, and in the previous year, Guntoor, in latitude 16° 17′ north, longitude 90° 32′ east, underwent a more disastrous visitation from these merciless destroyers of peace and civilization. The Marquis of Hastings, in 1817, took the field against the Pindaries and their abettors, the Mahratta Confederacy, at the head of an army which presented a strong contrast to the handful of British troops which Lords Clive and Lake had commanded; it consisted of 81,000 regular infantry, 33,000 cavalry, and a numerous and efficient artillery, altogether forming a force the like of which had never been seen on the plains of Hindostan.

The events which followed afford matter for voluminous history: suffice it to say, that before the grand army under the noble Marquis and his gallant and sagacious coadjutors, Generals Malcolm, Smith, Hislop, Doveton, Keir, &c. broke up in 1819, the Pindaries were utterly annihilated, the Mahratta Confederacy destroyed, and the following territories added to the Bengal Presidency, by conquest as well as by subsequent arrangements. Districts on the Nerbudda river to the extent of 29,800 square miles; Sumbalpore and some pergunnahs on the north-west frontier of Bengal; Khandah in Bundelcund; Ajmere, and part of Mairwarrah; part of Nimah; Bairsea, Shoojawulpore, and the fortress of Hatrass in Alighur; while the following states of Central India became tributary to the East India Company, receiving protection and guarantee in acknowledgment for British supremacy, viz. Jyepore, Joudpore, Oudeypore, Boondee, Kotah, Pertabghur, Rutlana, Banswarra, and Doongurpore. The peace of the north-west provinces of India has ever since remained undisturbed, with the exception of a disturbance in Bhurtpore, in March, 1825, when Durjunt Sal took forcible possession of the infant Rajah, murdered his uncle and followers, and notwithstanding the repeated mild persuasions of Lord Amherst, who appears to have been desirous of following the policy of Lord Cornwallis, treated the British power and authority with the utmost contempt. Those who know any thing of the nature of the English dominion in Hindostan, will admit the necessity of removing instantly an unfavourable impression from a people who are too apt to consider concession or mildness as the result of indecision or fear. To prevent any thing like the resistance which Lord Lake met with in 1805, Lord Combermere was ordered to attack this strong fortress with an army of 25,000 of the most efficient troops, and a powerful train of battering artillery. His Lordship invested Bhurtpore 23rd December, 1825; the works since the former attack had been considerably strengthened, and it was soon found that the largest cannon balls made no impression on mud walls sixty feet thick; a mine was therefore sprung, by which a breach was effected on the 17th January, 1826, and the fort stormed and carried the following morning, after a desperate but ineffectual resistance, in which the British had sixty-one Europeans and forty-two natives killed, and 283 Europeans and 183 natives wounded; while the loss of the garrison was 4000, almost all killed. The State of Bhurtpore was charged with the extra expenses of this contest, amounting to 2,439,173 rupees, and the young Rajah (who is a promising prince) was installed on the 5th February, 1826. The fortress (as regarded its principal bastions, curtains, and other important parts) was razed, and with its fall terminated a series of intrigues for the destruction of the British power which had been some time organizing in the north-west provinces.

Burmese Conquest.—It became a matter of self-preservation to humble another Asiatic power ere Bengal was secure from invasion. During half a century a kingdom had been gradually rising and extending on the south-eastern frontier, named Birmah, whose tone, always haughty to the English, became at last insulting and menacing. The origin of this nation is thus traced:—In the middle of the sixteenth century, the regions which lie between the south-eastern provinces of British India, Yunan in China, and the extremity of the Malacca peninsula, were occupied by four powerful nations, known to Europeans as Birmah (or Ava), Pegu, Siam, and Arracan. Devastating wars were carried on between these states, particularly between the Peguers (or Talliens) and the Burmese. During the seventeenth century the Burmese held the Peguers in complete subjection; but, in 1751, the Peguers, aided by the Portuguese and Dutch, conquered the Burmese, and took final possession of Ava. Headed, however, by the celebrated Alompra, the Burmese again subdued the Peguers, and the Alompra dynasty was established in Ava. In 1767, an army of 50,000 Chinese was destroyed on its entrance into the dominions of Ava, and from that period the Burmese continued extending their conquests, having captured Cassay and Munipoor in 1774; Arracan in 1783; and from the Siamese, in 1784 to 1793, the provinces of Tavoy, Tenasserim, Junk-Ceylon, and Mergui Isles. These acquisitions so inflated the vanity of the Burmese, that the most extravagant schemes were entertained of the conquest of Hindostan, and the utter expulsion of the English from India. Intriguers were sent by the Burmese to excite the north-west provinces of India to revolt against the British supremacy; and, in 1814, a confederation of all the native princes of India was attempted to be effected by the Burmese, the object of which was the destruction of the English power in the east: the King of Ava gave out that he intended to make a pilgrimage to Gaya and Benares, at the head of 40,000 men; emissaries were despatched into the Seik country, *via* Dacca, while the Shabundar of Arracan visited Madras and Trincomalee, to gather information as to the politics of the south of India. These projects were defeated, but the Burmese went on extending their conquests over the petty states south of the Brahmaputra, and establishing a strong and permanent military force along the north-east quarter of the Bengal province, ready at a moment's warning to commence an inroad on the unprotected British possessions. Indeed, from 1795, when the Burmese monarch marched 5000 troops across the Bengal frontier, to capture some of his refugee subjects who had fled from his tyranny, to the year 1822, when His Majesty set up a claim to the petty isle of Shapuree, in the province of Bengal, on the Chittagong frontier, recriminations had been going on between the two governments. The intended invasion of the Burmese, in 1795, was foiled by General Erskine; and in 1818, the Marquis of Hastings, by his policy, diverted another attack. While we were engaged in the Mahratta and Pindarie war, the Marquis of Hastings received a rescript from the Burmese monarch, requiring us to surrender all provinces east of Bagrutty; Lord Hastings sent back the envoy, stating, that an answer should be sent through another channel; a special messenger was therefore despatched to the King of Burmah, to declare that the Governor-General was too well acquainted with the wisdom of His Majesty to be the dupe of the gross forgery attempted to be palmed upon him, and that he therefore transmitted to the King the document fabricated in his august name; hoping, also, that those who had endeavoured to sow dissensions between the two powers would be condignly punished: the subsequent defeat of the Mahrattas prevented the repetition of this insolent threat.

On the retirement of Lord Hastings, the Burmese threatened to march into the Bengal provinces with fire and sword, to the plunder of Calcutta. In 1825, the unprovoked aggressions of this turbulent nation were met by a force at Chittagong, while a large British armament proceeded to Rangoon, the naval capital of Burmah (latitude 16° 35′ north, longitude 96° 25′ east), captured it, and after a series of hard fought actions, and much privation and distress, forced the Burmese to sue for peace in 1826, when the English troops were almost within sight of the capital (Ava). By the treaty of Yandaboo, the Burmese resigned all claim to the conquests which for years they had been making in Assam, Cachar, Gentiah, and Munipoor; the provinces of Arracan, Ye, Tavoy, Tenasserim, and Martaban, south of the Saluen River, comprising 50,000 square miles, together with the islands Cheduba and Ramree, were ceded to the East India Company; and 10,000,000 of rupees in cash were paid to the Company by instalments, as part indemnity to defray the expenses of war, which the rash ambition of his Burmese Majesty had provoked.

CHAPTER III.

MADRAS PRESIDENCY—WARS WITH HYDER, TIPPOO SULTAUN, &c.

The Southern Indian Presidency is called after the name of its capital, on the Coromandel coast, in latitude 13° 5′ north, longitude 80° 21′ east, which, to the extent of five miles along shore, and one mile inland, was ceded to the East India Company, A.D. 1639, by the reigning Prince of Bijanagur, with permission to erect a fort, which was immediately commenced under the designation of *Fort St. George*. In 1653, Madras was raised to the rank of Presidency, the military force of which was only twenty-six soldiers, which the Court of Directors, in 1654, ordered to be still further reduced to *ten*. The native population soon assembled round the English fortress; and, in 1687, the census of the inhabitants of the fortress of Fort St. George, the city of Madras, and the adjacent villages within the Company's boundaries, amounted to 300,000 persons. In 1702, Madras was besieged by Daoud Khan, one of Aurungzebe's generals; but a more formidable power was soon to contest the footing of Englishmen on the Coromandel coast. The war which broke out between England and France, in 1744, was carried on as fiercely in the east as in the west; and the ambitious, unprincipled, but talented Monsieur Dupleix spared no efforts, either by intriguing with the native princes, or by actual force, to root the English out of all their factories in India. A strong military and naval French force, under the command of the brave and high-minded Labourdonnais, besieged Madras on the 7th September, 1746, when the English garrison amounted to but 200 soldiers. After a severe bombardment of five days, capitulations were entered into, that Labourdonnais might enter within the four ill-constructed bastions which defended the town; but that, after taking possession of the Company's goods, &c., Madras should be restored on payment of a ransom. This stipulation was broken by Labourdonnais's superior, Dupleix (then Governor of Pondicherry), and Madras remained in the occupation of the French until the peace of Aix-la-Chapelle, when it was restored to the East India Company in 1749.

While Madras was in the occupation of the French, the Presidency of the East India Company was carried on at Fort St. David, or Negapatum, a fortress on the sea-coast of the Carnatic, sixteen miles south of Pondicherry, and 100 miles south-south-west from Fort St. George, or Madras; latitude 11° 45′ north, longitude 79° 50′ east. At this station the East India Company had established a factory in 1691, and they subsequently purchased a tract of territory larger than their settlement at Madras. M. Dupleix next attempted to drive the English out of Fort St. David; but his army of 1700 Europeans was defeated by about 200 British, among whom was *Ensign* (afterwards Lord) Clive, who, after the capture of Madras, escaped in the disguise of a Moor to Fort St. David.

Several severe contests between the French and English took place, until, as before stated, peace in Europe allowed the Company to resume possession of their Presidency at Madras; but, although hostilities had ceased between the rival nations in Europe, it was far otherwise in India, where the French and English alternately struggled and gained the ascendency in the native councils and contests of the Carnatic. This vast territory, formerly comprising the dominions and dependencies of the Nabob of Arcot, extends from 8° to 16° north latitude, stretching from the southern frontier of Guntoor Circar to Cape Comorin, a distance of 500 miles, with an unequal but average breadth of seventy-five miles. Heretofore the Carnatic was held by a number of petty Rajahs, with whom the French alternately intrigued in their efforts for complete supremacy—a point, indeed, which the wily Dupleix all but gained. The French long maintained the upper hand, until the daring genius of Clive, and the skill of Major Laurence, contributed materially to diminish it; while, in the Deccan, M. De Bussy obtained firm possession of an extensive country, 600 miles in extent, reaching from Medapilly to the Pagoda of Juggernaut, with an annual revenue of nearly 1,000,000*l.* sterling.

On the breaking out of the war in 1756, between France and England, the celebrated and unfortunate Lally was sent out as Governor of Pondicherry, with a large armament, for the purpose of utterly extirpating the English in Hindostan; and the very night Lally landed, he directed the march of troops for the attack of Fort St David, which was taken and razed to the ground, on the 1st of June, 1758, after which the conqueror proceeded with 3500 European, 2000 sepoy infantry, and 2000 European and native cavalry to the siege of Madras, which, defended by 1758 Europeans, and 2424 native troops, withstood the most desperate attacks for two months, until relieved by the arrival of six English ships, with 600 fresh troops. During the siege the fort fired 26,554 rounds from their cannon, 7502 shells from their mortars, 1990 hand grenades were thrown, 200,000 musquetry cartridges expended, and 1768 barrels of gunpowder; thirteen officers were killed, fourteen wounded, and four taken prisoners; of the European troops, upwards of 200 were killed, and 140 made prisoners: of the sepoys and lascars, 145 were killed, and 440 deserted.

The French retreated precipitately from before Madras, and the English in turn became assailants. Colonel Coote pursued and defeated Lally at Wandiwash[1], from whence the remnants of the French sought shelter in Pondicherry, which, in September, 1760, was closely blockaded by the East India Company's troops and his majesty's vessels by land and sea; the trenches were opened under Colonel Coote, 12th January, and, on the 14th, Lally and his garrison were prisoners. From this period the downfal of French influence was progressive, while that of the English became as rapidly ascendant.

In 1763, the East India Company obtained from the Nabob of the Carnatic, in return for services rendered to that prince and his father, a district in the Carnatic of 2460 square miles, called the "*Jaghire* (Chingleput), which is bounded on the east by the bay of Bengal, between Nellore and Arcot. The country was rented to the Nabob, on renewed leases, until 1780, when the entire management was placed under the Madras government.

The next territory acquired by the East India

[1] In the Carnatic, seventy-three miles south-west of Madras, latitude 12° 30′ north, longitude 79° 37′ east.

Company in the south of India, was that of Guntoor, comprehending an area of 2500 square miles (the fifth district in the northern circars) which was acquired from the Mogul, in 1765; but not taken possession of by the British authorities until 1786, and then only on the payment of an annual tribute to the Nizam of 600,000 rupees, which the East India Company finally redeemed in 1823, by the payment of 1,200,000 rupees to the Nizam at Hydrabad.

The wide spreading and devastating ambition of a fierce adventurer, in his endeavours to expel the English from the Carnatic, became the means of further extending the territorial dominions of the East India Company. Hyder Ali, the founder of the Mysore dynasty and kingdom, was originally a private soldier in a corps raised by his elder brother; and, for his gallantry at the siege of Deonhully (twenty-three miles north-north-east from Bangalore), he was entrusted with the command of 500 infantry and fifty horse. His character is described to have been a composition of courage, cunning, and cruelty; equally prodigal of faith and of blood—equally victorious in the use of intrigues and of arms. He could neither read nor write; but his memory was so tenacious, and his sagacity so great, that no secretary would venture to practise a deception on him[1]. His father died in

[1] The following anecdote of Hyder Ally is truly characteristic of the shrewdness and ability of that determined foe to the British power in India. In the war which was waged against him in 1768 by the East India Company, it was found impossible to bring him to a pitched battle. The Madras government endeavoured to equip Colonel Wood's army with a light

1734, in the humble situation of a naick of revenue Peons, leaving his family destitute and friendless; but

train of artillery, and a picked body of sepoys, in the hope that, by the velocity of their movements, they might bring Hyder to action. All Colonel Wood's efforts, however, to attain that object, were futile. At length that officer, completely harassed and weary of the pursuit, adopted a very singular expedient to effect his purpose. He wrote a letter to Hyder Ally, stating that "it was disgraceful for a great prince, at the head of a large army, to fly before a detachment of infantry and a few pieces of cannon, unsupported by cavalry." Hyder Ally's caustic answer to this very *naïve* proposition ran thus: —"I have received your letter, in which you invite me to an action with your army. Give me the same sort of troops that you command, and your wishes shall be accomplished. You will in time understand my mode of warfare. Shall I risk my cavalry, which cost a thousand rupees each horse, against your cannon ball, which cost two pice[1]? No! I will march your troops until their legs shall become the size of their bodies. You shall not have a blade of grass nor a drop of water. I will hear of you every time your drum beats, but you shall not know where I am once a month. I will give your army battle, but it must be when I please, and not when you choose."

Hyder Ally kept his word to the letter. He laid waste the country, and destroyed the wells and tanks as Colonel Wood advanced, so that the latter was frequently obliged to retreat for want of forage and water. Finally, Hyder surprised Colonel Wood's force, worn out with fatigue and privation, at Manbagul. He brought the Colonel to an engagement, in which the latter lost all his artillery, and nothing saved his little army but the advance of Colonel Smith, who reached the place in time to compel Hyder to fall back, at the moment when Colonel Wood's troops were on the point of being entirely defeated.

---

[1] A piece of copper equal to a penny.

Hyder Ali came on the stage when anarchy reigned in Mysore, and when he who was the strongest and the most cunning and daring, might easily usurp the highest station in the kingdom. From the command of a few hundred men, he quickly raised his force to 2000 horse and 5000 foot, with a small artillery. By degrees he obtained assignments of more than half the revenues of the kingdom, and ultimately taking advantage of the feeble state of the government, he proclaimed himself ruler in Seringapatam, reduced the Rajah of Mysore to the condition of a pensioner, shut up his enemies in cages, strengthened his fortresses, raised a large army, and vigilantly superintended the administration of the kingdom, whose affairs he had usurped the government of. Like Napoleon, he had an inveterate hostility to the English, because they treated him as an usurper: and he owed the ruin of his family to military co-operation with the French, for the destruction of the British in India.

After conquering every independent Hindoo state in the south, or raising them into hostile confederacy against the British power, Hyder approached close to Madras to attack it in 1767; but, deterred by its strength, the tyrant desolated the Company's Jaghire, or territory (Chingleput), in 1768, when he ravaged it with fire and sword, leaving little indication of its ever having been inhabited, save in the unhappy spectacle of the bones of massacred thousands strewed over their smouldering habitations. In June, 1780, Hyder marched from his capital of Seringapatam, at the head of the finest army ever before seen in the south of India. It consisted of 28,000 cavalry, 15,000 regular infantry, 40,000 irregulars, 2,000 French rocket men, 4,000 pioneers, and 400 Europeans. His avowed purpose was the annihilation of the English; and, before the latter were aware of their situation, columns of smoke, arising from the desolated Carnatic, were seen approaching Madras. The success of Hyder was nearly as complete in the south as that of Surajee Dowlah had been at Cossimbuzar and Calcutta; with a velocity and daring like that of Napoleon Buonaparte, Hyder interposed his whole force between the small armies of Colonel Baillie and Sir Hector Munro, who were endeavouring to join each other; Colonel Baillie was defeated by the Mysorean cavalry, Sir Hector Munro retreated, and Hyder reduced Arcot, 3d November, 1781, and laid siege to Wandiwash, Vellore, Chingleput, and other strongholds in the Carnatic.

The Bengal presidency now afforded to Madras a return for the assistance which the latter had sent, under Clive, for the re-capture of the Fort of Calcutta. Sir Eyre Coote, with 560 Europeans, and a party of sepoys, were ordered by Warren Hastings for the relief of the sister presidency. The war was carried on for some time with little decided advantage on either side, notwithstanding Hyder had received a valuable reinforcement of 3,000 French troops from Europe, with the most skilful officers at their head.

The East India Company struggled not for conquests, but for existence, and, on the death of Hyder in 1782, (after reigning twenty-one years,) a peace was concluded with his son Tippoo Saib, whose throne, although the most powerful in the east, began now to be shaken by the Mahratta chieftains. The wily Sultan, after defeating the latter, made a peace, and turned his arms towards the subjugation of Travancore, situate between the 8th and 10th degrees north latitude, which, amidst every shock, had hitherto maintained its independence and neutrality. A treaty of alliance, offensive and defensive, having been entered into between this little state and the English, the unprincipled and faithless disposition of Tippoo became so apparent, that Lord Cornwallis resolved on putting a stop to the ambitious designs of a man whose words were as false as his cruelty was odious. After a desperate and hazardous campaign, during which Tippoo shewed the most daring courage, Lord Cornwallis invested the formidable fortress of Seringapatam, in February, 1792, with 11,000 Europeans, 30,000 regular sepoys, forty-two battery guns, and forty-four field pieces, and in front of which Tippoo gave battle, with 50,000 chosen infantry, and 5000 cavalry strongly intrenched and defended.

The British, as usual, notwithstanding their inferior numbers, carried all before them, from the commencement of a moonlight attack, at eight p.m. and the morning's dawn beheld the Mysorean tyrant a fugitive, with the loss of 23,000 of his troops, in killed, wounded, and missing. Tippoo was glad to sue for and accept peace, by the surrender of half his dominions, the payment of 4,000,000*l.* and the delivery of his two sons as hostages for the quiet fulfilment of the conditions imposed.

By the treaty signed 18th May, 1792, the Company

obtained possession of the frontier territory of Baramahal on the east, in the south Dindigul, on the west a great part of Malabar, including Telicherry and Calicut, and part of Camara, &c. But the restless spirit of Tippoo was not to be quenched by misfortune; in 1794 he received back his children, and immediately commenced secret negociations with the French (then at war with England) for the renewal of his purpose of "utterly destroying the English in India [1]."

The new governor general (Marquess Wellesley) saw previous even to his arrival in India (1798) [2] that although his most positive instructions from the Company were, if possible, not to wage war with any native prince, nor to extend the British dominions in the east, yet that if our existence were to be preserved, particularly in the south of India, the coalition between Tippoo and the French must be broken, and a blow struck that would prevent the former continuing to stir up all the native powers against the English. Tippoo, under the promised aid of men and arms from the French Directory, and with the hope that Napoleon's expedition to Egypt would not be fruitless as regarded its ultimate destination, had joyfully hailed the planting of a tree of liberty in

[1] Language of Tippoo's secret intercepted circular to the different Courts of India while professing the greatest friendship for England.

[2] See the first volume of the Marquess Wellesley's despatches (published in 1836). His Lordship's letters from the Cape of Good Hope in February 1798, are the production of a statesman of the highest range of intellect and of the noblest principles.

his capital surmounted by the '*bonnet rouge*,' while his jacobinical friends hailed the Mysorean despot on his own public parade as 'Citizen Tippoo!'—To have waited the consummation of the anticipations of the crafty son of Hyder would have been political idiotcy; the governor general therefore declared war against Mysore in February, 1799, previously causing by a most able course of diplomatic policy the disarming of a French organized army of 14,000 men at Hydrabad without the shedding of a drop of blood—and by a series of the most complete diplomatic negotiations that the eastern or western world can display. The army under General Harris, consisting of 4381 European, and 10,695 native infantry—884 European, 1751 native cavalry; 2400 Lascars and pioneers, 608 artillery, and 104 pieces of cannon, besides 6000 foot and 10,000 horse, under the Nizam's British officers, together with 6000 soldiers which advanced from Malabar under General Stuart, was in a fine state of equipment, and had in its ranks one who ever after carried with him the fortune of the day, and who now in his very first attack on Tippoo's right wing evinced well merited confidence in the British bayonets, which he has always proudly boasted have won him every victory. Colonel Wellesley led the attack on the Sultan's army which lay encamped within thirty miles of Seringapatam; a large column of Tippoo's best disciplined troops advanced to meet him in noble style; the British infantry under Wellesley stood fast, receiving their opponents' fire until they arrived within sixty yards, when the English rushed to the charge with an impetus which it was impossible for the Mysoreans to withstand; they quivered under the dreadful shock for a moment, then broke their ranks and were completely routed by General Floyd with the cavalry. Tippoo made little further resistance in the field, but threw himself into his strong capital with the *elite* of his forces; and on the 5th of April, the British encamped on the western side of the far-famed fortress of Seringapatam, situate at the west end of a small island (latitude 20° 25′ north, longitude 76° 45′ east) four miles long by one and a half broad, surrounded by the river Cauvery, occupying about a mile in extent, and principally remarkable for exhibiting the long, straight walls, square bastions, and high and steep glacis of the Hindoo engineers. The siege of Seringapatam went forward with determined rapidity, though peace was offered to Tippoo when he solicited terms on the 26th of April, which, however, he subsequently rejected:—On the 4th of May, at 1 p. m., the breach being completed in the curtain, a storming party of 4000 British, led by the gallant General Baird, moved to the attack; Baird had been four years a prisoner in the fortress under Hyder's tyranny, and was in some measure acquainted with the *locale*:—the parapet was speedily gained,—'*Come, my brave fellows,*' said their heroic leader, in the presence of both armies—'*follow me, and prove yourselves worthy the name of British soldiers!*' The appeal was nobly answered: after a desperate but useless resistance, the Mysoreans were totally routed; and when the terrible conflict had ceased, the lifeless body of Tippoo Saib was found buried beneath a piled heap of wounded, dead and dying men and horses, and the dynasty of Hyder Ali had ceased to reign. The Marquess Wellesley took possession of the fortress for the East India Company, also the sea coast of Canara, the district of Coimbatore and the passes of the Ghauts; and of a portion of the recent Mysore kingdom a native state was founded, at whose head was placed the ancient and much respected Rajah of Mysore's family, who had long lingered in obscurity and poverty. The native state then formed has continued to nearly the present period a protected one by the British Government; but of late years, particularly since 1810, and the death of its Dewan Purneah, its internal administration had become so bad, and the disorders and unhappiness of the people so great, that the Court of Directors, by a despatch dated 6th March, 1833, authorized the Madras government to bring under the *direct* management of the servants of the Company the whole of the territories of Mysore[1]. In 1800, the fruitful districts of Bellary and Cuddapah, which fell to the Nizam on the conquest of Tippoo, were ceded by his Highness to the East India Company by treaty; and in 1801 the Nabob of the Carnatic ceded to the Company the districts of Palnaud, Nellore (7930 square miles), Angole, Arcot province (13,620 square miles), the Pollams of Chittoor and the divisions of Satiraid Tinnevelly (5700 square

[1] It will so remain I understand for ten years.

miles), and Madura, (10,700 square miles [1]). These possessions, together with those mentioned in the foregoing pages, the then seaport fortress of Negapatam, captured from the Dutch in 1781, but now dilapidated, and some minor places, containing altogether an area of 142,000 square miles, and a population of upwards of fifteen millions, form the large dominion under the government of the Madras Presidency.

CHAPTER IV.

BOMBAY PRESIDENCY—THE MAHRATTA CONFEDERACY, &c.

THIS presidency derives its name from the small

[1] Tanjore, forming a small state of 4000 square miles in the south of India, was a part of the kingdom of Bejapoor which ceased to exist in 1683, and the estate (Jaghire) was confirmed by the renowned Sevajee, in the possession of Venkajee, the son of the Mahratta General Shajee, who was in the service of the king of Bejapoor; Venkajee agreeing to pay half his revenue to Sevajee. Ameer Sing, the reigning Rajah on the Musnud of Tanjore, agreed by a treaty dated 10th April, 1787, to pay four lacks of pagodas into the East India Company's treasury annually, towards defraying the military peace establishment, and that four-fifths of the whole fiscal revenues should be applied to defray such expenses in the event of a war and during its continuance: eleven years arrears of tribute from Tanjore to the Newaub of the Carnatic were transferred to the East India Company. In 1792 the subsidy was reduced to 350,000 pagodas, and the tribute was suspended for three years; by this treaty the Company were empowered to assume the management of certain districts equal to the tribute in the event of the Rajah failing to pay it.

island or barren rocks of Bombay[1], situate on the Malabar coast in latitude 18° 56′ north, longitude 72° 57′ east, being about ten miles long and three broad. It was formerly under the Mogul dominion, but ceded to the Portuguese in 1530, by whom a fort was erected on the south-east extremity of the island, its fine harbour indicating it as a desirable place for establishing a factory. In 1661 the island was ceded by Portugal to Great Britain, as a portion of the Infanta Catharine's fortune on her marriage with Charles II. The mortality of the king's troops was so great, and there being no advantage derived by the crown from the possession of Bombay, the expenditure being greater than the receipts, his Majesty, in 1668, transferred the island to the Honourable East India Company in free and common soccage as the Manor of East Greenwich, for which the East India Company became bound to pay the annual rent of 10*l.* in gold on the 30th of September in each year. In 1681, Bombay was a dependency of the East India Company's settlement of Surat, but in 1683 it was erected into a presidency, and in 1686 became the head station of the English on the western side of India, the seat of government being transferred thither from Surat, the capital of Gujerat, (in latitude 21° 11′ north, longitude 73° 7′ east,) where the East India Company had their principal factory since 1612. Until the beginning of the eighteenth century, the settlement of Bombay languished in consequence of the ravages of the

[1] Called by the Portuguese Bom Bahia (good bay).

plague, civil dissensions among the authorities, and the piracy carried on by Englishmen not in the service of the East India Company, which, indeed, caused the Mogul's admiral to invest Bombay in 1688, by whom it was very closely pressed, Mahim, Mazagong and Sion being captured, and the governor and garrison besieged in the fort. Submission, however, being made to Aurungzebe, his forces were withdrawn from the settlement. In 1776 the island of Salsette, (long possessed by the Portuguese, but wrested from them by the Mahrattas A. D. 1750, from whom it was captured by the British in 1773,) eighteen miles long and fourteen broad, (which has since been joined to Bombay by a causeway,) was obtained by cession from the celebrated intriguer Ragoba or Rugonath Rao, on condition of restoring him to the supreme power as Peishwa or head of the Mahratta confederacy. In order to understand the origin of the Mahratta war, it may be necessary to premise that this wily chieftain was uncle and guardian to Nareen Rao, a minor, who, on the death of his brother Madhooras Ballajee, (styled the Great) succeeded to the office of Peishwa, or head of the Mahratta confederacy of feudal barons or chiefs. The minor was murdered, as was said, at the instigation of his uncle Ragoba, who in turn became Peishwa for a few months, until it was discovered that the widow of the murdered youth was pregnant. A considerable number of the Mahratta chiefs then confederated —expelled Ragoba, and formed a regency until the accouchement of the widow should take place, and the son or daughter of Nareen Rao be enabled to assume the government. Ragoba fled to Surat, denied all participation in the death of his nephew, questioned the legitimacy of the widow's offspring, and solicited the aid of the English to recover the Peishwaship.

On the downfal of the Mysore dynasty in the south of India, it was deemed necessary by the Marquess Wellesley to break the confederated power of the Mahrattas under Dowlut Rao Sindiah, Holkar, and the Rajah of Berar. A few words respecting Sindiah and Holkar will, therefore, be necessary. Ranojee Sindiah, the founder of the Sindiah family, first distinguished himself as a leader of the Mahratta army in 1738, when its successes against the imperial forces of the Delhi Emperor, led to the foundation of the Mahratta states of Sindiah, Holkar and Puar. Mahadjee Sindiah was his fourth but illegitimate son, and on the death of his four brothers succeeded to his father's jaghire or estates. He died in 1794, and was one of the most powerful native princes of his day; his whole life was passed in the camp devoted to the improvement of his army; his infantry and artillery being formed on the model of the European troops, and his cavalry after the graceful manner of Mahomedans and Rajpoots. He was succeeded by his grand nephew and adopted son, Dowlut Rao Sindiah, whose army constituted a disciplined force of 45,000 infantry, divided into seventy-two battalions, under European officers, with a park of 500 pieces of artillery, and a numerous cavalry. He died 21st March, 1827, after having for thirty years played a prominent military part in Indian affairs :—

On his death, his army, at the lowest computation (inclusive of the British contingent and garrisons to forts) consisted of 14,000 infantry, 10,000 cavalry, and 250 pieces of ordnance, and he left territories capable of realizing 14,000,000 rupees per annum, if properly managed. Mulhar Rao Holkar, the originator of his own powerful dynasty, was the son of a shepherd, who, in addition to tending sheep, gained a livelihood as a weaver of cumlies (native blankets). From the command of twenty-five horse, under Kantajee Kuddum, he rose until we find him, in 1724, at the head of 100 horse in the Peishwa's service, whose principal leader he became in 1732, when for the support of his troops, Indore, &c. was assigned to him. He died in 1765, one of the most distinguished Mahratta leaders of his day, leaving possessions rated at a gross annual revenue of 7,500,000 rupees. *Jeswunt Rao Holkar*, the formidable chieftain alluded to under Western India, was the illegitimate son of Tokajee Holkar, whom the celebrated Ahlya Baye, widow of Khunda Rao, had raised to the command of her army although no relative. *Jeswunt Rao Holkar* raised himself to the Imperial power by poisoning his brother and nephew together with the wife of the former; he died mad in 1811. His invasion of the British possessions in Hindostan was at the head of an army of 90,000 men, of whom 19,000 were in brigades of disciplined infantry, and 7000 in artillery. It was against D. R. Scindiah and J. R. Holkar, that the Marquess Wellesley carried on the war of 1803-4-5.

The battle of Assye, which was fought on the 23rd

September, 1803, (in which General Wellesley with a force of 4500 men, of whom only 2000 were Europeans, attacked the confederate disciplined forces of Scindia and the Rajah of Berar, consisting of 50,000 men, assisted by a well organized French artillery and 10,000 infantry, disciplined and officered by Frenchmen), may be said to have given supremacy to the British influence in the west of India.

On the termination of hostilities in December, 1803, with the Mahratta Dowlut Rao Sindiah, the valuable districts of Broach, (1600 square miles) in the province of Guzerat, having the gulph of Cambay on the west, was ceded to the Bombay presidency; as was also the strong fortress of Ahmednugger,[1] in the province of Aurungabad, which had been previously captured by General Wellesley in August, 1803, together with some other places of minor importance. Cutch Province next claims attention: the government of this maritime district consists of a Rao, whose power is partly hereditary, and partly elective, at the will of the Jahrejah Blugad or brotherhood of chiefs. In 1801 and 1804 the Cutch state sent deputations to Bombay, but no alliance was then formed; in 1809, a wily adventurer had the control of the government, and it became the hot-bed of pirates and robbers, who were a serious annoyance to the

[1] Latitude 19° 15′ north, longitude 74° 55′ east, distant from Bombay 181 miles, and from Calcutta 1119 miles. The fort is entirely of stone, of an oval shape, and about one mile in circumference. There are a great many martello towers and a glacis to cover the base of the wall; the ditch is deep and broad, and the whole area within vaulted for stores.

British, and a treaty was entered into to prevent predatory incursions into our own and our allies' territories. From this period the contentions for the sovereignty and the disorders of the state became intolerable to the neighbouring powers; the unprovoked hostility to the British power by Bharmalja (the father of the present Rao) together with his tyrannous and oppressive conduct to the Jahreja chiefs, owing to inebriety and insanity, led to the combined operations of the British and Guickwar's troops, who reduced the fort of Angar, and subsequently the whole province was restored to order. This led to the treaty of Bhooj in 1816, by which for political motives, Mandavie the chief seaport of the Cutch province, (latitude 22° 50′ north, longitude 69° 33′ east) together with Anjar, &c. in the same province, was ceded by the governing power to the East India Company, and placed under the sway of the Bombay presidency; and in 1812, Cutch became a subsidized state, the English engaging to curb the plunderers from Wagur, whose depredations had been carried on with desolating vigour, and to keep the Sindeans and Khosas from their occasional invasions of the province.

The ambitious and treacherous designs of the Peishwa in 1817 against the British, by whom he had been elevated to power and supported in his dominions so long, was the means of extending yet more the territories under the Bombay presidency. The Mahrattas took advantage of the Pindarie war to commence hostilities, but the decisive conduct of the Marquis of Hastings, as previously stated, settled up to the present period the fate of western India, and in 1818, the northern and southern Concan, (12,270 square miles) Kandiah (12,430 square miles) Poonah, (20, 870 square miles) Dharwar, (9950 square miles) and various territories, &c. in Guzerat, became the dominions of the British in India; the whole of the Bombay presidency now forming an area of 64,938 square miles, and a population of 7,000,000 million souls.

CHAPTER V.

STIPENDIARY PRINCES—SUBSIDIARY AND PROTECTED STATES—AND FEUDATORY AND TRIBUTARY CHIEFTAINS OF BRITISH INDIA—EXAMINATION OF OUR SUBSIDIARY POLICY.

It will be seen from the foregoing details that a large portion of the British dominions in the east is made up of the possessions of princes who either themselves, or their descendants, now enjoy stipends paid to them out of the public revenues. These princes first became connected with us by subsidiary alliances, and ceded territories in return for military protection; others lost their dominions by the chances of war; while some territories were taken under our control from the absolute incapacity of the rulers, or their tyranny, which in mercy to the unhappy sufferers we could no longer permit to exist. The princes of the first and last classes are formally installed on the Musnud, allowed to exercise sovereignty over the tenants on their household lands,—they are exempted from the jurisdiction of the British courts of law, have their own civil and military functionaries, with all the insignia of state, and a British envoy usually resident at their court, whose duties chiefly relate to their pecuniary affairs, or the ceremonials of sovereignty. The following is an abstract in round numbers of their stipends.

When granted.	Titles of Princes.		Stipend. Rupees.
1803	Emperor of Delhi and Family		15,00,000
1801	Soubhadar of the Carnatic		11,65,400
——	Families of former Soubhadars		9,00,000
1798	Rajah of Tanjore		11,83,500
1770	Soubhadar of Bengal, &c...............		16,00,000
——	Families of former do. &c.		9,00,000
1795	Rajah of Benares		1,43,000
1799	Families of Hyder Ali and Tippoo ...		6,39,549
——	Rajahs of Malabar		2,50,000
1818	Bajee Row	Peishwa's Family.	8,00,000
1818	Chimnajee Appah		2,00,000
1803	Vinaeek Rao		7,50,000
1803	Zoolfikur Ali		4,00,000
1806	Himmut Bahadoor's descendants ...		60,000
1818	Benaeek Rao and Seeta Baee		2,50,000
1818	Gowind Rao of Calpee		1,00,000
1771	Nawaub of Masulipatam		50,000
	Total Rupees...		1,08,91,449
	Or at the rate of 2*s*. per Rupee, in sterling, £1,089,144		

A very able document, drawn up by Mr. B. S. Jones of the Board of Control, makes the amount of stipends paid in 1827-28, as follows,—

"Nabob of Bengal, S. R. 22,40,350.—Rajah of Benares 1.34,282,—Emperor of Delhi, 13,40,983,—Benaeek Rao, 5,79,866,—Nabob of Arcot, 17,53,965,—Rajah of Tanjore, 10,47,389,—Nawaub of Masulipatam, 52,671,—Families of Hyder Ali and Tippoo Saib, 6,38,858,—the late Peishwa, Bajee Rao and Chimnajee Appah, 22,42,023,—Nabob of Surat, 1,62,675. Total 1,09,92,557 or at 2*s*. the S. R. £1,019,255 sterling.

SUBSIDIARY ALLIANCES.—Nearly one half of the Hindostan territory is held by governments in subsidiary alliance with the British government; the general terms of the treaties with whom are, on the side of the English, protection against external enemies, and on the other, a submitting, in all political relations with foreign states, to the arbitration and final adjudication of the British government; a specific force is furnished by the East India Company, and a territory equivalent to the maintenance of the troops ceded by the former; the subsidizing state is also bound to keep on foot a specific contingent force to act in subordinate co-operation with the subsidiary. The protecting power is not to interfere with the internal administration of the protected state, but in cases of exigency it reserves the right in general to assume the whole of the resources of the protected state. The subsidiary force is liable to be called out to protect the legal succession to power, but not to be employed between the head of the government and its Zumendars or chiefs.

The following is given as a list of the princes [1], the military protection of whose territories is undertaken by the British government, together with the amount of subsidy paid by each, or the revenue on the territorial assignment in lieu of subsidy.

[1] See the Marquess of Wellesley's Despatches, volumes I. to V., published in 1836 and 1837, for copies of the treaties from 1798 to 1805 explanatory of many of our political relations in India.

Princes and their Capital Cities.	Population.	Area of Territory, sq. miles.	First Treaty.	First Subsidiary Connection.	Subsidiary Forces.		Gross Revenue.	Charges, &c.	Net Subsidy.
					Cavalry.	Infantry.			
	No.						£.	£.	£.
King of Oude* ....(Lucknow) ...	6000000	25300	1764	1773	at least	10000 m.	1813562	506222	1307340
Soubhadar of the Deccan (Hydrabad) ...	10000000	108800	1766	1795	1000	8000	610000	120000	490000
His Highness the Guickwar (Baroda)	6000000	36000	1773	1805	2000	4000	302726	147170	135626
Sindiah and others ....(Gwalior)	4000000	42400	1781	1803	—	—	2398104	836825	1561278
Holkar and others ....(Indore)		17600	1805	1817	Undefd.	Undefd.	273574	} 87299	420995
Rajah of Nagpoor ....(Nagpoor)......	3000000	64270	1779	1816	Ditto	Ditto	224720		
Rao of Cutch ....(Bhooj)		6100	1816	1819	—	1 Batt.	—	—	32400
Rajah of Mysore ....(Mysore)	3000000	27561	1799	1799	Undefd.	Undefd.	—	—	280000
Rajah of Travancore ....(Travancore)..	} 1000000	6731	1784	1785	—	3 Batt.	—	—	89498
Rajah of Cochin................(Cochin)		560	1791	1809	—	1 Batt.	—	—	22857
Totals......		279620							4339994

* Some accounts give the area of Oude at 17,008,000 acres, of which about one-tenth is jungle and forest.

Two of the foregoing (Oude and Mysore) can scarcely be styled stipendiary, the former being almost entirely dependent on the British government, and the latter recently ordered under the direct management of Madras presidency, owing to long misgovernment. Sindiah's territories should also of right be excluded, as, to a great extent, he is independent of our authority. The charges include revenue collection, political, judicial and police, maintenance of provincial battalions, customs, mint, &c.; the balance remaining after these deductions goes to the purpose for which the territories were granted—namely, the military protection of the government which assigned them.

Protected States.—Besides the foregoing governments, there are several minor principalities with whom engagements or treaties have been entered into agreeably to the peculiar circumstances of each, but with general stipulations applicable to all; namely, that the Protected State maintain no correspondence of a political tendency with foreign powers without the privity or consent of the British government, to whom the adjustment of its political differences is to be referred; they are perfectly independent in their internal rule, but acknowledge the supremacy of the British Government. When the interests of both powers are concerned, the troops of the protected state act in the field in subordinate co-operation to the British forces, the latter being empowered to avail themselves of natural or other advantages in the allied country against an enemy when necessary. No asylum for criminals or defaulters is permitted, and every assistance required to be given to effect their apprehension in the state. Europeans not to be employed without British permission. According to the resources of the protected state, a tribute is required, or a military contingent to be kept in readiness, or service to be rendered according to the means of the protected power. The states thus protected[1], but without subsidiary allowances, are—

1st, In the north-west Siccim and the Sikh and Hill States, on the left bank of the Sutlej—(the Sirdars are in number 150).

2nd, *Rajpoot States.* Bickaneer, Jesselmere, Jyepore, Joudpore, Oudepore, Kotah, Boondee, Serowey, Kishengurh, Dowleah, and Pertaubgurh, Doorapoore, Banswarra.

3rd, *Jaut and other States on the right bank of the Jumna.* Bhurtpore, Ulwar or Macherry, Kerowlee.

4th, *Boondelah States.* Sumpthur, Jhansi, Jaloun, Oorcha or Tehree, Dutteah, Rewah[2].

5th, *States in Malwa.* Bhopaul, Dhar, Dewas, Rutlaum, Silana, Nursinghur, Amjherra, &c. &c. &c.

6th, *States in Guzerat.* Pahlunpore, Rahdunpore, Rajpeepla, Loonawara, Soonth, the States in the Myhee Caunta, the Kattywar States.

7th, *States on the Malabar coast, (chiefly Mahratta.)* Sattarah, Sawunt Warree, Colapore, Colabba.

[1] The Protected States and Jagerdars in Bundlecund are in number 37; area in square miles, 12,918; number of villages, 5755; population, 1,378,400; revenue, rupees, 8,381,300; cavalry, 6087; and infantry, 22,430.

[2] Statement of Protected States and Jagerdars in Saugor, abstracted from the letter of the agent in the Saugor and Nerbudda

8th, *Burmese Frontier*. Cachar, Jyntia.

States not under British Protection. Scindia, the Rajah of Dholapore, Barree, and Rajakera (formerly Rana of Gohud), Runjeet Sing of Lahore, the Ameers of Scind, and the Rajah of Nepaul.

The following table exhibits the tributaries and territories acquired in India since 1813 :—

Nerbudda territories, dated 4th December, 1831. See Bengal Political Cons. 13th January, 1832, No. 56.

States.	Extent of Territory.	Number of Villages.	Population.	Revenue.	Military Force.	
					Cavalry.	Infantry.
Rewah	70 Coss, 3 miles N. to S. and 60 E. to W.	4000	1200000	2000000	4000	...
Ocheyrah...	10 Coss, E. to W. 7 ditto, N. to S.	404	120000	150000	50 or 60	300
Sohawul ...	Computed to own about half the quantity of Land that Ocheyrah possessed.	217½	80000	100000	...	...
Kothee	5 Coss, E. to W. 5 ditto, N. to S.	82	3 0000	50000	20 or 30	800
Myhur	15 Coss, E. to W. 10 ditto, N. to S.	700	100000	150000	200	1800
Shahgurh...	9 Coss, N. to S. 23 ditto, E. to W.	285	30000	69000	200	1000
Chimdea ...	....	Included in the Rewah State.		50000		
Simeria	....	Included in the Rewah State.		70000		

District.	State.	Date.	Particulars of Cessions, amount of present Tribute, &c.
Rajpotana.	Kotah	26 Dec. 1817	The Tribute paid to the Mahrattas (Rs. 264000) ....
	Boondee	10 Feb. 1818	The Tribute and Revenue paid to Scindia (Rs. 90000) ......
	Joudpore ...	6 Jan. 1818	The Tribute paid to Scindia (Rs. 108000) ....
	Oudepore ...	13 Ditto 1818	A Tribute of 1-4th of the Revenues for 5 years, and afterwards 3-8ths (Rs. 235000) ....
	Jyepore	2 April 1818	A Tribute increasing from 4 to 8 lacs for six years, and afterwards 8 lacs till the Revenues exceed 40 lacs, and then five-sixths of the excess (Rs. 800000) ....
Malwa ...	Sarowey	31 Oct. 1818	A Tribute of not more than three-eighths of the Revenue
	Pertaubgurh & Dowlea	5 Oct. 1818	The arrears due to Holkar, and Rs. 72700 Tribute (Rs. 60000) ....
	Banswara ...	16 Sept. 1818 25 Dec. 1818	A Tribute not to exceed three-eighths of the Revenue; also the Tribute paid to Dhar (Rs. 35000) ....
	Doongurpore	11 Ditto 1818	Ditto (Rs. 35000) ....ditto.........
	Rutlam ...... Sillana ...... All. Mohun	....	Tribute payable to Scindia and Dhar ....
	Scindia........	 1818	Cedes Ajmere and the Tribute of Rutlam, Sillana, and Allee Mohun (Rs. 444414)..
	Holcar........	6 Jan. 1818	Cedes the Tribute paid by the Rahjoot Princes; and all places within or north of the Boondee Hills; also his possessions in Candeish, and within and south of the Snutpoora Hills, and Umber and Ellora ....
	Dhar	10 Jan. 1819 18 Dec. 1821	Cedes the Tribute of Allee, of Banswara and Doongurpore
	Bhopaul	26 Feb. 1818	Tribute..
Guzerat ...	Guicowar ...	6 Nov. 1817	The farm of Ahmedabad ....
Deccan	Peishwa ...	13 June 1817	Cedes Ballapoor and other Districts, the Tribute of Kattywar, the Territories of Dharwar and Koosigul; also Rights and Territories in Malwa. Cedes also his rights in Bundlecund and Saugor, and Rights and Territories north of the Nerbudda, excepting those in Guzerat ...
		 1818	Cedes the whole of his possessions ....
	Sawunt Warree.	17 Feb. 1819 1820	Cedes Forts of Newtee and Rairee, and Districts and Coast from the Cartee to Vingorla, and thence to the Portuguese Territory, a portion of which was restored in 1820.
	Colapore......	15 Mar. 1829	Cedes Akevat and lands adjoining, equivalent to Rs. 10000 per annum..
	Nizam	12 Dec. 1822	Cedes Possessions on the West Bank of the Scena and within Ahmednuggur, estimated at four and a quarter lacs, for which he receives Territory in exchange ....
Berar.........	Nagpore	6 Jan. 1818	Cedes Territories North of the Nerbudda, and on the South Bank, also Ganslegiun, certain tracts in Berar; also Sirgoojah and Jushpore ....
		26 Dec. 1829	Tribute of eight lacs per annum................................
Nepaul	....	2 Ditto 1815	Cedes a considerable portion of Territory, much of which was given to the King of Oude and Siccim Rajah ....
Ava....	....	24 Feb. 1826	Renounces claims to Assam, Cachar, and Jyntea. Cedes Arracan, Ye, Tavoy, Mergui, Tenasserim. ....
Malay, St.	Johore	2 Aug. 1824	....
	Malacca	Mar. 1824	Ceded by the Dutch..

Acquired Territories, &c.	Gross Receipts*.	Mouths.	Sq. Miles.
....	Sur. Rs. 122360		
....	40000		
....	108000		
....	299219	15000000	350000
....	738000		
....	none		
....	76547		
....	85719		
....	117185		
See Rutlam, Sillana, and Allee Mohun.			
Ajmere	409278	....	400
Part of Candeish. See Paishwa.			
....			
....	160424		
....	1261969		
Collectorates of Poona	1351422	500000	4200
Ditto Ahmednuggur	2095292	650000	28000
N. Concan	1640359		
S. Concan	1285372	640857	7000
Part of Dharwar	(Total) 2710961	684193	6300
Candeish	(Total) 1716346		
Ramdroog, Kittoor, &c.	(Total) 645000	62000	
Saugor, Hutta, &c. See Nagpore.			
....			
....			
....			
Ceded Territory on Nerbudda	1855261		
Part of Saugor, Hutta, Rehly, and Mhairwarra.................	(Total) 1207863		
Kumaon	181173	300046	10967
Lower and Upper Assam ...... Arracan .... Ramree .... Sandoway	608374	100000	50000
Singapore		14000	
Malacca	44080	33132	1400

* The Net Receipts of the British Government, or the Sum which remains after paying the Expenses of Residencies, Agencies, Establishments, and Military Charges, incurred in consequence of the connexion with the several States, cannot be given with any accuracy.

British Feudatory Chiefs.—These chiefs so far differ from the former class, that, while the *protected* chiefs had treaties concluded with them as independent princes, the *feudatory* have had their allegiance transferred to Great Britain by their feudal superiors or by the events of war. In most cases, the lands which they held as a life tenure have been converted by our government into a perpetuity, and the chiefs are permitted a supreme control on their own lands. Among the number of these chiefs may be mentioned the Putwurdhun family, of which there are nine chiefs; the Soubahdar of Jansi, chief of Julaon and Calpee; family of Angria (the Mahratta pirate); numerous tributaries in Kattywar and in Gujerat; the Rajahs of Shorapoor and Gudwal; the Seedee of Jinjeera, and other Abyssinian chiefs. The Parliamentary Return of the area of Protected and Allied States is as follows:—

Dominions of the Rajahs of Travancore and Cochin, 9400 square miles; Nizam, 108,800; Rajah of Mysore, 29,750; King of Oude, 25,300; Dowlat Rao Scindiah, 42,400; the Rajah of Berar, including Nagpore, 64,270; Jeswunt Rao Holkar, 17,600; the Guicowar, including the detached Pergunnahs belonging to the British in Kattywar and Guzerat, 36,900; Rajah of Koorg, 2230; Nabob of Kurnool, 3500; Rajah of Sikhim, 4400; Nabob of Bhopal, 7360; Rajahs of Sattara, Colapore, Sewuntwarree, and the principal British Jaghiredars, 21,600; Rajah of Cutch, 6100; Soubedar of Jhansi, Rajah of Duttea and others, commonly known as the Bundlecund chiefs, 19,000. Territories under British protection west of the river Jumna, comprehending Jhodpore, Bikanier, Jessulmeer, Khotah, the Seikh country, the hill districts of Sirmoor, and other small states, 165,000. Of Assam, Jynteea, Cachar, and Muneepore, the boundaries are so undefined that it is difficult to form even an approximation to their superficial contents, but it is estimated at 51,000. Total, 614,610 square miles.

British Allies.—Independent of the foregoing states, the East India Company's government have general treaties with other surrounding nations, viz. with *Persia* the Company are in alliance, and have a resident at the court of the sovereign; with *Cochin China*, *Siam*, *Caubul*, *Nepaul*, and *Ava*, the intercourse of the Company is principally of a commercial nature, but they have residents established at Nepaul and Ava.

With the *Imaum of Muscat, and with other chiefs on the western shores of the Persian Gulf*, the Company have treaties for commercial purposes, and with a view to the suppression of the slave trade, and of piracy in the Gulph. In order to secure the fulfilment of the provisions of these treaties, the Company have established political agents on the shores of the Persian and Arabian Gulfs.

The area of the kingdoms and principalities of India has been computed by Captain J. Sutherland after a novel manner; the boundaries of each state having been marked off on a skeleton map, drawn on paper of equable texture, the whole were cut out with the greatest care, and *weighed* individually and collectively, as a check in the most delicate balance of the Calcutta Assay Office; the weights were noted to a *thousandth part of a grain*, the balance being sensible to the tenth part of that minute quantity. Before setting to work on the states, an index, or unit of 100 square degrees, cut from the same paper, was first weighed, to serve as a divisor for the rest. The weighing process commenced in the driest part of the day, taking the whole of the papers together; thus the continent of India weighed 127,667 grains troy: the sum of the *individual* weights of the separate states 127,773 grains troy: the addition was proved to proceed from the hygrometric water absorbed towards the evening, and corrections were applied to endeavour to neutralise this source of error: the following data must, however, only be considered as an approximation to truth in the absence of better information, owing to the imperfect data of Maps of India. By Captain Sutherland's weighing process, the area of the native states, in alliance with the British government, is 449,845 square miles. That of the territory under British rule, with the remaining small states and Jágérdars, 626,591, giving the superficial area of India 1,076,591 square miles, which nearly agrees with Hamilton's estimate of 1,103,000.

Captain Sutherland classes the native states of India under the three following heads, viz:—

1st, *Foreign*—Persia, Kabool, Senna, the Arab tribes, Siam, and Acheen: 2nd, *External on the frontier*—Ava, Nepal, Lahore, and Sinde: 3rd, *Internal* (to which the following areas refer), which, according to the nature of their relations, or treaties, with the British, he divides into *six* classes.

First Class.

	By Weighment.	By Hamilton*.	
1. Oude, square miles,	23,923	20,000	Treaties offensive and defensive; right on their part to claim protection external and internal from British Government, and right of the latter to interfere in internal affairs.
2. Mysore, do.	27,999	27,000	
3. Berar, or Nagpur, do.	56,723	70,000	
4. Travancore, do.	4,574	6,000	
5. Cochin, do.	1,988	2,000	

Second Class.

6. Hyderabad, sq. m.	88,884	96,000	Do. with the exception of the right of Britain to interfere in internal affairs, but empowered to require the aid of British troops for the realization of the sovereign's just claims on his subjects.
7. Baroda, do.	24,950	12,000	

Third Class.

8. Indore, square miles,	4,245	Treaties offensive and defensive, states mostly tributary; acknowledging the supremacy of, and promising subordinate co-operation to, the British Government, but supreme rulers in their own dominions.
Rajpoot States—		
9. Oudipore, (H. 7,300)	11,784	
10. Jeypúr,	13,427	
11. Judpoor,	34,132	
12. Kotah, (H. 6,500)	4,389	
13. Bundi, (H. 2,500)	2,291	
14. Alwar,	3,235	
15. Bikbanír,	18,060	
16. Jesalmír,	9,779	
17. Kishengurh,	724	
18. Bauswarra,	1,440	
19. Pertabgurh,	1.457	
20. Dúngarpúr,	2,005	
21. Keroli,	1,878	
22. Serowí,	3,024	
23. Bhurtpúr, (H. 5,000)	1,946	
24. Bhopal, (H. 5,000)	6,772	
25. Cutch, (H. 13,300)	7,396	
26. Dhar and Dewas,	1,466	
27. Dhólpúr,	1,626	
28. (In Bundlekund) Rewah,	10,310	
29. ——— Dhattea, Jhànsi, and Terhí,	16,173	
30. ——— Sawantwari,	935	

Fourth Class.

Ameer Khan—			Guarantee and protection, subordinate co-operation, but supremacy in their own territory.
31. Tonk,	1,103	1,633	
Seronj,	261		
Nimbahara,	269		
31. Patiala, Keytal, Naba, and Jeend,	16,602		

* Extracted from Hamilton's Hindostan by way of comparison.

FIFTH CLASS.

33. Gwalior,	32,944	— Amity and friendship.

SIXTH CLASS.

34. Sattara,	7,943	Protection, with the right of the British Government to control internal affairs.
35. Kolapúr,	3,184	

Of the above states Captain Sutherland enumerates four as *Mahomedan* (*i. e.* with Mussulman rulers I presume), viz.:—Hydrabad, Oude, Bhopal, and Tonk: of the *Hindoo* States eight are Mahratta, viz.:—Sattara, Gwalior, Nagpúr, Indore, Banda, Kolapúr, Dhar, and Dewas: nineteen are Rajput, viz.:—Oudipúr, Jeypúr, Judpúr, Búndi, Kotah, Cutch, Alwar, Bhikanír, Jesalmír, Kishenghur, Bánswára, Pertábgúrh, Dungerpúr, Kerolé, Serowé, Rewah, Dhattea, Jhansé, and Terhi: six are of other Hindoo tribes, viz.:—Mysore, Bhurtpoor, Travancore, Sawantwari, Cochin, and Dholpúr. Besides these allied states, there are the following inferior Rajships and Jágérdars, viz.:—Chota-Nagpúr, Singújer, Sumbhalpúr, Oudipoor, Manipúr, Tanjore, the Baroach family, Ferozpúr, Merich, Tansgaon, Nepani, Akulkote, and those of the Ságar and Nerbudda country, together with Sikhim, and the States of the Northern Hills.

Before closing the subject, it may be desirable to mention an independent chief of great talent, wealth, and power, with whom the British government is on terms of friendly alliance. I allude to Runjeet, or Ranajit Sing, whose country includes not only what is called the Punjaub, and the whole of the lovely and important valley of Cashmere, but also considerable tracts of territory beyond the Indus from Tatta on the south to Thibet on the north, and from Caubul on the west to beyond the Sutlej on the east. This formidable potentate possesses a large army (see *Military chapter*), an immense arsenal at Umritzar, and a vast treasury (his annual revenues are estimated at 18,000,000 rupees) at Govind Garrow.

CHAPTER VI.

STATE OF INDIA — CONSEQUENCES RESULTING FROM THE BRITISH CONQUEST OF HINDOSTAN.

THE motives which led to the acquisition of the British power in Hindostan, and the means by which it was acquired, have now, with as much brevity as possible, been brought to a close, and it is almost impossible, at this short distance of time, to contemplate coolly and impartially the important proceedings therein narrated: step by step, from the landing of Clive, in 1757, at Calcutta, for the re-conquest of the few acres of land possessed by the East India Company to the present period, the British power has gone on increasing in strength, and I trust in wisdom. There can be no doubt, that if the happiness of the great mass of the people be considered as paramount, the acquisition of the Indian provinces by Britain must be looked on as a most fortunate circumstance, for *peace*, the indispensable prelude to civilization, had not within record or tradition heretofore been known to continue for the shortest period among the unhappy inhabitants. The *Mahomedan dynasties* were built on usurpation, cemented with the blood of the feeble and innocent, and maintained by sequestrating the riches of the wealthy; the policy of the Moslems in Asia was complete subjugation, universal dominion, and uncontrolled despotism; their ruling principles avarice, sensuality, an imposing pageantry, and a conversion to the faith of the Koran.

The *Mahratta* conquests were considered as predatory acquisitions, to be held only by the sword; and such was the anarchical condition of the small principalities existing in different parts of India, that in the Carnatic for example, no less than twenty petty chiefs assumed at one time the title of *Nizam Ul Mulk* (Composer of the State), exhibiting a scene of boundless exaction and rapacity on the part of those claiming the government; no wonder therefore that the ploughman was armed at his rustic occupation, and the shepherd, while peacefully tending his herds, always prepared for the battle field. Property of every kind may well be supposed totally devoid of security; Mr. Orme, writing at the time, says (Book I. Ch. IV.) "the mechanic or artificer, under the government of the petty princes, will only work to the measure of his necessities—he dreads to be distinguished; if he becomes too noted for having acquired a little more money than others of his craft, that will be taken from him; if conspicuous for the excellence of his skill, he is seized upon by some person in authority, and obliged to work for him night and day." It is indeed on authentic record, that rebellion, massacres, and barbarous conquests, make up the history of India from the remotest annals; we read of thousands—twenty, seventy, a hundred, thousand persons being *slaughtered in one day*, without the slightest compunction;—unbounded perfidy and treason;—never ending assassination for personal revenge or public confiscation,—the noses and ears of thousands cut off at one time, justice openly sold, villainy practised in every form,—all law and religion trodden under foot,—the bonds of private friendship, of connexions, of society, broken,—every individual, as if amidst a forest filled with wild beasts, relying upon nothing but the strength of his own arm:—in fine, the work of war and blood was perpetual, living beings hewed or torn to pieces, hillocks of bodies and pyramids of human heads piled up for public show, the inhabitants of whole provinces hunted like wild beasts for royal amusement; the march of a monarch, whether Mussulman or Mahratta, tracked by gore, desolation, burning villages, famine, and pestilence.

It may perhaps be said that I have exaggerated these statements in order to uphold the sway of the East India Company, but let the reader peruse the following description of the former state of India, by Mr. Rickards, who did all in his power to destroy the Company, though compelled to admit their fitness for the government of India. Mr. Rickards, speaking of the *Mahomedan dynasties in India*, says, that 'Throughout the whole period of the Mahomedan ascendancy in the south of India, the same enormities, the never-failing accompaniments of their presence and power, are recorded to have been uniformly and unceasingly perpetrated, as in the northern provinces. To review the occurrences of this period would only be to give further examples of the same unprovoked and devastating warfare, the same struggles for power, the same unbridled thirst of conquest, the same *perfidy, treason, and private assassination;* the same disregard of any tie, whether of nature, of honesty, or of honour, and the same persecution, oppression, and massacre of the Hindoos.

'The scenes, indeed, of butchery and blood, are often mentioned as too horrid to relate—*thousands—twenty—seventy—a hundred thousand souls being sacrificed at one time,* without the least remorse; it was no uncommon thing for 50,000 and 100,000 souls to be massacred at once, in which neither sex nor age were spared; and of the blood of the most venerable priests, learned men, and citizens being used for tempering the earth with and plastering the city walls! Mahomed, son of Alla-ud-deen, one of those southern monsters, died, it is true, acknowledging 'all is vanity,' but not until after gratifying during his life every sensual passion, slaughtering 500,000 persons, and ruining and depopulating the Carnatic.

'The treasuries of the southern princes were always filled from the enormous plunder of their defenceless subjects; and the system of Mahomedan exaction, sometimes under the name of contribution, but permanently under that of revenue, being every where the same, with the power of rapacious armies every where to enforce it, the fate of the unhappy people was here, as in the north, stamped with the same wretchedness. There was no security for person or property; the latter more especially was always a fair object of seizure whenever it was known to exist[1], and the mass of the people were thus reduced to a state of poverty from which there was no escape, and of violence and oppression against which there was no redress[2].'

What a revolting description of despotism is the foregoing delineation of a Mahomedan dynasty! While perusing it the blood curdles in the veins, and the genial current which in general flows around the heart becomes almost frozen in its course. Yet let me proceed. The same authority asserts that the " loose principles of banditti were, on a larger scale, those of the Asiatic courts for seven or eight centuries; whoever has a taste for atrocities of this nature, for details of lawless rapine, and wholesale butchery of the species, for flaying and impaling alive, and every species of torture, *for hewing living bodies to pieces*, for massacring prisoners in cold blood, and making hillocks of their bodies, and pyramids of their heads for public show, for hunting down the inhabitants of whole provinces like wild

[1] Even to the present day the Hindoos have not entirely got over the dread of being known to possess money, or of having gold and silver utensils. Vast sums of money remain buried in the earth from generation to generation, and not unfrequently a sudden death deprives the inheritor of treasure of a knowledge where it lies concealed. Those who have conversed with wealthy natives can confirm me in this particular.—R. M. M.

[2] Rickard's India, vol. i. page 223.

beasts, with other like modes of royal amusement, may be feasted to satiety in the history of the Mussulman conquests and governments of the Deckan, which is little more than a continued series of those disgusting barbarities. Timour was justly denominated the 'firebrand of the universe.'" The Westminster Review, for July, 1832, says, he was "one of the greatest wholesale butchers of humanity ever heard of; he plundered and massacred in India, without distinction of religion or sex, and his track was marked by blood, desolation, famine, and pestilence!" Aurengzebe persecuted the Hindoos in a similar manner to the other Mahomedan tyrants; Tippoo Saib circumcised all the Brahmins he could get hold of, and, as the reviewer says, 'subjected 60,000 Christians to the same operation in a single province.'

Of the Mogul proceedings in India, Mr. Rickards observes, that "the prisoners taken were inhumanly massacred; insurrections in the provinces were also incessant, so that *the work of war and blood was perpetual;* massacres were common to every reign, when the butchery extended, not only to the parties immediately concerned, but to their vassals, dependents, and even acquaintances; not even weeping mothers, nor their smiling infants at their breasts, were pitied or spared! To prevent the accumulation of property in a few hands, the wealth and estates of Mussulmans and Hindoos were, without distinction, seized upon and confiscated; no man durst entertain his friends without a written permission from the vizier, and the different public offices were filled with men whose indigence and dependence rendered them implicitly obedient to the dictates of government!" Yet, strange to say, while narrating these horrifying facts, Mr. Rickards loads the English with opprobrium for their conquest of Hindostan, and pines over the downfal of the Great Mogul, and with him of the Mahomedan dynasties in India.

A Mahomedan historian, famed for his impartiality, named Golaum Hossein Khan, is, however, less tender than Mr. Rickards for the fate of the Great Mogul. In his able work, entitled "A View of Modern Times," he says, "when the Emperor Shah Allum was carrying on war against the English nation on the plains of Azimabad, it was made known that the Emperor designed to march thither in person. Although the inhabitants had received no benefits from him, they seemed to have but one heart and one voice on the occasion; but when he arrived amongst them, and they experienced from his profligate officers and disorderly troops the most shameless acts of extortion and oppression, whilst, on the other hand, they *observed the good conduct and strict discipline of the English army, the officers of which did not suffer a blade of grass to be spoiled, and no kind of injury done to the feeblest peasant*, then, indeed, the sentiments of the people changed, and the loyalty which they once bore to the Emperor was transferred to the English; so that when Shah Allum made his second and third expeditions, they loaded him with imprecations, and prayed for victory to the English." The quantity of plunder, and the value thereof, abstracted at various times from the Hindoos, is detailed with much minuteness by Mr. Rickards; and it must astonish every one where such immense treasures could be had, and how speedily they were re-collected, did we not know what a salient power there is in Hindostan, and how rapidly the most destructive disasters are recovered from by an industrious people, of commercial habits and few wants.

I turn now to Mr. Rickard's[1] description of the Mahratta governors, whom he states to have been "quite equal to the Mussulmans in the dreadful atrocities they perpetrated, and the devastating ravages with which they desolated the countries through which they passed; their route being easily traced by ruined villages and destroyed cultivation; plundering as they went along, and seizing, by violence or by treachery, all that was valuable or conducive to their present security or ulterior views; controlled by no fixed laws, and by no better sense of right than the power of the sword. The districts which resisted were overrun with fire and sword, the inhabitants tortured and murdered, and the country left a dreary waste, to forewarn others of their fate if not averted by ready compliance with these lawless exactions."

The annexed sketch of Mahratta barbarity affords a melancholy illustration of the dreadful state to which

[1] I have quoted Mr. Rickard's testimony, because although owing his fortune and station to the position he held in India in the service of the East India Company, yet he was their most violent, and, I will add, unjustifiable opponent.

the great mass of the people were reduced by the combined barbarities of the Mussulmans and the Mahrattas, from which, in a few years, they were so happily rescued by the East India Company:—'In 1759, Abdallah again turned his attention towards Hindostan, and in 1761, made himself master of its devoted capital, Delhi. He laid the city under heavy contributions, and enforced the collection with such rigour and cruelty, that the unfortunate inhabitants, driven to despair, took up arms. The Persian ordered *a general massacre, which, without intermission, lasted seven days*. The relentless guards of Abdallah were not even then glutted with slaughter; but the stench of the dead bodies drove them out of the city. A great part of the buildings were at the same time reduced to ashes; and many thousands, who had escaped the sword, suffered a lingering death by famine, sitting upon the smoking ruins of their own houses. Thus the imperial city of Delhi, which, in the days of its glory, extended thirty-four miles in length, and was said to contain 2,000,000 of people, became almost a heap of rubbish. But this was not all; for the *Mahrattas* had now marched towards Delhi, to oppose Abdallah, with an army of 200,000 cavalry. On their approach Abdallah evacuated the city, which the Mahrattas immediately entered, and filled every quarter of it with devastation and death. Not content with robbing the miserable remains of Abdallah's cruelty of every thing they possessed, they stripped all the males and females naked, and wantonly whipped them through the streets. Many now prayed for death as the greatest blessing, and thanked the hand which inflicted the wound. Famine began to rage among the unfortunate citizens to such a degree, that men fled from their dearest friends as from beasts of prey, for fear of being devoured. Many women devoured their own children, while some mothers of more humanity were seen dead in the streets, with infants still sucking at their breasts.'

Several formidable bands of Hindoos, who, like the Mahrattas, gloried in the 'inestimable advantage of having a finger in every man's dish,' afford ample scope for details of cruelty and devastation; such, for instance, as the desolating freebooting Pindaries, the bands of terrific robbers named Coolies, and professional murderers called Thugs; but my limits forbid me. I cannot, however, close this chapter without adducing the testimony of the author before me, respecting the governments of the minor princes; and who, according to Mr. Rickards and Colonel Wilks, are accused of privately assassinating 400 priests (the only number they could collect together who would trust them), while passing from the audience-hall into a pretended refreshment chamber, because they opposed themselves to the *moderate* request of a tax upon 'opening a door!'—or of surrounding with large bodies of cavalry any community of their subjects who showed the least resistance to oppression!

'The kingdom of Mysore, which arose out of the ruins of Vijeyanuggur, exhibits also a like origin in military adventure and blood, and in similar series of intriguing usurpations, murder, and conquest.

Each petty chief, by counterfeiting grants from Delhi, laid his claim to districts; the country was torn to pieces with civil wars, and groaned under every species of domestic confusion.'

Another set.—'The Polygars, like the northern zemindars, were originally military adventurers, or leaders of banditti, or revenue or police officers, employed under former governments, and who, availing themselves of times of weakness or distress, or the absence of a controlling force, established themselves in their respective districts. Each Polygar, in proportion to the extent of his jurisdiction and power, had forts and military retainers, and exercised within his own limits all the powers of an Asiatic despot. In the history of the Pollams (the districts governed by the Polygars), anarchy, misrule, lawless power, insurrection, civil and external wars, ravages and famines, are the most prominent features. When the contribution demanded by a Polygar, the amount of which depended on his conscience, was resisted or not quietly submitted to, it was enforced by torture and the whip; the whole village was put in confinement; every occupation interdicted; the cattle pounded; the inhabitants taken captive into the Pollam lands, or *murdered;* in short, every species of outrage continued to be committed, until the object of the Polygar was accomplished [1].'

Another specimen.—'In the northern circars, when they came into the Company's possession, not only

[1] This is just the state of Western Africa at present.

the forms but even the *remembrance of civil authority seemed to be totally lost;* the zemindars had all forts and armed forces for their defence, the more powerful using their force as opportunities favoured to extend their possessions, and swallow up minor zemindaries.'

One more instance.—'The jaghire (now called Chingleput, a district 2440 square miles in extent, and in the immediate vicinity of Madras), was twice invaded by Hyder Ali—once in 1768, and again in 1780. In the latter, more especially, fire and sword seemed to contend for pre-eminence in the work of havoc and destruction. At the close of the war in 1784, the country exhibited few signs of having been inhabited, save in the bones of murdered bodies, or the naked walls of villages and temples, the melancholy remains of an almost universal conflagration. To the miseries of desolating war, succeeded a famine: death and emigration nearly depopulated the country.'

But why continue details at which the heart sickens?—why relate further instances of 100,000 men being put to death, in *cold blood,* in one day?—why depict streets of cities made impassable by heaps of slain?—why describe the pitiless slaughter of thousands of mothers, with their smiling infants at their breast)—why picture the fury of respectable citizens, who, beholding the pollution and ravishment of their wives and daughters, their wealth seized by the hand of rapine, and they themselves insulted, beaten, and abused, with one consent shutting the gates of their cities, murdering their consorts and children, setting fire to their houses, and then rushing out like madmen against their enemies?—why, I ask, narrate any more of scenes such as these, which everywhere crimson the page of Indian history prior to our conquest? A Christian and a philanthropist would say, that any power, European or Asiatic, interfering to put a stop to such harrowing scenes would be entitled to the highest approbation which man could bestow. If the East India Company had never added one shilling to the wealth of England, one inch of dominion to her crown, or one leaf of laurel to its glory, the mere circumstance of establishing peace in a country such as India, which for countless ages had been a prey to every species of atrocity which degrade men far below the level of the brutes, and which, under a less genial clime, and fertile territory, would have converted the whole land into a howling wilderness,—they would most assuredly deserve to be ranked amongst the noblest benefactors of the human race. Let therefore those who condemn the British conquest of Hindostan reflect whether Providence acted wisely in putting a stop to scenes which harrow up the soul on bare perusal, making England the means of introducing tranquillity, civilization, and Christian precepts into a country whence incalculable blessings may flow, to cheer and gladden many hundred million of human beings scattered throughout the vast territories of the Eastern Hemisphere.

AREA, PARALLEL, MERIDIAN, AND PHYSICAL ASPECT OF EACH POSSESSION IN BRITISH INDIA.

Districts.	Area in square Miles.	Parallel.		Geography and Physical Aspect.
		Lat. N.	Long. E.	
		° ′	° ′	
Bengal Province.				
Calcutta	4722	22 23	88 28	Level with the sea, rivers, salt lakes and dense jungles, soil sandy.
Hooghly	2260	22 54	88 27	Low, flat, well watered, rich alluvial soil, along Hooghly river.
Nuddea	3105	23 25	88 24	Ditto, ditto, light soil, Jellinghy and Cossimbazar rivers, fertile.
Jessore	5180	23 7	89 15	Ditto, salt marshy isles, rich soil, embouchures of the Ganges.
Backergunge	2780	22 42	89 20	Very low, part of the Sunderbunds, alluvial soil, ditto.
Dacca	4435	23 42	90 17	Covered with lakes, and intersected by the Ganges and Brahmaputra.
Tipperah	6830	23 30	92 20	Wild hilly regions, fertile tracts on Megna with marshes, dense forests.
Chittagong	2980	22 0	92 0	120 miles along the bay of Bengal, hilly, productive lands, islets numerous.
Sylhet	4000	24 55	91 40	N. E. hilly, S. flat and inundated, W. conical hills, and fine vales.
Mymensing	6988	24 30	90 20	Valley of Brahmaputra, low, flat, and innumerable streams.
Rajeshaye	3950	24 30	89 0	Intersected by the Ganges, and flat with extensive lakes.
Moorshedabad	1870	24 11	88 15	Intersected by the Jellinghy, flat and fertile, well irrigated.
Jungle Mehals	6990	23 20	87 10	Wild, forest, hilly country, beautifully picturesque and dry.
Birbhoom	3870	24 0	87 20	Hilly, jungly, and dry land, with hot mineral springs
Dinagepoor	5920	25 37	88 43	Hilly, to S. waving valleys, numberless streamlets and lakes.
Rungpoor	7856	25 43	89 22	Do. to E. forests, watered, Garrow mountains 3000 ft. clusters of lakes.
Burdwan	2000	23 15	87 57	Rising land, rich soil of a thirsty nature, jungly, coal and iron.
Bahar.				
Ramghur	22430	24 30	84 30	Hilly, mountainous district, two-thirds waste, very rocky and mineral.
Boglipoor	7270	25 13	86 58	Clusters of fertile hills and swelling valleys, hot springs, iron.
Bahar	5325	25 10	85 20	Hilly and rugged to S., flat near the Ganges, dry valleys, nitrous soil.
Patna	667	25 37	85 15	Ganges' banks for 9 miles, river 5 miles wide, very picturesque.
Shahabad	4650	25 0	84 0	Picturesque along the Ganges, hilly to S., good roads and rivers
Purneah	7460	25 45	88 23	Marshy to S., alluvial country, sinking towards the Ganges.
Tirhoot	7732	27 10	86 0	Elevated, but not hilly, extensive wastes to the N , well watered.
Sarun	5760	26 0	84 56	Ditto irrigated, rich flats along Gunduck, majestic forests.
Sumbhulpoor	....	21 8	83 37	Hill and dale, picturesque, intersected by Mahanundy.
Orissa.				
Midnapore	8260	22 25	87 25	Cultivated plains, with good roads, and dense jungles.
Hidjellee	....	51 50	88 10	Embanked against the tides, and intersected by rivers.
Cuttack	9000	20 30	86 0	Delta of rivers, elevated, then hilly, and next mountainous.

(Continued.)

AREA, PARALLEL, MERIDIAN, AND PHYSICAL ASPECT OF EACH POSSESSION IN BRITISH INDIA. (*Cont.*)

Districts.	Area in square Miles.	Parallel. Lat. N.	Long. E.	Geography, and Physical Aspect.
		° ′	° ′	
Ultra Gangetic. Arracan.	11500	20 30	92 5	Isthmuses, islands, swamps, sea-coast; jungles, hills, mountains, inland.
Assam, &c.	15900	26 28	90 96	Valley of the Brahmaputra, 60 miles wide by 350 long.
Tavoy	15000	10 8 to 16 0	97 0 to 99 0	Dense forests and jungles, sea coast, low islands.
Ye				Numerous rivers, rice plains and forests, rocky coast.
Tenasserim				Mergui Archipelago, interior hilly, little known.
Mergui Isles				Chain of high bold isles in triple lines, with harbours and wide channels.
N. West. Provinces of Hindostan, Benares	350	25 30	83 0	The holy city situate on the Ganges, highly cultivated.
Ghazeepore	2850	25 35	83 33	Gently undulating lovely groves, Ganges on the S., Goggra on the E.
Azimghur	2240	24 6	83 10	Elevated flat, jungly, sandy but fertile, Goggra river.
Goruckpoor	9250	26 46	83 19	Base of hills low, intersected by rivers, forests, Nepaul, ms. to N.
Juanpoor	1820	25 20	84 30	Slightly undulating surface, well cultivated, N. & S. Goggra, E. Ganges.
Allahabad	2650	25 27	81 50	Ganges and Jumna Delta, 800 feet above Calcutta, flat sandy loam.
Banda	4685	25 30	80 20	Elevated table land, high hills in parallel ranges, and few rivers.
Kalpee		26 10	79 41	Along Jumna, flat, rising towards Panna mountains; diamond mines.
Futtehpore	1780	25 56	80 45	Ganges and Jumna valley, rising from either bank, picturesque.
Cawnpore	2650	26 30	80 13	Segment of vast plain from bay of Bengal to the mountains, fertile, dry.
Etawah	3450	26 47	78 53	Flat, but intersected by ravines, naked soil, Chumbul river.
Furruckabad	1850	27 24	79 27	The Doab is in general flat and divested of lofty trees, dry and clayey soil.
Shahjehanpoor	1420	27 50	79 48	Flat and intersected by N. mountain streams, well cultivated.
Saidabad	1000	27 30	78 0	Highly cultivated, many water courses, retentive brick clay.
Allyghur	2300	27 56	77 59	Low dark jungle, loneliest part of the Doab, many watercourses.
Saiswan	1800	28 0	79 0	Highly cultivated, many watercourses.
Bareilly	2000	28 23	79 16	Generally level, watered by the Ganges, Kosila, &c. Kumaon ms. N.
Peelibheat	2300	28 42	79 42	Pleasantly situate on the Gurrah, very fertile.
Moradabad	5800	28 51	78 42	A varied moist soil, inundated along the Ganges, Gerwhal ms. Nd.
Agra	3500	27 11	77 53	Table land, Chumbul and Jumna, 60 feet high, light dry soil.
Delhi	9600	28 41	77 5	Ditto, 800 feet above the ocean, thirsty saline soil, canals.
Sarahunpoor	1420	29 57	77 32	Quite flat to base of hills at N. and E., which rise abruptly, fertile.
Kumaon, &c.	7200	30 6	79 0	Succession of high mountainous ridges, elevating to 7000 feet.

(*Continued.*)

AREA, PARALLEL, MERIDIAN, AND PHYSICAL ASPECT OF EACH POSSESSION IN BRITISH INDIA. (*Cont.*)

Districts.	Area in square Miles.	Parallel. Lat. N.	Long. E.	Geography, and Physical Aspect.
		° ′	° ′	
Nerbudda District.	85700	23 0	80 0	Deep ravines, fertile valleys, and dense forests, Nerbudda delta.
Madras Presidency.				
Gangam	3700	19 21	85 0	Low sea-coast, large fertile plains, hilly to W.
Vizigapatam	5600	17 42	83 24	Mountainous lofty ridge, parallel with and frequently close to the sea.
Rajamundry	4690	16 59	81 53	Bounded by the Godavery, extensive delta, high hills, delta 500 sq. miles.
Masulipatam	4810	16 10	81 14	Mountainous, W. low sea-coast, lakes and streams, good harbour.
Guntoor	4960	16 17	80 32	Ditto, ditto, ditto, watered by Krishna, to N. and Gondegama to the S.
Bellary	12703	15 5	76 59	Stupendous wall of mountains, rising abruptly from low lands, like a terrace, a vast level, and fertile plains.
Cuddapah	12752	14 32	78 54	
Nellore	7478	15 0	80 0	Picturesque even to the sea, groups of small hills, &c.
Arcot	13620	12 14	79 22	Varied surface, mountainous to the North, clothed with verdure.
Chingleput	3020	12 46	80 0	Includes Madras, low, with large masses of granite in a sandy soil.
Salem	7593	11 37	78 13	To N. 5000 feet above the sea, 3 divisions of hills, the last table land.
Coimbatore	8392	11 0	77 20	Undulating table land, 900 feet high; to the N. 6000 feet, Neilgheries.
Trinchinopoly	3169	11 0	78 10	More elevated, waving valleys, and abrupt eminences.
Tanjore	3872	10 11	79 11	Delta of Cauvery one flat sheet of rice cultivation to the East.
Madura	7656	9 11	78 30	Flat to S. and E., hilly and mountainous, N. & W. forests, fertile valleys.
Tinnivelly	5590	8 10	78 0	Ridge of mountains W. open country to the sea, few hills, rivers.
Malabar	4900	10 12	76 0	200 miles sea-coast, low hills, separated by narrow valleys from W. Ghauts.
Canara	7477	12 15	75 0	180 miles ditto, rocky and mountainous, W. Ghauts.
Bombay Presidency.				
Conkan, N. & S.	12270	16 20	74 0	225 miles along sea, congeries of steep mountains, 2 to 4000 feet Ghauts.
Dharwar	9122	15 16	75 0	Elevated to the W. isolated eminences, flat summits.
Poonah	20870	18 30	74 2	Irregular and intersected by many rivers, fertile valleys.
Kandeish	12430	20 22	75 0	Interspersed with low hills to S., and numerous streams.
Surat	1449	20 21	73 0	Hilly and jungly to the E. and S. flat to N. and along the coast fertile.
Baroach	1351	21 22	73 14	Flat, well cultivated and peopled along the Gulph.
Kairah	1850	22 23	72 18	Intersected by the Karee river, level, well watered, good soil.
Ahmedabad	4072			
Kattywar	1728	22 30	72 0	Unequal hills, jungles, and reddish rocks, rude coast.

CHAPTER VII.

PHYSICAL ASPECT OF BRITISH INDIA—AREA AND GEOGRAPHY OF EACH PROVINCE—MOUNTAINS—RIVERS AND LAKES—PRINCIPAL CITIES—TOWNS, &c.

No language would do justice to the varied and magnificent scenery of Hindostan, partaking as it does of the richly luxuriant and wildly beautiful; *here* interterminable plains, intersected with deep and mighty rivers: *there* inaccessible mountains, whose unmeasurable summits are wreathed in eternal snow;—on the one hand an almost boundless landscape, verdant with the softness of perpetual spring—on the other alpine *steppes*, ruggedly romantic, and fringed with vast and towering forests: mountainous ranges or ghauts on *this shore*, presenting a stupendous barrier to the Indian ocean,—while on *that*, a low and sandy alluvium seems to invite the further encroachments of the deep and stormy Bengal Bay. Indeed the features of British India are so varied that, although despairing to convey an exact idea of their peculiarities, I must distinguish the country by provinces, as offering the most simple mode of delineating this immense section of the British empire, whose sea-coast line (extending from Cape Negrais to the frontiers of Sinde) is 3622 English miles, with a territorial breadth (from Surat to Sinde) of 1260 miles: premising, however, that the leading geographical features are the Himalaya Mountains, along the northern and eastern frontier; a range of ghauts, rising at the southern point of the peninsula, running north along the coast until receding at the parallels of 20° to 22°, when they branch off in ridges of different elevations across the continent of India, until lost in the table land of Malwa and Allahabad; while on the eastward the mighty *Ganges,* and on the westward the nearly equal *Indus,* roll their impetuous and lengthened torrents from the Himalaya snows to the sultry coasts of Bengal and Cutch, giving off in their progress an infinity of tributaries, which are ramified in every possible direction over the whole peninsula.

Physical Aspect of the Bengal Presidency.—Although it might be naturally supposed that in a territory extending over so great an extent of surface as that of the province of Bengal, a diversity of physical aspect would exist, there is with few exceptions a remarkable monotony of scenery. The province of Bengal proper, containing 100,000 square miles, has scarcely a hill of any elevation, and the few eminences which are to be found are confined to a small area on the eastern boundary.

No country in the world is better irrigated than this flat alluvial province, which has long been considered the granary of India; the Ganges, Brahmaputra, Hooghly, Teesta, Roopnarain, Dummoodah. Kooram, Korotoya, Cosi, Manas, Conki, and Jhinaya, with their innumerable tributaries, everywhere intersect Bengal, and owing to the lowness of the river banks, and those banks being composed of a sandy, *clayey soil,* large streams are frequently changing their beds, and causing stagnant marshes of considerable extent, by which the boundaries of property are annihilated, and the erection of stable edifices materially impeded.

The province of Bahar, containing 54,714 square miles, situate between 22° and 27° north latitude, is, with the exception of the northern division (which is an uninterrupted flat), a beautiful hill and dale country; the former extending in ranges, and in some places, as at the Rajmahal hills in the neighbourhood of Boglipoor, assuming the features of a celtic region. The soil is fertile, unless where saltpetre is in excess, but the province, it may be supposed, is not so well watered as Bengal; it is only, however, in tracts south of the Ganges, where artificial irrigation is much required. The principal rivers are the Ganges, Sone, Gunduck, Dummodah, Caramnassa, and Dewah.

The province of Allahabad (including the rich district of Benares[1], is in the neighbourhood of the

[1] Benares, or the Holy City, stands upon the northern bank of the Ganges, where the sinuosity of the sacred river forms a magnificent semicircle, of which its site occupies the external curve. The ground upon which it stands is considerably elevated, particularly towards the centre, from which point the rows of buildings descend in terraces, like the seats of an amphitheatre, to the water's edge. From the opposite shore, which is low and level, and projects itself inward between the horns of the half moon, the whole of this vast city, studded with innumerable pagan temples of remarkable beauty, and crowned by a lofty Mahommedan mosque, may be viewed at a single glance, rising, stair above stair, on the circular slope of the hill, or reflected with all its grandeur in the broad glassy surface of the Ganges. But, like Constantinople, and almost every other Oriental city, the interior of Benares falls very far short

great rivers Ganges and Jumna, flat, well watered, and exuberantly fertile; but to the south-west the

of what the picturesque beauty of its external appearance would seem to promise. The streets are crooked and dirty; and the houses, though in many cases six stories high, and built of stone, lose, by the narrowness of the streets, much of the effect which their bold irregular architecture is well calculated to produce.

"The number of temples," says Bishop Heber *, "is very great, mostly small, and stuck like shrines in the angles of the streets, and under the shadow of the lofty houses. Their forms, however, are not ungraceful, and there are many of them entirely covered over with beautiful and elaborate carvings of flowers, animals, and palm branches, equalling in minuteness and richness the best specimens that I have seen of Gothic or Grecian architecture. The material of the building is a very good stone from Chunar, but the Hindoos here seem fond of painting them a deep red colour, and indeed of covering the more conspicuous parts of their houses with paintings in gaudy colours of flower-pots, men, women, bulls, elephants, gods and goddesses, in all their many-formed, many-headed, many-handed, and many-weaponed varieties. The sacred bulls devoted to Siva, of every age, tame and familiar as mastiffs, walk lazily up and down these narrow streets, or are seen lying across them, and hardly to be kicked up (any blows, indeed, given them must be of the gentlest kind, or woe be to the profane wretch who braves the prejudices of this fanatic population), in order to make way for the Tonjon. Monkeys, sacred to Hanuman, the divine ape who conquered Ceylon for Râma, are in some parts of the town equally numerous, clinging to all the roofs and little projections of the temples, putting their impertinent heads and hands into every fruiterer's and confectioner's shop, and snatching the food from the children at their meals. Fakirs' houses, as they are called, occur at every turn, adorned

* Narrative of a Journey, &c. vol. i. pp. 272, 273.

country becomes more elevated, and in the Bundlecund district assumes the form of table land diversified with hills. The principal rivers are the two before-mentioned and the Goomty and Caramnassa, with their numberless branches. A canal, seventy-five miles long, is now being executed between the Goomty and Ganges. The territory under the sway of the King of Oude is here situate, amounting to 21,000 square miles, with a population of 6,000,000, spread over one of the most fertile parts of India, but immersed in poverty and wretchedness. The capital is termed Lucknow, built on the Goomty, (a branch of the Ganges) in latitude 26° 51′ north, longitude 80° 50′ east, and with its numerous gilded cupolas, minarets, turrets, arches, temples, and pinnacles, presenting an extraordinary picture of oriental magnificence. Its population is nearly half a million, whose mean and filthy tenements present a melancholy contrast to the splendid palaces and temples of their rulers and priests. Constantia, the residence of the late General Claude Martin, by whom it was built, at a cost of 150,000*l.*, stands in the neighbourhood. Lucknow contains a mixture of enterprising adventurers from various parts of Europe, who expect and

with idols, and sending out an unceasing tinkling and strumming of vinas, biyals, and other discordant instruments; while religious mendicants of every Hindoo sect, offering every conceivable deformity, which chalk, cow-dung, disease, matted locks, distorted limbs, and disgusting and hideous attitudes of penance can show, literally line the principal streets on both sides."

generally obtain employment from the king; it is distant 650 miles, by the nearest road, from Calcutta.

Bundlecund presents in its physical features a remarkable configuration; the mountains run in continuous ranges parallel to each other, each successively supporting a table land one above the other. *Bindhyáchal*, the first of these ranges, commences at *Kesóghar*, five miles north of *Sëunda* on the *Sindhe* River, making a circuitous sweep by *Narawá*, *Chandri*, *Hirapur*, *Rajghar*, *Ajeyghar*, and *Calanjara*; they cease near Barghar to belong to Bundlecund, and continue their course by *Bindhyavasini* and *Tárá*, until they approach the Ganges at *Surajghara*, and again at *Rajmahl*. Nothing, says Captain Franklin, can be more striking as a topographical feature than the plains of Bundlecund, which resemble a vast bay of the ocean formed by these natural barriers, crowned with the fortresses above-mentioned; and what is somewhat remarkable, the progressive elevation of the soil from the bed of the Jumna is towards the apex of this bay: hence the diminished altitude of the range at that point, being scarcely 300 feet above the surface, whilst at *Calyanghar* the same range is 800 feet. The most elevated summit does not exceed 2000 feet above the ocean level. The picturesque, numerous, and isolated hills which appear to stand alone and unconnected with other mountains, are portions of ranges which alternately appear and disappear, sometimes in the form of isolations and sometimes in continuous ranges; but they all radiate from the apex of the bay as if from a common centre, and diverge from it like the sticks of a fan. *Panna*, the second parallel range, preserves a distance of ten miles from summit to summit. The *Baudair*, or parallel range, is the most elevated portion of the province, and its contour describes in miniature the greater curves of the lower ranges, as if it were the nucleus on which they were formed. The range resembles an acute spherical triangle, the apex of which is near *Nagaund*, the area being table land, and the sides of the triangle having their abrupt faces outwards. This range gives rise to the *Ken* and *Patni* rivers. The *Kaïmur*, or *Vindhyana* mountains do not properly belong to Bundlecund, but they run parallel to the foregoing ranges, and form part of the tropical zone of mountains which run across India, a tract which comprises several ranges nearly parallel. The vast province of Allahabad, as also those of Agra and Delhi, are divided into collectorates, the territories under which have an area of 66,510 square miles.

Agra province, situate between 25° and 28° north latitude, extending in length 250 miles, and in breadth 180 miles, is to the north-east flat, open, and rather bare of trees, but hilly and jungly to the south, and rather more so on approaching the western frontier, with hills of various elevations in the north-west. The soil, dry and sandy, is but imperfectly watered by nature, deep wells and canals affording the chief supply of the indispensable element of cultivation. The principal rivers (which become smaller as they approach their source) are the Ganges, Jumna, Chumbul, Sinde, and Kohary.

Agra, built on the south-west of the Jumna, latitude 27° 11′ north, longitude 77° 53′ east, is a large and strongly constructed fort, of a red kind of very hard sandstone, quarried at Futtehpoor (nineteen miles distant): the fosse is of great depth with double ramparts, the inner one being sixty feet above the level of the river: well constructed bastions are placed at regular intervals, and the fortress is one of the keys of Western India, particularly from its commanding the navigation of the Jumna, which in the month of June is half a mile broad, and never fordable at any time at this spot. The moslem buildings in the fort are numerous and splendid, in particular the Tauje Mehal, built of marble resembling Carara, the Mootee Musjeed, or pearl mosque, built of small white marble, of singular purity of design: the great Chowk contiguous to the principal gate of the fort, the tomb of Etimaund ud Dowlah, &c., all attest the splendour with which the Mahomedans sought to captivate the weak minds of their Hindoo serfs, well knowing that, owing to the infirmity of our nature, regal pomp and magnificence often reconciles a feeble race to the despotism of foreign conquerors. The Moslems in Spain, as well as in India, expended the taxes of their subjects in erecting splendid structures, which, after the lapse of centuries, remain as monuments of the daring genius of the conquerors, and of the slavish submission of the conquered. The imperial palace, which has been denominated one of the finest edifices in Asia, was erected by the emperor Akbar. Like the city it is in the form of a crescent, and stands on the edge of the river, with a terrace in front, reaching down to the water's edge: here, during the flourishing days of Agra, pleasure boats and barges were unceasingly pouring forth their motley crews. The great square of the palace, planted with rows of plantain trees, and surrounded by a beautiful gallery, was adorned by six triumphal arches, which served as the entrance to six noble streets. Along the facade of the palace ran two immense galleries, adorned with twenty-four columns of white marble, springing from pedestals of blue granite, and terminating in capitals of yellow mica. Of the interior, as it exists at present, Bishop Heber says, " The hall, now used as the Dewanny Aum, or public court of justice, is a splendid edifice, supported by pillars and arches of white marble, as large and more nobly simple than that of Delhi. The ornaments, carving, and mosaic of the smaller rooms, in which was formerly the *zenánah*, or ladies' apartments, are equal or superior to any thing which is described as found in the Alhambra. The view from these rooms is very fine; at the same time that there are some adapted for the hot winds, from which light is carefully excluded. This suite is lined with small mirrors in fantastic frames; a cascade of water, also surrounded with mirrors, has been made to gush from a recess at the upper end, and marble channels beautifully inlaid with cornelians, agates, and jaspers, convey the stream to every side of the apartment.

The census of the city of Agra has been lately estimated as follows: houses 29,788, viz. Pukha, 25,536, and Kutcha, 4952; inhabitants, 96,597, viz. Hindoos, 65,011 (males, 35,085, females, 29,983),

Moosoolmans, 31,579 (males, 16,059, females, 15,520[1]).

Delhi, 800 feet above the ocean level (embracing the north part of the inclined slope which forms the plains of Hindostan, extending from the Himalaya to the Bay of Bengal), between 28° and 31° north latitude, is more hilly and sandy than Agra; it is level in the centre, clear and cultivated in the south-west, hilly in the north-west, and covered with dense jungles and forests; the chief rivers are the Ganges, Jumna, Caggur, and Chitting; but the thirsty soil soon imbibes the greater part of their contents in the dry season; Bareilly excepted, which is level and well watered.

Delhi, the ancient capital of the Patan and Mogul empires, latitude 28° 41′ north, longitude 77° 5′ east, according to popular tradition, covered a space of twenty square miles, and the ruins at present occupy nearly as great an extent. The new city of Delhi was founded by the Emperor Shah Jehanabad, in 1631, on the west bank of the Jumna; it is about seven miles in circumference; the walls are faced along their whole extent with substantial masonry constructed of huge blocks of sparkling granite; martello towers stand at intervals, flanking the defences, and the city has seven gates all built of freestone. The principal street, leading from the palace to the city gate, is 1100 yards long and 30 broad; the second, leading from the palace to the Lahore gate, is

[1] A similar census ought to be prepared for every town in India.

a mile long by 40 yards broad. Until 1011 A.D. Delhi was governed by Hindoo Rajahs, but in that year Mahmoud the Ghaznivede captured and plundered it, but subsequently restored it to the Hindoo Rajah, making him a tributary prince. In 1193, Cuttub ud Deen, the slave of Mahomed Ghauri, took final possession of the city from the Hindoos, and commenced the series of Afghan or Patan sovereigns, which reigned until the invasion of Baber, the grandson of Timour. It was pillaged by Timour in 1398, and in 1516, Sultan Baber finally overthrew the Patan, and founded the Mogul dynasty; the descendant of whom, after fourteen sovereigns intermediate, now resides in Delhi as a nominal prince, without a shadow of power, but enjoying a yearly income of nearly 150,000*l*. During the era of its splendour, Delhi is said to have covered a space of twenty square miles, and in fact its ruins are at this day very little less in extent. What its population may have amounted to, when it was the capital of the Mogul empire, cannot now be ascertained[1]. Hamilton is of opinion

[1] In the time of Bernier, Delhi was doubtless a magnificent city. 'Whatever Asia could furnish of barbaric pomp or gorgeous show, was there collected together, and disposed with as much taste as Mogul or Persian art could give birth to. Domes of vast circumference and fantastic swell crowned the summits of the mosques, and towered above the other structures of the city; palaces, cool, airy, grotesque, with twisted pillars, balustrades of silver, and roofs of fretted gold; elephants moving their awkward and cumbrous bulk to and fro, disguised in glittering housings, and surmounted with golden howdahs; and gardens shaded and perfumed by the most splendid trees and

that the number does not exceed two hundred thousand. The modern city contains many magnificent ruins, and a great number of mosques still in good preservation; of which the principal is the Jumna Musjeed, erected by the Emperor Shah Jehan. But the great ornament of Delhi is the imperial palace, constructed of red granite, in a beautiful style of architecture. Its interior is adorned with gold, azure, and other splendid ornaments. The stables were erected to contain ten thousand horses. In the vast suburbs of Delhi, among other striking buildings, is the *Godaïe Kotelar*, the principal apartment of which, called the "Hall of Embassies," was lined throughout with crystal, and adorned with a lustre of black crystal, exquisitely wrought, which, when lighted up, caused the apartment to present on all sides the appearance of a conflagration. In this hall a peacock throne was still preserved in the time of Legoux de Flaix[1], wholly different from that described by Bernier, and which was carried away by Nadir Shah[2].

sweetest flowers of Asia: such were the principal features of Delhi.'—*Lives of Celebrated Travellers*, vol. i. p. 204.

[1] Essais sur l'Indoustan, tom. i. p. 193.

[2] 'Il y avait," says the historian of Nadir, " entre autres (trésors) un trône en forme de paon, qui sembloit renfermer tous les trésors de Kaikavus et les richesses de Dekianous, et dont les joyaux dans les temps des anciens empereurs des Indes étoient évalués à deux crores, chaque crore (selon la computation Indienne) valant cent mille lacs, et chaque lac cent mille roupies. Il y avoient de plus des perles si parfaites et des diamans si brillans, qu'on n'avait jamais vu de semblables dans les trésors d'aucun monarque du monde; et le tout fut transporté dans celui de Nadir Chah.' Works of Sir

It was of an oval form, and placed under a palm-tree, which overshadowed it with its foliage. A peacock perched upon a branch near the summit extended its wings like a canopy over the throne. Both the palm-tree and the peacock were of gold, and the wings and leaves so delicately and exquisitely formed, that they appeared to wave and tremble at the slightest breeze. The rich green of the peacock's feathers was represented by superb emeralds; and the fruit of the palm-tree, formed of brilliant Golconda diamonds, mimicked nature so admirably, that the observer might easily have been tempted to pluck them.

The gardens of the Shalimar, a mile in circumference, formed by Shah Jehan at an expense of one million sterling, are now, like all his other works, in ruins; and from these the view southward, as far as the eye can reach, is covered with the wreck of mosques, pavilions, and tombs, all desolate and decayed. About nine miles south of Delhi stands the Kuttub Minar, a remarkable column, two hundred and forty-two feet high. Four balconies sweep round the pillar at different heights from the ground, and an irregular spiral staircase leads to the summit, which is crowned with a majestic cupola of red granite. It seems to have been intended as a minaret to a

William Jones, vol. ix. p. 459. 'The throne was supported upon six large feet of massive gold, set with rubies, emeralds, and diamonds. But its principal ornaments were two peacocks, whose feathers were imitated by a crest of pearls and jewels. The real value of this throne could not be exactly ascertained, but it was estimated at four crores, or forty millions of rupees.' —*Lives of Celebrated Travellers*, vol. i. p. 202.

stupendous mosque never completed, and was erected about six hundred years ago by the Afghan Emperor Kuttub Shah, whose tomb, a humble and inconsiderable building[1], stands a few hundred yards to the west of it. Kuttub Shah died in A.D. 1210. Delhi is distant from Calcutta, by the Birboom road, 976 miles.

The British provinces in Berar are wild, rugged, and hilly, with steep water-courses, dense jungles, and impassable ravines; their area is 55,900 square miles, and they are but little explored. Hussingabad, the key to the British possessions in this quarter, is situate south of the Nerbudda river, latitude 22° 40′ north, longitude 77° 51′ east, 135 miles north-west of Nagpoor. The romantic valley of the Nerbudda, formed by the Vindhyana range of hills on one side, and the Gundwana on the other, extends in length from Gurry Mundelah to Hindia through a space of nearly 300 miles; the distance from one mountain chain to the other being on an average from fifteen to twenty miles, and the river holding its course through the valley more to the north or Malwa side. The aspect of the valley (with the exception of the middle part) is rude and uncultivated in the extreme; forests of deep jungle extending on both sides, and rising to the summits of the adjoining hills. The soil consists of a dark, coarse earth, denominated

[1] Asiatic Researches, vol. iv. pp. 223—228. Tieffenthaler speaks of the tomb as that of "a Mohammedan hypocrite," tom. i. p. 132. Bishop Heber, describing the Kuttub Minar, observes, "it is really the finest tower I have ever seen, and must, when its spire was complete, have been still more beautiful."—*Narrative*, &c. vol. ii. p. 307.

regur or cotton soil, the product of decomposed trap and amygdaloids, which must have existed in great abundance in these districts. The source of the Nerbudda river (which performs a known journey of 700 miles) is not yet explored. The natives say it rises in Omerkuntuck in Gundwana, 2463 feet above the sea, close to the source of the Sone; it has fewer curvations than most India rivers, but its passage is obstructed by rocks and shallows and beautiful cataracts. At Hussingabad the bed of the Nerbudda is much broken, and about 900 yards broad; but there are thirteen fords within fourteen miles of the town.

The Malwah territory belonging to Britain occupies upwards of 8000 square miles, and is situated on an elevated plateau, averaging 2000 feet above the level of the sea, diversified by conical but table-crowned hills and low ridges, watered with numerous streams, which flow over a deep, rich black soil of unsurpassed productiveness.

The great province of Ajmere, or Rajast'han, is bounded on the north by Lahore, on the east by Delhi and Agra, on the south by Malwah and Guzerat, and on the west by Mooltan. It is about three hundred and fifty miles in length, and about two hundred miles upon an average in breadth. Rajast'han is the collective and classical denomination of that portion of India which is "the abode of princes." Its surface is exceedingly varied. From the summit of Mount Aboo (which, after the Himâlaya, is one of the most elevated spots in Hindostan), the eye glances from the blue waters of the Indus on the west, to the withy-covered Betwah on the east. In this latter direction is the chain of the Aravulli hills, stretching north and south throughout the whole length of Rajpootana, from the Vindhya mountains to the confines of Delhi, and dividing Mewar and the other mountainous districts of eastern Ajmere from Marwar and the sandy deserts of the west. The Aravulli mountains, which, for scenes of savage grandeur, rival or surpass the western Ghauts, repose upon a basis of nearly sixty miles in breadth. From the Aravulli, eastward, the country is a lofty table-land, or rather a succession of steppes, resembling those of Tartary. At Rinthumboor the plateau breaks into lofty ranges, their whole summits sparkling in the sun; cragged, but not peaked, and preserving the characteristic formation, though disunited from the mass. Distinguished as is this elevated region in the surface of Central India, its summit is but little higher than the general elevation of the Vindhya, and upon a level with the valley of Oodipoor and base of the Aravulli. The slope or descent, therefore, from both these ranges to the skirts of the plateau, is great and abrupt, of which the most intelligible and simple proof appears in the course of these streams. Few portions of the globe attest more powerfully the force exerted by the action of waters to subdue every obstacle, than a view of the rock-bound channels of the streams in this adamantine barrier. Four streams, one of which, the Chumbul, would rank with the Rhine and almost with the Rhone, have here forced their way, laying bare the stratification from the water's level to the summit, from 300 to 600 feet in height perpendicular, the rock appearing as if chiselled by the hand of man[1].

KUMAON PROVINCE.—Mr. Trail, the commissioner for the affairs of Kumaon, says, that Kumaon, with the annexed territory of Gerhwal, forms an almost equilateral parallelogram facing north-east and south-west. On the north, where separated from Tartary by the Himalaya, the frontier extends from longitude 79° 51′, latitude 31° 4′, to longitude 80° 45′, latitude 30° 10′, giving a line of about 100 miles: the east boundary, which is formed by the river Kali or Sarde, gives a line of 110 miles, extending from latitude 30° 10′, longitude 80° 45′, to latitude 26° 2′, longitude 80°. On the west the province is divided from the Raj of Gherwal by the rivers Kali and Alakananda, with a line of frontier of about 110 miles, stretching from latitude 31° 4′, longitude 78° 10′, and on the south the province joins on Rohilcund, the line of demarcation being nearly parallel and equal to that on the north. Within the boundaries above detailed the horizontal superficies of the province is about 10,967 square miles, of which there are

Snow $\frac{4}{15}$—2924 sq. miles. Cultivated $\frac{3}{15}$—2193 sq. miles.
Barren $\frac{5}{15}$—3655 sq. miles. Uncultivated $\frac{3}{15}$—2193 sq. miles.

The whole province is numerous ranges of mountains, the general run of which are in a parallel direction to the north and south line of position. The peaks and ridges necessarily vary in height; commencing from the plains of Rohilcund (500 feet

[1] Colonel Tod.

above the level of the sea), the first mountain range gives an elevation of 4300 feet, while the second range, the Ghagar, attains 7700 feet. The intervals between the mountains are extremely small, and the whole country, when viewed from a commanding position, exhibits the appearance of a wide expanse of unconnected ravines rather than a succession of regular chains of mountains. The valleys (if the narrow interstices between the mountains merit such an appellation) are lowest on the banks of the largest rivers, and it is in the same situations that the greatest portion of level land is generally to be met with. These spots, however, in no instance exceed, and in few cases equal, half a mile in breadth. The site of the town of Shrinagur, latitude 30° 14′ north, longitude 78° 37′ east, on the banks of the Alakananda, is of this description, and is only 1500 feet above the level of the sea. The *tarai* or forest land of saul, sissoo, and bamboos, included in the province, is very unequal in extent. Under the Gherwal pergunnas it averages only from two to three miles from the foot of the hills, while in Kumaon Proper it is nowhere less than twelve or fifteen miles broad. From Kotedwara, longitude 78° 20′ to near Bhamouri, longitude 79° 20′, the *tarai* is divided from Rohilcund by a low range of hills, which contain numerous passes, some practicable for wheel carriages; the remainder is wholly open to the plains. Where there is sufficient soil the sides of the mountains are cut in terraces (supported in front by slight stone abutments, as in Ceylon and in Italy) rising above each other in regular succession. There are several lakes, but of no great extent; the depth, however, is considerable (some in the higher Himalaya are stated to be *unfathomable*) and the base of every mountain has a stream of more or less magnitude flowing silently or rapidly according to the elevation of the country. The country about Almorah (latitude 29° 24′ north, longitude 79° 39′ east, built on a ridge of mountains 5400 feet above the level of the sea) is extremely bleak and naked. Mr. Trail has furnished a very interesting paper in the seventh volume of the Transactions of the Asiatic Society of Bengal, on the Bhotia Mehals (districts) of Kumaon, Bhot signifying that part of the Himalaya range which once formed about a third part of the Tibet province of Bhot, fifteen parts of which consist of snow or barren rocks: the minimum elevation in the passes of the Himalaya is here 6000 feet above the sea. These tracks or paths are along branches of the Ganges and Goggra, and roads of communication through the Himalaya unite the passes from east to west; but they are buried in snow, except for a few days in the year. The interior of the Himalaya mountains (of which a full account will be found in a subsequent page), except at these passes and paths, is almost inaccessible, and they are becoming daily more and more so. The Bhotias now point out ridges never free from snow, which, within the memory of man, were clothed with forests, and afforded periodical pastures for sheep.

The kingdom of Nepaul is one of the most interesting divisions of Hindostan. To the north it is separated from Tibet by the Himalaya mountains; on the south bounded by the British territories in the provinces of Delhi, Oude, Bahar, and Bengal (with the exception of about sixty miles intervening, which belong to Oude); to the east, the Nepaulese territories are separated from those of the British by the river Mitchie; from thence to the Himalaya mountains they are bounded by the principality of Sikhim, which stretches north to the Chinese frontier; to the west the limits are accurately defined by the course of the river Cali (the western branch of the Goggra), beyond which is the British district of Kumaon. The lowest part of the ancient Nepaul kingdom, stretched into the great plain of Hindostan; the great valley of Nepaul whose northernmost boundary lies about 27° 50′ north latitude, is twenty-two miles from east to west, and twenty miles from north to south. Nepal in its extreme length may be estimated at four hundred and sixty, and its breadth at one hundred and fifteen miles. This singular country consists of three parallel belts, of which the first, about twenty miles in breadth, is a portion of the Gangetic plain. Next succeeds a region of nearly the same width, consisting of a series of small hills rising behind each other like a succession of terraces, until the more elevated gradually unite with the more lofty mountains of the Himâlaya. Through the rocky valleys or chasms which separate these hills, numerous streams, springing from the southern faces of the mountains, descend and spread fertility and verdure throughout the country. Magnificent forests of *saul* (Shorea robusta), mingled with *sisoo* (Dalbergia sisoo) and *toon* (Cederela toona) trees, stretch along the declivities of the minor eminences for a considerable distance into the adjacent plains. As you ascend, the forests exhibit a greater variety, gradually putting on more and more of Alpine features, as the sombre pine mingles more freely with the mimosa and other trees of the plain. Parrots, parroquets, and many other species of birds, abound in these woods, and are caught and taught to speak by the natives, who export them into Bengal, as the inhabitants of the Tyrol export Canary birds to all parts of Europe. Between the hills and the Himâlaya fine cultivated valleys are sometimes met with; but, though fertile, they are generally neglected on account of their extreme unhealthiness. Some of these wild glens produce rattans and bamboos of enormous dimensions; in others nothing but pines and oaks are found, while a third class ripen the pine-apple and the sugar-cane. Others again produce barley, millet, and many similar grains. Peaches grow wild by every rill, but never ripen; and the vines, requiring more care than is bestowed upon them, produce but inferior grapes. But the orange, which ripens in winter, is found in the greatest perfection in Nepaul. Ginger, cardamoms, and grain of every kind are abundant. Cat'hmandoo, the capital, stands on the east bank of the Bishenmutty, 4,784 feet above the plains of Bengal. It is of inconsiderable extent. The most remarkable objects it contains are a great number of wooden temples, which as well as those constructed of brick, appear to be in the Chinese style of architecture, with three or four sloping roofs. None but the priests and princes are admitted within the shrine. The houses are three or four stories high, an indication that earthquakes are not frequent; and the streets, which are exceedingly narrow, rival those of Benares in filth. The population may amount to about 20,000.

The principality of Sikkim, a small and little explored province, lying between Nepâl and Bhotan, is situated entirely among the hills; and its productions, both vegetable and mineral, entirely resemble those of Nepâl. "According to native authorities," says Hamilton, "there are on the Konki two marts, named Bilasi and Majhoya, to which the traders from the plains carry rice, salt, extract of sugar-cane, hogs, dry fish, tobacco, spirituous liquors, and various cloths. Before the Ghorkha conquest they also took oxen for the slaughter; but that tribe, being Hindoos, prohibited such sacrilege. The traders procured in return from the mountaineers cotton, Indian madder, musk, and Tibet cow and bull tails. At Dimali, on the Balakongyar river, there is a mart or custom-house, consisting of a square surrounded by buildings, into which the merchants and their commodities are received, there being no other dwellings except those of the collector and his assistants. To this place the dealers from the low-country take up salt, tobacco, cotton cloths, goats, fowls, swine, iron, and occasionally broad-cloth; and in return bring back mungeet or Indian rubber, cotton, bees' wax, blankets, horses, musk, cow and bull tails, Chinese flowered silk, and rhinoceroses' horns[1].

The city of Sikkim stands on the west bank of the

[1] Description of Hindostan, vol. II. p. 270, 271.

Jamikuma river, which rises on the south side of the Snowy mountains, and, opposite to the town, separates into two branches, that flow round an immense mountain, upon the summit of which there is a stronghold named Tasidong.

The river Tista, which comes from the mountains in about 88° 32′ east longitude from Greenwich, divides Sikkim from the territory of Bhotan, a mountainous tract, situated like Nepâl on the southern declivity of the Himâlaya chain; the highest part of which separates it from Tibet and the Chinese empire. The country is about 240 English miles in length, from east to west; the width of Bhotan Proper does not probably exceed forty or fifty miles. South from that is a hilly, but lower tract of perhaps ten or fifteen miles in width, which is occupied by Cachharis, Mech, and other rude tribes; and south from thence is a plain, which in different parts varies from ten to twenty miles in width, and which is chiefly occupied by Coch or Rajbangsis. The inhabitants, called Bhoteas, are Buddhists. A person who is considered as an incarnation of God, and who is named Dharma-Raja, is their nominal head, but the government is carried on by the Deva-Raja, his vicegerent. Let us now turn to view the

Sea Coast of the Bengal Presidency, and the territories to the east and southward. The sea coast of Bengal province is, for many miles, scarcely elevated above the level of the sea, and where the sacred Ganges and mighty Burrampooter, with their hundred mouths, rush to join the parent fountain, a vast extent of country (30,000 square miles) called the *Sunderbunds*, extending for 180 miles along the bay of Bengal, is an interminable labyrinth of salt water lakes, rivers, and creeks, interspersed with mangrove islets of shifting mounds of sand and mud.

CALCUTTA, on the banks of the Hooghly, latitude 22° 23′, longitude 88° 28′, distant from the sea 100 miles, and from the *Sandheads* about 130 miles, has a very intricate navigation through the banks of the sand and mud which occasionally shift their beds in the Hooghly river as well as in the other branches of the Ganges [1]. It is, however, very favourably situated for internal navigation, as the Ganges and its subsidiary streams permit the transport of foreign produce to the north-west quarters of Hindostan over a distance of upwards of 1000 miles, and the day may not be far distant when the Indus and the Ganges navigation will be united by a canal. Diamond har-

[1] In 1829, the author when sailing on the Hooghly off Chandernagore, tried the depth of water at various periods, and did not find sufficient to float a four hundred ton ship. The whole channel of the Hooghly is shoaling fast, and the other embouchures of the Ganges are deepening. There is a native prophecy, that the Ganges (or Hooghly, which is merely a name for a branch of that mighty river) will flow over the spot where Calcutta with its million and a half of inhabitants now dwell; and certainly, to stand at Chandpaul Ghaut, and watch the rising of the river in the rains almost to a level with the houses on the 'Strand,' one would think the prophecy on the eve of fulfilment. If the waters ever pass the strand road banks, the whole city is lost, for they would overwhelm it in joining the low salt water lake at the opposite extremity of the metropolis.

bour, about thirty miles below Calcutta on the east bank of the Hooghly, has a draught of water sufficient for the largest Indiamen, but ships of 600 tons anchor quite close to the grand promenade (entitled the *Strand* road and *Esplanade*) of the 'City of Palaces.'

This metropolis and commercial emporium of the east (now containing *upwards of a million* of inhabitants), was so late as 1717 a small straggling village, with a few clusters of huts, to the number of ten or twelve, the inhabitants of which were husbandmen, endeavouring to reclaim the surrounding forests and swamps, which extended even to where Chandpal Ghaut now stands. The city is divided into streets at right angles with each other, with large and handsome squares throughout, particularly in the European part of the metropolis, each square having in its centre an extensive tank or reservoir of the Ganges water, with verdant sloping banks planted with evergreen shrubs. The residence of the Governor General is of equal magnitude to any palace in Europe. The country is indebted for its erection to the taste, munificence and patriotic spirit of the Marquis Wellesley. The architecture is of the Ionic order, with arcades all round on a rustic basement. The palace has four wings connected by circular passages, in order to secure a free admission of air from whatever quarter the wind may blow. The grand entrance is to the north, where there is an immense arch of steps, beneath which carriages drive up to set down; on the south side is a circular colonnade with a splendid dome. In the centre of the building are two magnificent state rooms, the lower paved with dark grey marble, supported by numerous Doric columns, resembling Parian marble; the upper or ball-room is floored with exquisitely polished dark grained woods, supported by beautiful Ionic pillars. The Vice-regal canopy and chairs of state are of light and beautiful construction. The apartments are lit by a profusion of cut glass lustres suspended from a painted ceiling with gold mouldings. The entrance gates are of a grand and imposing appearance, and the square around the palace is tastefully laid out. Several of the other public buildings, such as the Mint, Colleges, &c. are on a noble scale, and the private mansions are built in the fascinating style of Grecian architecture.

The stupendous fortification of Fort William was commenced by Lord Clive after the battle of Plassy, and has cost the East India Company 2,000,000*l.* sterling. Situated on the margin of the river Hooghly (about one-fourth of a mile below Calcutta), and on a level with the surrounding country, which is a perfect flat for many miles, it does not make an imposing appearance, indeed its strength is scarcely perceptible; nevertheless it is superior in strength and regularity to any fortress in India, and requires from 10,000 to 15,000 men to man the works. The form is octagon, five sides being regular and three next the river according to circumstances. The river flows up to the glacis, the citadel towards which has a large salient angle, the faces of which enfidale the whole sweep of the water; indeed the guns of the faces bear upon the city until crossed by the fire of the batteries parallel to the river. This salient angle is defended by several adjoining bastions and a counterscarp that covers them. The bastions on the five regular land sides have all many salient orillons, behind which are retired circular flanks extremely spacious, and an immense double flank at the height of the berme; the double flank would enable the besieged to retard the passage of the ditch, as from its form it cannot be enfiladed; the orillon is effective against ricochet shot, and is not to be seen from any parallel: the berme opposite the curtain serves as a road, and contributes to the defence of the ditch like a fausse-brave. The ditch is very wide and dry, with a cunette in the middle which receives the water of the ditch by means of two sluices that are commanded by the fort. The counterscarp and covered way are excellent; every curtain is covered by a large half moon without flanks, bonnet, or redoubt, but the faces each mount thirteen pieces of heavy ordnance, thus giving a defence of twenty-six guns to these ravelins. The demi-bastions which terminate the five regular fronts on each side are covered by a counterguard, of which the faces, like the half moons, are pierced with thirteen embrasures. These counterguards are connected with two redoubts constructed in the place of arms of the adjacent re-entering angles, the whole faced, and palisaded with great attention to neatness as well as strength. The advanced works are executed on an extensive scale, and the angles of the half moons being extremely acute, project a great way, so as to be in view of each other beyond the flanked angle of the polygon, and capable of taking the trenches in the rear at an early period of the approach. The interior of this admirable fortress is truly beautiful,—large grass-plots surrounded by rows of shady trees, beneath which are well gravelled promenades,—with here and there piles of balls, bombshells, and parks of artillery. The barracks are spacious, and will contain 20,000 men. The wells are numerous, and there is an immense reservoir for rain water. The church is of an elegant Saxon style of architecture with enamelled glass, and the residences of the commandants of corps, and the principal staff officers, on an extensive scale. For a quarter a mile round the fort no tree or house is permitted, and the ships pass so close to the fort that they may be hailed from the glacis.

Cuttack sea coast is similar to the contiguous Delta of Bengal (which closely resembles the Missisippi Delta) except that the flat shore does not extend more than from five to fifteen miles inland from the Black Pagoda to Piply on the *Subanrekha*, while that of the Sunderbunds extends nearly 200 miles. The town of Cuttack (latitude 20° 27′ north, longitude 88° 5′ east), 251 miles travelling distance from Calcutta, containing 6512 houses, and a population of 40,000 souls, is advantageously situated, politically and commercially speaking, on a tongue of land or peninsula near the bifurcation of the Mahanuddy river (which is here two miles across) with a pleasing and picturesque prospect from the environs of the hilly country of *Rajwarra*. The town is defended from the encroachments of the river by stone revetments which front two of its sides. Within from two to five leagues of the sea coast of Cuttack the land rises into swelling undulations, extending over a space of from fifteen to fifty miles, gradually becoming more elevated, when the surface assumes a hilly shape with a dry and fertile soil and magnificent forests of every description of timber. This hilly region, which is termed the Mogulbundy, has a soil of a whitish appearance, and often for miles the surface is strewed with a thin sprinkling of lime-stone concretions. This description of country extends from north of the Mahanuddy to Midnapore. The Mogulbundy is finely cultivated, and has a most picturesque aspect. At Balasore, (where the Dutch had a settlement in 1660) latitude 21° 32′, longitude 86° 56′ east, a group of fine hills of this district project forth to within fifteen miles of the shore of the Bay of Bengal. The principal rivers are the Mahanuddy, (which during the rains may be navigated 300 miles from the sea) Brahmini, Biturini, Solandy, Kausbans, Burabalang, Subanrekha, &c.

The Chilka lake, thirty-five miles long by eighteen wide, is separated from the sea for many miles by a narrow strip of land, or rather sand, sometimes not more than 300 yards broad. The native historians say it was formed by an irruption of the ocean at a period corresponding with the third century of the Christian era; it is scarcely more than five feet deep, and is filling up from the sand and mud brought into it by various streams. Cuttack however is but little known; the hilly region is said, by Mr. Hamilton, to reach as far west as Gundwana in Berar, in breadth probably 100 miles, in length 200 miles: the greatest height of the hills seen from the Mogulbundy, or central district, is supposed to be 2000 feet, their general elevation from 300 to 1200, chiefly of granite formation resembling sand-stone, and containing a variety of valuable minerals (rich iron ore is abundant) and curious precious stones. The rivers in the lowlands are embanked with immense bunds or mounds of earth, some sixty feet in breadth, and nearly twenty feet high, the necessity of which will be understood when it is known that in *one* night the Cajori river, one mile and a half broad and thirty or forty feet deep, rose in height *eighteen feet!* In the cultivated country the banks of the rivers are extremely picturesque. Mr. Stirling observes that the granite rocks of Cuttack are highly indurated and denuded of vegetation, presenting a bold and varied outline with frequent and sharp peaks and abrupt craggy faces; they are in many parts curiously intersected by trap veins, which seem to consist chiefly of green stone, approaching often to basalt and hornblende rock. In company with these rocks *talc* slate, *mica* slate, and chlorite schist passing into serpentine and pot stone are found in abundance. A variety of corundum and steatite in the shape of a remarkably pure white powder are plentiful. The British district comprises an area of 9000 square miles.

The maritime province of Arracan, situate between the 18° and 21° of north latitude, presents for a short distance from the sea an aspect similar to that of Bengal and Cuttack, but the ocean barrier being of a firm argillaceous nature with a limestone formation, exhibits, instead of an interminable marsh, a series of islands, peninsulas, and isthmuses, which are peopled and cultivated. About thirty miles inland, conical hills arise to the height of 500 feet, intersected by jeels (small lakes) or rivers, and about twenty miles further to the east a range of mountains from 2000 to 5000 feet high, run north and south nearly parallel with the sea-shore. The town of Arracan (latitude 20° 35′ north, longitude 93° 32′ east) distant, in a direct line from the sea, about fifty miles, has a navigable river running close up to it, and then dividing into several smaller branches which flow through the town in every direction. The average rise of tide is about eight feet, spring tides of course rise higher. Arracan bears north-east from the mouth of the river, and from the town are visible three distinct and parallel ranges of hills; the former being situate with respect to the general line of the first range nearly as the apex of a triangle to its base, but from the number of insulated hills and slight curvatures in the range, it appears nearly embayed in a recess of the hills. The height of the highest hill in the first range is 550 feet, and of the second and third ranges from 2000 to 4000 feet. The hills, generally speaking, are abrupt, and many of them insulated. About a quarter of a mile from the north-west angle of the fort, is a large lake, extending several miles among the hills, the structure of which latter is principally schistus, no granite having as yet been observed; the soil is luxuriantly rich, and beyond the hilly range is a magnificent champaign country, with navigable streams and particularly healthy.

The principal rivers of Arracan are the Mayoo, Kaladyne, Arracan, Monjee, and Lemonkrong: the Mayoo is the most northerly, and running in a south-west direction along the base of an extensive range of hills, empties itself into the bay a little to the north of the Arracan river. The largest river in the south division of the province is the Lemonkrong or Lembroo, which after a winding course to the north-west flows into the Bay of Bengal, among the numerous detached rocks which extend along the coast between Ramree and those high insulated hills to the north of the Arracan river called the Broken Islands. All the rivers to the south, and many to the north, are intimately connected with each other. The islands of Ramree and Cheduba (dependencies of Arracan) lie within the 19° north latitude. Ramree is mountainous and jungly, and separated from the mainland only by a creek; Cheduba is larger, more completely insulated, rather a low island, but dry and sandy; pretty free from jungle, and healthy. The little island of Aykab, at the mouth of the Arracan river is similar to Cheduba on a small scale.

The Assam territory, between 26° and 28° latitude, and 90° and 96° longitude, is formed of the valley of the Brahmaputra, which is about forty miles wide, by 150 long, bounded to the northward by the mountainous ranges of Bootan[1], Anka, Dophla, and Meree, and to the southward by the Garrow Hills. Lower Assam, comprehending 4100 square miles, is bounded on the north by the Bootan Mountains, on the south by the Garrow and Kossya Hills, on the west by Monass river, and on the east by Bissanath; it is a

[1] At the foot of these mountains there is a plain of thirty miles broad, clothed with most luxuriant vegetation, like the *taria.*

rich and valuable country; about sixty rivers flow through it, which have in general a sufficient depth at all seasons to admit of commercial intercourse. The soil is fertile and well watered; the rivers being numbered to the extent of twenty-six, the principal of which are the Brahmaputra, Dihong, Dibong, Dikho, and Dikrong. The Brahmaputra river is stated by some European authorities to have been traced to 25° 54′ north latitude, and longitude 25° 24′ east, when its navigation was impeded by a mass of rocks; its channel was then 150 yards across; the natives describe it as running easterly, and stated its sources to be the snowy mountains, from whence the Irrawaddy proceeds.

The country of Cachar is as yet little known. Southern Cachar, which is the most valuable part of it, contains about 2500 square miles of level land, generally from 200 to 300 feet above the sea, intersected by detached hills and low wooded ranges, and bounded on three sides by mountains, some of which have an altitude of 5000 or 6000 feet. The soil is eminently fertile, and has been found by experiment to be perfectly well adapted to the production of wheat, barley, gram, potatoes, tobacco, and sugar cane, as well as that of rice, kulaie, sursoo, &c. which latter alone are commonly raised. The population of Cachar is small, and out of all proportion to its extent, but it is very various, consisting of Cacharees, Bengalees, Munnipoorees, Assamese, Nagas and Kookies.

Cachar enjoys an uninterrupted water communication with Calcutta, besides which it will soon have the advantage of a high road, which is now in progress and more than half finished, by order of government, throughout the country, from Banskandee to the town of Sylhet, from which place it is to be hoped it will ultimately be prolonged either to Dacca or Commillah, and thus complete an interior line of communication along the whole frontier northwards from Arracan, which cannot fail to be of immense value in a commercial point of view, enabling also the government at any time easily to occupy in force the important pass which Cachar forms from Burmah, and which renders it in fact the gate of our possessions in the eastern part of Bengal.

The Ultra Gangetic provinces of Tavoy, Ye, and Tenasserim, ceded to the British after the Burmese war, form a strip of land on the eastern side of the Bay of Bengal, extending from latitude 10° 35′ north, to 15° 30′ north, 340 miles long, by an average breadth of forty-four miles, and embracing a surface of 15,000 square miles. The shore is full of creeks, rivers, and rocky islets, but it is not of the swampy nature of Bengal or Cuttack. The country is diversified with hill and dale, rising towards the Siamese Mountains on the eastward with ranges of hills, clothed with forests of teak shelving towards the sea, the valleys of which form conduits for the mountain streams.

The province of Martaban on the same line of coast as the preceding districts, extends from 15° 30′ to 16° 30′ north, comprehending a surface of about 6000 square miles, and its physical aspect bears a general resemblance to the contiguous provinces of

Tavoy, &c. Three large rivers, the Saluen, Gain, and Athran, rising in the eastern mountains of Siam, and navigable for small craft to a considerable distance from the ocean, join their embouchures in forming an expanse of water seven miles broad, opposite to Martaban, the chief town, which stands on the north or Burmese side of the river Saluen.

PHYSICAL ASPECT OF THE MADRAS PRESIDENCY.—The territories under the government of this presidency present no vast alluvial plains like the deltas of the Ganges, Jumna, and Burrampooter, nor is the sea coast of that marshy nature which characterises Bengal, Arracan, or Cuttack. The province of the Northern Circars on the west side of the bay of Bengal extends from 50° to 20° north latitude, comprising an area of 18,800 square miles. The coast, as viewed from sea-ward, appears mountainous to the beach; it has, however, a strip of sandy waste along its whole extent, stretching interiorly about three miles, when the land rises into detached hills, which separate the province from the Hydrabad territories. From Coringa to Nellore the shore is flat and sandy, as indeed it is throughout the lower Carnatic, extending 560 miles along the Bay of Bengal, as far as Cape Comorin, but from this point up the Malabar coast the aspect is totally different.

The southern part of the Asiatic peninsula is, within a few feet, as high as the extremity of the African peninsula at the Cape of Good Hope. At Cape Comorin the promontory begins to lessen in height a few miles from the sea, and as it approaches the ocean, runs out into a low green headland, something like Green Point at Table Bay. From Cape Comorin, through Dindigul and Tinnivelly, the scenery combines the magnificent and the beautiful: the mountains assume every varied form, and are clothed with stupendous forests, while the smaller hills, which skirt the plain, are here and there graced with temples and choultries, exhibiting exquisite specimens of architecture: winding streams flow from every hill, and the soft and lovely valleys are in striking contrast to the dark and mighty forests which overcap them.

The little State of Travancore, extending from the Cape 140 miles to the northward, by forty miles inland, presents along the sea-shore valleys clothed with perennial verdure; then a lovely and picturesque scene of hills and dales, the latter richly cultivated, while further inland are seen the gigantic western ghauts, crowned to their very summits with immense forests of teak, bamboo, &c., the *tout ensemble* forming the most splendid picture of tropical scenery to be witnessed in any part of the globe. Pondicherry, French factory, distant from Madras 100 miles, from Seringapatam 260, from Hydrabad 452, from Poona 707, from Nagpoor 773, from Calcutta 1130, and from Delhi 1400 miles, is now an insignificant settlement, on a sandy plain, not far from the sea shore, producing only palm trees, millet, and a few herbs. As a commercial town, it has no natural advantages, and cannot be considerəd as any benefit to France. So long as we sought or seek to maintain supremacy in India, it should not have been restored to the French; and it is wise for the French now to negociate for the final cession of Pondicherry and Chandenagore to the British government. In the event of hostilities between the two nations, the latter would immediately seize on the former; it would be be better, therefore, for the French to make some compromise in time.

The British province of Malabar, extending 120 miles along the sea coast, embracing an area of 4900 square miles, has in general a similarity of feature to the Travancore coast, but in some parts a sandy plain, of three miles wide, runs along shore, with numerous inlets of the sea, or low downs covered with cocoanut trees, and the sea coast hills are separated from the western Cordillera by narrow, steepsided, but fertile valleys. In the adjoining British province of Carnara, extending 230 miles along the sea coast, and comprehending within its territory 7477 square miles, the ghauts in many places run close to the sea shore, or hills, with naked tops, are laved by the waters of the Indian ocean.

The eastern and western ghauts connected by the *Neilgherries*, a range of mountains, extending from west to east thirty-four miles, and from north to south fifteen miles, elevate a vast extent of table land, from 2000 to 5000 feet above the level of the sea, partaking in its general features the aspect of the table land of Spain on which Madrid is situated, or perhaps bearing a more decided resemblance to the extremity of the South American continent, the Andes and the Ghauts of India offering a striking similar conformation, if the greater height of the former be excepted.

The *Nil-ghiri*, or Blue Mountains, are of various elevations, and almost insulated from the east and west Ghauts. Jackanairi is 5659 feet; Jackatally, 5976; Dimhutti, 6041; Ootacamund, 6416; and Moorchoorti Bet, 8800 feet above the ocean level. These hills, or mountains rather, are remarkable for being free from jungle, and in general in a high state of cultivation. The rivers Myar and Bhavani rise among the highest peaks. Coimbatore, the capital of the province, is in 10° 52′ north latitude, 77° 5′ east long, 120 miles south by east from Seringapatam, and 306 from Madras. The country about Coimbatore is not more than 1000 feet above the sea, but to the north it shoots up rapidly, the scenery blending the wild and beautiful.

The extensive table land of southern India is, for the greater part, under British dominion, and contains some of the most fruitful districts in the Madras presidency; viz. Bellary, embracing an area of 12,703 square miles[1]; Cuddapah, of 12,752 square miles; and Coimbatore, 1392 square miles,—three districts possessing a population of 3,000,000 souls. In so elevated a region, there are no large rivers, nor indeed are there any throughout the south of India[2], to compare with those of Bengal: but the small rivers which descend from the plateau are numerous, and fertilize a great portion of country. The Mysore territory, situated between 11° and 15° north latitude, in length

[1] *Bellary* proper has 8695 square miles, Harpunhully 666, and Kurnool 3342; *Cuddapah* proper has 11,852 square miles, Punganoor 652, and Banaganpully 248.

[2] Nor in the southern peninsulas of Africa, Europe, or America.

from north to south 234 miles, breadth east to west 264 miles, with an area of 27,561 square miles, consists of an elevated plateau or table land, from 2,000 to 2,500 feet high, enclosed on two sides by the east and west Ghauts. The kingdom of Coorg, which has lately occupied our attention, is situate to the westward of Mysore, of small extent, being comprised within the twelfth degree of north latitude, and the seventy-fifth and seventy-sixth degrees of east longitude. It is sixty miles long by sixty broad, with an area of 2,165 square miles. Surrounded by lofty mountains, for the most part inaccessible, it contains many others, scattered over the interior surface, forming a succession of wild rugged hills and highly cultivated valleys; and, as if this were not sufficient to confirm its title to the appellation of a "strong country," the natives have divided the whole interior into squares,—those where no streams or marshes are contained being generally about a mile in width, with an enormous ditch and high mound or bank, formed by the original contents of the ditch, and covered inside and out with deep jungle, in which are included many enormous forest trees. Some of these enclosures have four apertures for ingress and egress, one in each face, particularly those through which the principal roads pass, and which consequently present so many strong barriers against an approaching enemy. Every hill and mountain is also covered with jungle: the finest teak, jack, mango, and other large trees, growing spontaneously in a country watered by numerous streams, and continual fogs and misty clouds, which, from its great height, even above Mysore, are attracted by the hills, and cover them during the night. At Bangalore, a plateau of sixty miles by fifty, the surface is undulating, and nearly 3000 feet above the sea; to the north, after passing Nundydroog, the country falls rapidly, and towards Seringapatam the surface has a sudden descent. Siva Gunga, the highest mountain in Mysore, is 4600 feet above the sea. The rock basis of the country is a kind of syenite, composed for the most part of quartz, felspar, horneblende, and mica; the principal rivers are the Cauvery, Toombudra, Vedavatti, Bhadri, Arkanati, Pennar, Palar, and Panaur; there are no lakes of magnitude; several excellent roads exist through the province, and the bridges erected over the Cauvery river, by a native gentleman (at his own expense) named Ramaswamy, deserve the highest commendation. One of these magnificent structures, completed in 1821, is 1000 feet long, with a road-way of thirteen feet, and a height of twenty-three feet, supported by 400 pillars of stone; the whole fastened with iron pins and mortar.

The Hydrabad territory, embracing an area of nearly 100,000 square miles, consists principally of lofty granite ranges, and in the plains and valleys are found elevations, which are miniature features of the loftier ranges. These are few in number, and remarkably interrupted and irregular; their extension inconsiderable, and their height above the level of the sea 2500 feet. The mountains are bare and rugged in their outline, and consist of piles of rock heaped on one another in irregular succession. The country is watered by the Godaveri and Kistna, which, like all the other Indian rivers, are subject to great variations in the quantity of water, and dependent on the periodical rains. Their banks vary from thirty to fifty feet in height, and about fifty miles from their embouchure they both pass through the chain of granite mountains, which extend from Gantur to Gundwana. The inundations of the Godaveri are the most extensive, varying from six to three miles on either side of the river. The rivers take their rise in the Western Ghauts, and disembogue within sixty miles of each other.

PHYSICAL ASPECT OF THE BOMBAY PRESIDENCY.—The Northern and Southern Concan, forming the more southern sea-coast territories of the Bombay Presidency, extend along-shore from Damaun to Malabar, about 220 miles, by 35 miles inland, embracing an area of 12,270 square miles, and presenting a congeries of steep, rocky mountains, rising in some places to the height of from 2000 to 4000 feet, as abrupt as a wall, while in most parts the table land to the eastward is of difficult, if not of impracticable access for wheeled carriages. The Ghauts, in general, gradually decline towards the sea, possessing in some places fertile rice tracts, irrigated by numerous mountain streams. The coast is indented with small bays and shallow harbours or coves, with rocks, ravines, and chasms.

Bombay Island (containing eighteen and a half square miles, including Colaba and Old Woman's island) is little more than a cluster or double bank of once detached whinstone rocks, through which the sea and Goper river flowed, but which the retreating ocean from the western side of India has now permitted the consolidation of into an islet, by means of two sand-belts at the northern and southern extremity of each ledge of rocks ; and these natural causeways, now changing into rock, are rendered more secure by the construction of artificial dams, by which at spring-tides the ingress of the sea is prevented. On the cession of Bombay by the Portuguese to England, in 1661, its population did not exceed 16,000 souls, the refuse or outcasts of the natives of India ; it now contains a population of 229,000 persons, inhabiting 15,474 houses, which are valued at 3,606,424*l*. sterling ! The fort is extremely strong towards the sea, which surrounds it on three sides, and the view from thence is singularly beautiful, consisting of verdant isles, and on the mainland lofty and curiously shaped hills and mountains. Admirable roads have been formed throughout the island, the causeway communicating with Salsette widened, a great military road from Panwell to Poona (seventy miles) with several bridges over rapid rivers, and a road cut with great labour over a high range of mountains, have been constructed. Among the numerous buildings at Bombay, the town-hall and mint are conspicuous for the elegance and convenience of their structure.

There are no rivers of magnitude on the Concan coast ; when ceded to the British, in 1818, almost every hill had a fortification, and every rock of an inaccessible nature a fortress, all of which are now rapidly crumbling into decay.

Captain Hughes, under whose superintendence the

road from Panwell to Poona has been constructed, thus describes the country :—' The Bhore Ghaut is formed of a succession of lofty eminences, towering above each other, the last of which attains a height of 2000 feet above the level of the sea. Its outline at a distance is bold and imposing; it presents a plane or table summit, with ranges of stupendous hills beyond, with the sublimity of which Europe possesses little that is analogous. At its foot stands the small and romantic village of Campolee, which has a noble tank appertinent and a Hindoo temple, both built by Nana Furnavese, (the Peishwa's prime minister,) at his individual expense. Entering upon the scene, language can very imperfectly describe the beauty of this mountain—the luxuriant and variegated foliage by which it is clothed; or faithfully contrast that feature with its dark and fearful chasms: its high and impending rocks. Plants of great variety, and rich in colour, and all those graceful and stately trees which adorn an Indian forest, particularly the palm and feathery cocoa-nut, are scattered over it in gaudy profusion. The views obtained from commanding points in ascending this Ghaut (particularly from the Durwazu or Gateway) are of that order which may be termed the *magnificently picturesque ;* commencing in the foreground, with Campolee, its tank and temple, and tranquilly unfolding a *riant* and cultivated plain of very considerable extent, watered by the silvery and sinuous course of a mountain stream, which, during the Monsoon, swells into a broad and rapid river. The road which has been carried over this Ghaut has had the effect of changing the mode of transport between Panwell and Poonah (a distance of seventy miles), from the back of a bullock and shoulders of a man to a four-wheeled waggon; of reducing the hire of conveyance to at least *one-half;* of abridging the time occupied by *one-third;* and, lastly (no trifling consideration), of drawing to the purse of government a revenue of 40,000 rupees per annum. Already there is a surprising increase in the number of carts in Panwell; from 50 or 60 they amounted to upwards of 300 within the short interval of two years. One habit of industry begets another.'

The districts of Surat (1350 square miles), of Broach (1600), of Ahmedabad (4600), and of Kaira (1850 square miles), all in the province of Guzerat, cover an extensive portion of wild sea-coast, as well as hilly, jungly, and mountainous country, with many fertile tracts, cultivated and waste, watered by several noble rivers, such as the Nerbudda, Tuptee, Mahy, Mehindry, and Sabermutty, not available for commerce like the Ganges. Guzerat peninsula, 200 miles long by 140 broad, between 21° and 23° north latitude, projects between the Gulfs of Cutch and Cambray into the Indian Ocean. It is a flat country, very rich and fruitful; the fields in the eastern districts inclosed, and the prosperity of the peasant marked by his dress, the comfort of his dwelling, and the high cultivation of his fields.

The Bombay government possesses a political control in the rich mineral province of Cutch, a district 140 miles in length, by about ninety-five in breadth, bounded on the east by Guzerat, on the north and west by Ajmere and Mooltan, and on the south by the gulf of Cutch and the Indian Ocean; it consists of two remarkably distinct portions, the one an immense salt morass called the *Runn*, the other an irregular hilly country completely insulated between the Runn and the sea. This latter division is deficient neither in fertility nor verdure, and whenever industry is unrepressed by the tyranny of the government, is sufficiently productive. 'Throughout the interior it is studded with hills of considerable elevation, mostly covered with jungle, where the petty chiefs erect their strong holds and dens, and from whence they look down on, protect, or plunder the intervening valleys. The principal towns are Bhooj, Mandavie, Anjar, Tharra, Cuntcote, and Cutarra. There are many mountain streams, but no navigable rivers; and all along the coast of the Runn, the wells and springs are more or less impregnated with common salt, and other saline ingredients[1]'. In general, however, there is a deficiency of water, and the productions of Cutch have consequently never been equal to the consumption of its inhabitants. Mines of coal and iron have been recently discovered.

The Runn, which forms the second division of Cutch, is a vast salt morass, the total superficies of which may be estimated at 8000 square miles. Commencing at the extremity of the gulf of Cutch, of which it would appear to have been at one time a continuation, it sweeps round the whole northern frontier of the province, to the vicinity of Lacpat Banda, on the Sankra or eastern branch of the Indus. Like

[1] Hamilton. Description, &c. vol. i. p. 585, 586.

the Bahr[1] Faraouni, or Lake Tritonis, near the Lesser Syrtis, this prodigious fen may be traversed in certain directions, while in others its plashy or tremulous surface, yielding to the slightest pressure, presents insurmountable obstacles to the passage of caravans or armies. Though for the most part barren and uncultivated, the appearance of the Runn is distinguished in the dry season by an extraordinary variety of phenomena. Diminutive lakes of shallow water, long ridges of barren sand, patches of verdant pasturage, fields susceptible of cultivation, and extensive sheets of saline incrustations, which in many places resemble a fresh fall of snow, alternate with each other, and render this morass one of the most striking and extraordinary spots in the world. Here the *serâb*, or "false water of the desert" (*mirage*), exhibits, during the dry season, its most magnificent illusions. The stunted saline shrubs and bushes are magnified to the size of lofty forest trees, waving, separating and uniting again; armies seem to march over the flat; peaceful hamlets, shady groves, castles with embattled towers, rise, disappear and reappear in rapid succession on the salt bed of the morass, deluding or terrifying the way-worn solitary traveller. During the monsoons, or when the wind blows up the gulf, the whole of this immense plain is inundated, and resembles an arm of the sea; and on the retiring of the waters, myriads of dead prawns, mullets and other fish, are seen strewed over the surface of the mud. On the physical agents engaged in the for-

[1] Dr. Shaw's Travels, 4to. p. 126.

mation of the Runn opinions are various, some supposing it to be effected by the overflowing of the Loni, while others, with more probability, regard it as the bed of a gulf, which, by some convulsion of nature, has been raised above the level of the ocean. The accumulated deposits of soil brought down perpetually by the rivers will probably at no distant period exclude the waters entirely, the Loni here performing the part which the Nile has so successfully performed in Egypt. On the banks and in the small oases of the Runn, the wild ass exists in untameable fierceness, breeding in the wastes, and issuing forth in droves in the months of November and December, when the brackish and stunted vegetation of the desert is exhausted, to ravage the corn fields in the plains. Apes, porcupines, and vast flights of large birds constitute, with the wild ass, the sole inhabitants of this dreary and desolate region[1].

At a distance of about fifty miles from where the Loni falls into the Runn of Cutch, about the latitude of 24° 30′ it sends off numerous branches, which pursue a meandering course through a valley, and again form a junction with the river before entering the Runn. The portion of the country under irrigation from these rivers is called Nueyur. It is fertile in wheat, very populous as compared with the neigh-

[1] Colonel Tod, Annals of Rajast'han, vol. i. p. 17, 18; Fifteen Years in India, p. 349—352. Lieutenant Burnes's Memoir on the Eastern Branch of the River Indus and the Runn, in the transactions of the Royal Asiatic Society, vol. iii. p. 550—588.

bouring countries, and studded with villages. The district is subject to the Raja of Joodpoor[1].

The district of Parkur, situated under the 24° north latitude, and near 71° east longitude, is nearly enclosed on all sides in the Runn. It is now ruled by two Rajpoot chieftains, but its possession has often been a source of contention between the surrounding governments. There is no river or running stream in this district; but water and pasture are abundant, and the inhabitants subsist by tending herds and flocks, with which they wander from one place to another, as their wants can be most readily supplied[2].

Bhooj, the capital of Cutch, is a strong but irregular fortress, surrounded by a wall, flanked with round and square towers, defended by heavy artillery. Within, each house is a fort, standing in a lofty inclosure of stone, terraced, provided with loopholes, and generally enfilading the streets and approaches. Even the villages are fortified, and though they might not present very formidable obstacles to a regular army and artillery train, are impregnable to the impetuous but undisciplined forces of the natives[3].

The province of Mooltan, which, in making the circuit of the empire[4], follows next after Cutch, is

[1] Burnes, Journal of Geographical Society, vol. iv. p. 102—106.

[2] Ibid. vol. iv. p. 92—102.

[3] Hamilton, vol. i. 585—595.

[4] I have given the topography of some of these districts, although not, properly speaking, part of the empire; but as our natural boundary is the Indus, they will sooner or later be ours altogether.

bounded on the north by Lahore, on the east by the great desart of Ajmere, on the west by the course of the Indus, and on the south by the Indian Ocean. Its greatest length falls little short of 600 miles, and in breadth it varies from seventy to about 150 miles. Within these limits are contained Bahawulpoor, Bhakar, Sinde, Tatta, and Chalehkaun.

The north-west quarter of the ancient district of India, termed the "Deccan" or Dukhun, is under the administration of Bombay, and affords, in its general features, a complete resemblance to the European kingdom of Hungary, and like the latter, though of exceeding fertility in some places, yet in many parts, owing to the mountainous and rocky nature of the country, it is exceedingly barren. The Deccan, (embracing altogether 44,987 square miles,) is by the natives divided into the Mawhuls or hilly tracts, and the Desh or flat country, the former situate along the face of the Ghauts, and the latter extending to the eastward, in very extensive plateaus descending by steep steps. In travelling southward through the Deccan there are chains of flat-topped hills, occasionally assuming a conical form, but scarcely ever exceeding the moderate height of 1500 feet; their sides are neither abrupt nor sloping, and are covered with numerous blocks of trap rock, which in the interior of the mountains appear to have a tabular arrangement, giving them at a distance a fortification-like aspect, as if one circumvallation contained within another ascended from below. Between these hilly chains narrow valleys are formed, some of which are extremely rich, and romantically situate.

On approaching the banks of the Krishna, the country is one extensive plain to the south-east and north-west, whilst the ridges of hills on the north and south side are at a distance barely visible. From the Krishna river at Yervoi to the Ghatpurba at Argul, the country undulates, and presents here and there hilly ranges of broken basalt and extensive plains. On the Ghatpurba banks the hills of Pádasbápúr become visible, running from east to west, surrounded by fine valleys opening to the north and south, in which direction the Ghatpurba flows to form the falls of Gokauk,—a cataract formed by the descent of the Ghatpurba (here 180 yards wide) over a perpendicular quartz rock of 176 feet. Near Belgaum the country again becomes undulating—the landscape diversified by low sloping hills. The Collectorates of Poona and Ahmednuggur embrace an area of 20,870 square miles, of an irregular country, elevated 2000 feet above the level of the sea, intersected by many rivers and streams, flowing through the most lovely valleys the sun ever shone on, overtopped by hills 1,000 feet high, of the trap formation, with the scarped summits peculiar to that species of mountain, and crowned by native fortresses of a highly picturesque aspect.

Candeish, another British settlement in the Deccan of 12,430 square miles in extent, is an extensive, fertile, well watered plain, interspersed with low barren hills, at the base of which run numerous ever-purling limpid rivulets flowing from the table land into the Tuptee; a large extent of country is still under jungle. The only remaining territories to be noticed of the

Bombay presidency are the Collectorates of Darwar, Sattarah, and the Southern Jagheers, containing 9950 square miles, situate in the south-west quarter of the Deccan. The western districts in the vicinity of the Ghauts are in many parts extremely rugged. Lieutenant-Colonel Sykes states that along the Dharwar, the Satarrah, and Poona frontier, and part of Ahmednuggur, there is a depth of from thirty to fifty miles of mountainous valleys, studded with clumps of forest trees; and that there is also a good deal of jungle. The eastern tracts are less alpine, affording more level country where the rocks, which in some places stud the surface, are buried in a rich black mould. The Ghauts along this district are not so much broken into masses, but present to the view continuous lines of mountain forests, and along the course of the principal rivers Krishna, Toombuddra, Beema, and Ghatpurba, the country is exceedingly rich and picturesque.

RIVERS.—The vast territory, of which a brief delineation has now been completed, is distinguished above all other parts of the known world by two of the most striking natural phenomena,—the loftiest mountains on the surface of the globe, and rivers of such magnitude, that compared with them the Thames is but a rivulet.

The Indus is 1700 miles long, and for the distance of 780 miles there is sufficient water to sail a 200 ton vessel, and in some places it is from four to nine miles wide. From the sea to Lahore there is an uninterrupted navigation (for fleets of vessels) of 1000 miles[1] British. The waters of the Indus enter the Arabian gulf in two great branches, forming a rich delta of alluvial land 125 miles wide at the base, and eighty in length from thence to the point where they separate about six miles below Tatta. At seventy-five miles from the sea, the tides are scarcely perceptible, and at full moon the rise at the mouth is about nine feet; the tides ebb and flow with great violence, particularly near the sea, where they flood, and abandon the banks with incredible violence: there are no rocks or rapids to obstruct the ascent, the slope is gentle, and the current does not exceed two and a half miles an hour: when joined by the Punjaub it never shallows in the dry season to less than fifteen feet, the breadth being half a mile: the Chenab or Azesines has a minimum of twelve feet, and the Ravee or Hydrastasis is about half the size of the latter: the usual depth of the three rivers cannot be rated at less than four, three, and two fathoms. Lieutenant Burnes found the *Indus* at Tatta (latitude 24° 44′ longitude 68° 17′,—from the sea 130 miles distant) 670 yards broad, running with a velocity of two and a half miles an hour, and a depth of fifteen feet; these data give 110,500 cubic feet per second, but estimated in April so low as 80,000 cubic feet of water per second; it exceeds by four times the size of the Ganges in the dry season, and nearly equals the Mississippi. The

[1] The passage down of 1,000 miles was made in fifteen days; a steamer might average six knots an hour in opposition to the stream. Mr. Howell, in unison with my advice, is now projecting an inland steam navigation company for India, the Indus being one of the rivers on which it is intended to ply.

much greater length of course of the *Indus*, its tortuous direction and numerous tributaries among towering and snowy mountains (the Sutledj rises in lake *Manosawvara* in Tibet, 17,000 feet above the sea) leads to such a result. While the Indus receives the torrents of either side of that massy and snow-girt chain swollen by the showers of Caubul and the rains and ice of Chinese Tartary, the Ganges and its subsidiaries take their origin from the south face of the Himalaya.

The Ganges is 1500 miles long, and 500 miles from the sea the channel is thirty feet deep when the river is at its lowest during the dry season, and its width makes it appear an inland sea. At 200 miles from the ocean the Ganges separates into two branches; the south-east retaining the name of *Ganges*, and the west, assuming the appellation of the *Hooghly*, the delta between the two being termed the *Sunderbunds*. This magnificent river, like its compeer, rises amidst the perpetual snows of the Himalaya, in the 31° of north latitude 20,000 *feet above the level of the sea!* The arch from beneath which it issues is 300 feet high, composed of deep frozen layers of snow—probably the accumulation of ages, surrounded by hoary icicles of gigantic magnitude. Mr. Colebrooke has given, in the Asiatic Researches, Vol. XI. pages 429—445, an interesting history of the attempts which have at various times been made to explore the sources of the Ganges, Of these geographical expeditions the first was undertaken in 1711 by two Lamas, who were commissioned by the Emperor of China to travel into Tibet for the purpose of constructing a map of the country from Si-miy to Lasa, and thence to the source of the Ganges, some of the water of which they were instructed to bring back with them to Peking. From the materials which they collected the map of Tibet, published by Duhalde, was prepared.

Wars and revolutions, however, prevented them from completing their task, and the best information they were able to acquire was exceedingly imperfect. The Catholic missionaries at the court of Pekin being desirous of submitting this map to some European geographer, D'Anville undertook to examine and correct it. But he was not in possession of sufficient materials for the purpose; and accordingly his labours, like those of the Lamas, were full of errors. These were animadverted on, but not corrected, by Major Rennell and Anquetil Duperron. Other attempts to determine the point, whether the Ganges actually rises on the northern or southern side of the Himalaya, were equally unsuccessful, until in 1818 an expedition, projected by Colonel Colebrooke and conducted by Captains Raper and Hearsay, settled the long agitated question. The party arrived on the 1st of April at Haridwâra, but did not themselves proceed to Gangotri, owing to the near approach of the rainy season. An intelligent native was sent forward, who arriving at Gangotri, the place where the river issues from the Himalaya, found the breadth of the stream to be about forty cubits, and not exceeding two in depth, with scarcely any current. From this point he continued to ascend the stream, occasionally perceiving the course of the river in the snow; but at the distance of three miles its channel was so encumbered with snow that it could neither be seen nor heard, while the superincumbent snow appeared somewhat like a cultivated field. Proceeding 500 yards further, he again saw the sacred stream appear; but here his progress was stopped, for in front arose a steep mountain like a huge wall, from an angle of which the Ganges appeared to issue; but this was only conjecture, as the goddess (so the Ganges is called) here veils her head in an impenetrable mass of snow. This spot was found by observation to be 12,914 feet above the level of the sea. This is the most sacred source, and it is here that the offerings of the pilgrims are made; but the Dauli and Alacananda rivers, which, with this, the Bhâgîrat'hî, form the Ganges, have a longer course, and rise still higher in the snows of the Himalaya. The source of the Alacananda, explored by the English officers themselves, was very similar to that of the Bhâgîrat'hî. Vast beds of snow, seventy or eighty feet in thickness, obstructed the ascent, and sometimes concealed the river. 'We are now," say the travellers, " completely surrounded by hoary tops, on which snow eternally rests, and blights the roots of vegetation. The lower parts of the hills produce verdure and small trees. About midway the fir rears its lofty head; but the summits, repelling each nutritious impulse, are veiled in garments of perpetual whiteness. At twelve o'clock we reached the extremity of our journey, opposite to a waterfall called Barsû Dhârâ. It falls from the summit upon a projecting ledge, about 200 feet high, where it divides into two streams, which descend in drifting showers of spray upon a bed of snow, where the particles immediately become congealed. The small quantity that dissolves undermines the bed, whence it issues in a small stream about 200 paces below. This place forms the boundary of the pilgrims' devotions; some few come hither for the purpose of being sprinkled by this holy shower-bath.—From this spot the direction of the Alacananda is perceptible to the south-west extremity of the valley, distant about one mile; but its current is entirely concealed under immense heaps of snow, which have most probably been accumulating for ages in its channel. Beyond this point travellers have not dared to venture; and although the Sastras mention a place called Alacapura, whence the river derives its source and name, the position or existence of it is as much obscured in doubt and fable as any other part of their mythological history[1].' From Calcutta to Allahabad the distance on the Ganges through the Sunderbunds is 1000 miles, and thither steam vessels are now continually passing. The height of the river at Allahabad above the level of the sea is 348 feet, and the maximum and minimum known rise is forty-five and thirty-four feet. There are other rivers, such as the Brahmaputra (which in some parts is from *four to six miles wide!*) Sutledj (which is 900 *miles long* before its junction with the Indus)

[1] Asiatic Researches, vol. xi. p. 524.

Jumna, Jhylum, &c. which would be considered vast rivers in Europe.

The length of course of some of the principal rivers to the sea is in English miles—Indus, 1700; Ganges, 1500; Sutledj, (to Indus 900) 1400: Jhylum, (ditto 750) 1250; Jumna (to Ganges 780) 1500; Gunduck (to Ganges 450) 980. In the Deccan and south of India—Godaveri, to the sea 850 miles; Krishna, 700; Nerbudda. 700; Tuptee, 460; Cavery, 400. Taking the limit of the Ganges and Jumna to the west and south, and the Brahmaputra and Megna to the east, the country, completely intersected by navigable rivers, may be computed to cover an area of not less than *forty square degrees.*

The quantity of alluvial matter which these vast rivers carry down to the ocean is immense

The Rev. Mr. Everest has furnished us with some interesting observations and experiments on the River Ganges, which he recently made at Ghazepore in the province of Benares.

Velocity of the stream in feet in an hour.—July 3rd 6,810, 7th, 11,520, 23rd, 21,000; August 8th, 4,200, 22nd 34,560; September 6th, 21,600, 24th, 13,320; October 8th, 10,800, or 20,200 average of the four months—equivalent to about four miles an hour.

Depth of the river.—June 22nd, 19 feet 6 inches, 30th, 22 feet 6 inches; July 7th, 25 feet 6 inches, 14th, 28 feet, 23rd, 30 feet; August 1st, 35 feet 6 inches, 8th, 44 feet, 13th, 47 feet 6 inches, 22nd, 42 feet, 31st, 36 feet; September 6th, 38 feet, 15th, 37 feet 6 inches, 24th, 28 feet 6 inches; October

1st, 26 feet 6 inches, or an average of 33 feet for the four months.

Insoluble matter contained in a given quantity of Ganges water.

	Wine Quart.	Cubic Foot.
July 3rd, ...	1 grain.	30 grains.
7th, ...	8	240
23rd, ...	10	300
August 8th, ...	58—10	1740
13th, ...	37	1110
22nd, ...	26	780
September 6th, ...	17	510
24th, ...	8	240
October 8th, ...	6	108

On an average nineteen grains of insoluble matter for every wine quart, during the four rainy months, that is from the 15th June to 15th October, to which must be added for soluble matter, say two grains, making the whole equal to twenty-one grains, or about 630 grains of soluble and insoluble materials carried into the sea in every cubic foot of water of this magnificent river.

Mountains.—The principal mountain ranges are the Himalaya, the eastern and western Ghauts, and the Vindhya chain, which run through the centre of the Peninsula parallel to the course of the Nerbudda. The Himalaya range, or, as its name signifies, *the abode of snow*, elevates its lofty peaks from 20,000 to 27,000 feet above the level of the sea, forming an alpine belt eighty miles in extent from Hindostan to Tibet. The principal chain of the Himalaya, running from north-west to south-east, rises in a ridge, with an abrupt steep face against the plains of 6000 feet in height; there is then a slope from the crest of the ridge towards the north. The mountains on the side of the snowy range consist of a series of nearly parallel ridges, with intermediate valleys or hollows; spurs are thrown off in all directions into the hollows, forming subordinate valleys. There is nothing like table land (perhaps in the whole of the mountains, with the exception of Nipál), and the valleys are broad wedge-shaped chasms, contracted at bottom to a mere water course; for this reason the quantity of level ground is inconsiderable. On the flank of the great chain there is a line of low hills (the *Sewalik*), which commence at Roopur on the Sutlej, and run down a long way to the south, skirting the great chain. In some places they run up to and rise upon the Himalaya, in others they are separated by an intermediate valley. Between the Jumna and the Ganges they attain their greatest height, viz. 2000 feet above the plains at their feet, or 3000 above the sea, rising at once from the level, with an abrupt mural front. To the east of the Ganges and west of the Jumna the Sewalik hills gradually fall off. They are serrated across their direction, forming a succession of scarcely parallel ridges, with a steep face on one side, and a slope on the other; the slope being, like that of the great chain (see *Geology*), towards the north, and the abutment towards the south. These hills may be considered an upheaved portion of the plains at the foot of the Himalaya, and formed of the debris of the mountains, washed down by rains and other natural causes. They are covered with vast forests of saul, toom, and fir, and are uninhabited, and, as on the Himalaya, the dip or slope being towards the north, and the abutment towards the south, the great mass of vegetation has a northern exposure, and the south faces are generally naked. Twenty thousand feet have been barometrically measured and trigonometrically confirmed; at this height huge rocks in immense detached masses lie scattered about or piled on each other, as if realizing the Titanic fable of giants climbing to heaven. Beds of decayed sea shells are found, and lichens and mosses, the last link in vegetable life, struggle through a stunted existence beneath the verge of perpetual snow. At 16,800 feet north side, campanulas and ammonites have been found by enterprizing Englishmen,—at 13,000 feet the birch, juniper and pine appear, and at 12,000 feet the majestic oak rears its spacious head, towering amidst the desolation of nature. The cultivated limits of man have not passed 10,000 feet on the south slope, but on the north side villagers are found in the valley of the Baspa river at 11,400 feet elevation, who frequently cut green crops, and advancing further the habitations of man are found as high as 13,000 feet, cultivation at 13,600,—fine birch trees at 14,000, and furze bushes for fuel thrive at 17,000 feet above the ocean level! At 11,000 feet elevation Captain Webb found extensive fields of barley and buckwheat, and 11,630 feet above Calcutta his camp was pitched on a clear spot surrounded by rich forests of oak, pine and rhododendra; a rich rank vegetation as high as the knee, extensive strawberry beds and beautiful currant bushes in full flower (21st June) and a profusion of dandelions, buttercups, crocusses, cowslips, and every variety of wild European spring flowers. In the skyey villages of Kunawar, although the soil is poor and rocky, apples, pears, raspberries, apricots, and other fruits, are abundant, and above them is a forest of gigantic pines, the circumference of which is stated to be 24 feet and the height 180. The summer heat is so great as to uncover whole mountains of their snowy covering, and the cold of winter frequently so intense as to split and detach vast masses of rock, which roll from mountain to mountain with terrific uproar. Captain Gerrard in crossing the Charang Pass (17,348 feet high) describes the neighbouring mountains to be all of blue slate, naked to their tops, and exhibiting decay and barrenness in their most frightful form; and the natives declare that volcanoes exist amidst the regions of perpetual snow. A severe earthquake occurred on the north of the great Himalaya range, which was experienced throughout the greater part of Western India, on the 26th August, 1833; the vibration was from north-east to south-west. There were three principal shocks; the first at 6.30, P.M.; the second at 11.30, P.M.; and the third, or most severe shock, within five minutes to twelve (Calcutta time). The second shock was particularly noticed at Calcutta by the stopping of an astronomical clock, and is thus compared with other places:

	Observed.	Dif. L.	Cal. Time.	
	H. M.	M.	H. M.	
Katmandu (Nipal)	10 45	+ 12	= 10 57	Effects very severe; loud noise.
Rungpur	11 20	− 2	= 11 18	Ditto; many houses injured.
Monghyr	11 27	+ 7	= 11 34	Noise heard; walls cracked.
Arrah	11 15	+ 14	= 11 29	Ditto, ditto.
Gorakpur	11 20	+ 19	= 11 39	Ditto, ditto.
Bancoorah	11 30	+ 4	= 11 34	None such since 1814.
Calcutta			11 34 48	No injury done.

At Katmandu nineteen persons were buried under the ruins of their houses, and at Bhatgaon, east of Katmandu 300 souls perished. The earthquake commenced gradually, though travelling with the speed of lightning towards the west; it increased, until the houses, trees, and every thing on the surface of the ground seemed shaken from their foundations; full-grown trees bent in all directions, and houses reeled like drunken men; the earth heaved most fearfully; in a dead calm a noise, as if from a hundred cannons, burst forth; and, to add to the impressiveness of the scene, a general shout arose from the people in every direction, and the murmur of their universal prayer was carried from the city to the British cantonment, a mile distant. Slight vibrations were felt towards Katmandu during the twenty-four hours.

Although the limit of eternal frost had been fixed by theory at from 10 to 12,000 feet, yet Samsiri, a halting place for travellers on the banks of the Shelti, is 15,600 above the sea[1]; the landscape is there beautiful,—verdant hills and tranquil rivulets, with flocks of pigeons, herds of deer, and lovely banks of turf and shrubs, adorn this extraordinary scene.

[1] That is three miles and a half high.

A village has been found at a height of 14,700 feet; in the middle of October, the thermometer on two mornings was 17°; yet the sun's rays felt oppressive[1], and all the streams and lakes which were sheeted with ice during the night, were free and running by two o'clock. The finest crops of barley are reared here, and to irrigation and solar heat are the people indebted for a crop. The barometer gave for the highest field 14,900 feet of elevation, which verifies the observations, or rather inferences, as to the limit of cultivation in the upper course of the Sutledj, and it is quite possible and even probable, that crops may vegetate at 16,000 or 17,000 feet. The *yaks* and shawl goats at this village seemed finer than at any other spot in the mountains. On the north-eastern frontier of Kunawar, close to the stone bridge, a height of more than 20,000 feet was attained without crossing snow, the barometer showing 14,320, thermometer 27° at 1 p. m. Notwithstanding this elevation, the sun's rays were oppressive, though the air in the shade was freezing. The view from this spot is grand and terrific beyond the power of language to describe. It comprises a line of naked peaks, scarce a stripe of snow appearing.

At *Simla* (lat. 31° 06′ north, long. 77° 09′ east) 7,486 feet above the sea, where the Bengal Government have founded a delightful station, the view of the Hima-

[1] This corroborates the opinion which I entertain, that heat is a product and not an element; it being the result of solar electricity and of terrestrial magnetism, when the rays are brought into vertical opposition to each other.

laya Mountains is magnificent. The portion visible is a depressed continuation of the chain, extending from the emergence of the Sutlej through the snow, to an abrupt limit bordering close upon the plain of the Punjab, near the debouche of the Ravee; few, if any of the detached peaks rise beyond 20,000 feet; the crest of Jumnotree may indeed be seen from the highest point of Simla, which is a conical hill named Jucko, formerly in undisputed possession of the bears and hogs. This insulated point Jucko, besides being crowned by garnets, throws the waters of its corresponding declivities towards the Bay of Bengal on one side, and the Gulph of Cutch on the other; the former by the intersections of the Giree, the Tons, and Jumna, to the Ganges[1]; the latter by the medium to the Sutlej, and that magnificent river the Indus; even the road itself here marks the divergence of twin streamlets, which are latterly separated 1,500 miles.

There are none of those giant peaks visible from Simla, which we hear of aspiring to 25 and 28,000 feet, threatening heaven with their points and earth with their fall; but the gelid array is sufficiently grand to excite astonishment in the minds of people in their noviciate, who behold the primeval summits

[1] The Ganges and Brahmapootur may also be considered as adjunct rivers; but they part to meet again, as Rennel observes. The two streams are as different in character as masculine is from feminine; one creeps slowly through fertile plains, under the pressure of superstitious reverence for gods and cows; the other rolls over rugged and barren wastes, where beef is worshipped by keen appetites.

sheeted in drapery of perpetual whiteness. The boundary is still very lofty, perhaps not under 13,000 feet upon the plainward slope, while the dark rock stares through the snow in the highest regions. But it is on the cessation of the periodical rains that the scene is most striking; the tops only remaining covered, glare their radiant snow at the powerless sun in calm, desolate grandeur. Greater part of the bare rock is then disclosed, and the vast dim mass, just crowned by gelid points, appears like the curling crest of an enormous wave rising out of a sea of mist. The marginal limit has then receded to its maximum elevation, and may be determined as a fixed point; traces of snow extend down the hollows, and accumulations repose far below, while steep cliffs project their bare sides even to 18,000 feet, but the belt is very precisely defined, and if geometrically measured, will be found to have an uniform level beyond 15,000 feet[1].

The pines upon the slopes of the snowy chain are taller and more symmetrical than elsewhere; whole forests occur, where individuals measure twenty-four to twenty-six feet round. The maximum girth in one instance was twenty-nine feet. Close to the same spot were numbers of the same magnificent barrels, like gigantic masts, each rising as if in rivalry, and all at a level verging upon 10,000 feet, a limit beneath which on the equator (according to Baron Humboldt) the larger trees of every kind shrink; a

[1] The descriptions of the Himalaya I have been obliged to obtain from various authorities.

limit which various writers have placed close to the marginal snow in the region of the torpid lichen; but the Himalaya peer over the Andes, and laugh at theorists and closet speculators[1].

Dr. Gerard crossed the Himalaya range to the skirts of the Ladak capital. After traversing the table land of Roopshoo, Dr. Gerard descended into the valley of Speetee, opening upon the Sutlej at the monastery of Kanum. The Sutlej was crossed in July by a rope bridge, where the bed of the river has an extreme elevation of 2500 feet. The mountain state of Cooloo, tributary to Runjeet Sing, was traversed by a route successively varied by ridge and valley. It being the season of rain, the landscape was obscured with mist—the roads being bad and quaggy. The lofty boundary ridge, which throws the streams from opposite sides to the Sutlej and Beas, was crossed at a height of nearly 10,700 feet. On the 27th of July, Dr. Gerard came in sight of the ancient Hyphasis, at the ferry of Koortor, where the river has an expanse of bed which he little expected to find so near its source. At Sultanpore, the Capital of Cooloo, he encamped near the margin of the river, upon a green sward shaded by magnificent elm trees. Sultanpore is populous, and frequented by a considerable number of foreigners. Good roads, however, are totally unknown. The physical configuration of this alpine tract is gigantic,

[1] We are still in the infancy of physical science, and our great object should be to accumulate facts rather than to frame theories; it will require many years of investigation before we have sufficient data to form just and permanent conclusions.

and its frontiers well defined. The Sutlej is southward, the Hyphasis on the western skirt, while the Himalayan crest forms a magnificent limit on the north, and opens into countries of which we scarce know the name. Leaving Sultanpore, he crossed the Beas by a double bridge, connected by an island.

On the 8th of August, he pitched his tent on the slope of the Himalaya, at an altitude of 10,000 feet, surrounded by luxuriant vegetation and flowering herbs. The road up is one long stair to the crest, and was constructed by a fakir. On the 9th, they crossed the Himalaya by Rotang Pass, turning a little to the right to the consecrated rills of the river, which are collected in a small basin, walled round for the purposes of ablution. Here is the source of the Beas, which, at the distance of only five days' march, presents a formidable expanse: the extreme altitude of this spot appears to be about 13,000 feet. Descending into a ravine, the bed of the Chandera-Baga, or *River of the Moon*, was crossed by a cradle bridge. The traveller is now struck with the change of the climate, and the alteration in the appearance of the inhabitants. The configuration of the country assumes a new form, and the eternal snow gradually recedes to the summits of the mountains: even the skies have a deeper and more resplendent blue. Nothing was green but the crops; the vegetation being scanty and arid, and the sun's rays powerful. In the former part of their route they had been daily shrouded in rain and mist: vegetation was luxuriant, and the slopes were fringed with pine forests: here, however, not a tree was visible but the drooping willow, which is planted. The soil was quite destitute of verdure, and the air felt dry and elastic. On the 13th of August, Dr. Gerard reached Tandeh, upon the bank of the Soojur-Baga (*River of the Sun*). The passage of the stream was by a fragile bridge of osier twigs. It has an altitude of 10,000 feet. The temple of Tilaknath is two long days' journey down the river. The valley of the Chenab, or Acesines, is under the dominion of Runjeet Sing, but the government officers seldom shew themselves so high up as Tilaknath. The whole country abounds in ancient gigantic ruins.

On the 29th of August, Dr. Gerard resumed his journey along the course of the Sooruj Baga: and on the 2nd of September, he reached the last inhabited spot of the country, at an elevation of 11,000 feet. The valley was prettily enamelled with villages and cultivation. The inhabitants, however, appeared poor, greasy, and ragged. He was greeted by one of the Thakoors (chiefs) of the country with a present of ardent spirits, distilled from malt, some rice, atta, and butter. It was now constant sunshine, and the temperature increased with the elevation, though they were still in the vicinity of enormous masses of snow. Darcha is the last village in the dell, and the sun's rays reflected from the barren sides of the rocks raise the temperature to 84° in the shade.

On the 8th of September, Dr. Gerard crossed the Paralasa chain, at an elevation of 16,500 feet, and traced the Sooruj Baga (which the party had been following) to its source, in a lake only 300 feet lower. Dr. Gerard remarked, 'that its surface was at its extreme ebb; thus almost verifying Moorcroft's similar observation respecting Mansarowar, a fact which Mr. Colebrooke and reviewers were puzzled at, and actually discredited; but it would appear that the lakes, at least in the Trans-Himalaya regions, are highest in spring, when the ice first breaks up and thaws.' In crossing this lofty ridge, the wind blew piercingly on one side, while the sun's rays were scorchingly ardent on the other. The extremely thin, dry, and cold air checks the vital energy with fearful rapidity. On the sixth day's journey from the inhabited limits, they ascended the Laitchee long range, which rose up abruptly, like a vast wall, from the bed of the Chander-Baga. Along this tract are found marine fossil remains. At length, after a most toilsome journey over rugged and sterile mountains and rocky tracts, Dr. Gerard, for the first time, pitched his camp upon the plateau of Tartary, where the barometer indicated an elevation of nearly 16,000 feet! In front was a black ridge, having the uniform height of 3000 feet above the camp; yet there was no snow on its summit. The soil was almost without any vegetation, baked, hard, and thirsty. The skies were of the most resplendent indigo tint, and the air highly transparent. The attendants, who expected to enter upon a fine flat country, after crossing three successive ranges, viewed with consternation interminable alps upon alps arise. They saw a wild horse, at which one of the party fired; but hardly any report was heard, sound being so feeble in the rarified air. A pack of wild dogs (quite red) were also seen stealing along a gully.

On the 17th of September, his progress was arrested by the Wuzeer of Ladak. His interview with this person was highly agreeable; his deportment, dress, and address were showy, his conversation frank, and his appearance altogether prepossessing. The day after he invited Dr. Gerard to dinner. The Wuzeer seemed, on the whole, to be a jolly *bon-vivant*. In impeding Dr. Gerard's further advance, he appeared to rely more upon that gentleman's good feeling than any exertions of his own; remarking that he would not oppose it by rude interference, but that the consequence would be discredit and disgrace to *him*. The three days Dr. Gerard passed in the Wuzeer's camp were far from uninteresting: yet, notwithstanding his kind familiarity, he seemed quite uneasy till Dr. Gerard decided upon turning his face southward, and his eagerness to equip and transport him into Speetee, by a route skirting the Chinese confines, evinced his extreme anxiety to get him fairly out of his sight, and away from the precincts of the capital.

On the morning of the 19th of September, the yaks being ready, after the ceremony of smoking pipes together, our traveller and the Wuzeer parted. His route now became excessively uncomfortable, owing to exposure to the cold night air in such a savage country. He met several groups of wild horses, which they endeavoured in vain to chase. Southward, towards Speetee, the landscape appeared very sharply peaked, and in clusters of white tops;

but in the north-east the mountains were of a vast contour, and the snow more uniformly defined. At length they encamped in a dell which opened upon Lake Chimorerel. From this spot were seen numerous herds of shawl goats, sheep, horses, and yaks. The dell, save towards the lake, was land-locked on every side; and Lake Chimorerel itself spread out its blue expanse to the foot of very precipitous mountains, forming a sharply defined and lofty boundary to the valley of Speetee, through the windings of which the route of the party lay.

On the 27th of September, their path skirted the shore of the lake, the whole circumference of which is embayed by mountains; but hill-ward on its north-eastern shore, the mass of elevated land rose very abruptly from the water's edge, and entered the regions of snow, which had an uniform margin of 19,000 feet. Neither this nor the other lake has any efflux, and were we less acquainted with the course of the Sutlej, we should have here at least a verification of the fact, which Mr. Colebrooke, and reviewers, received with cautious credence, and even actually discredited, of Mansarowar being entirely land-locked, conceiving that in so elevated a region evaporation was insufficient to carry off the supplies derived from the neighbouring snow; thus forgetting, or not knowing, that the absorbing power of the atmosphere is infinitely increased by its rarefaction, and in tracts so singularly arid, that the traveller beholds ice permanent and unthawed in a temperature of 50°, torrents frozen fast in their fall in a medium often 20° warmer than the graduated freezing point. Throughout India, in July and August, though the thermometer often points above 90°, evaporation is checked in spite of this heat; such being the density of vapour at so low a level that a damp mouldy surface is thrown over everything. Upon the table-land of Tibet the air is so dry that frost is not visible upon the soil, or grass, though the thermometer may stand at the zero of the scale. Few and inconsiderable streams pass into the Chimorerel at this season, but the dry channels of water courses were crossed, which shewed an expanse of bed that argued their powerful body at some period of the year. The highest water-mark upon the shore did not appear to exceed five feet.

The frozen zone in the tropics, which the reader is now examining, is yet but imperfectly explored, and doubtless every additional information which can be obtained and placed on record will be desirable. Mr. H. T. Colebrook, whose learning and zeal for the honour of his country has been productive of so much advantage to the Asiatic hemisphere, has furnished some valuable extracts from Captain A. and Mr. J. G. Gerard's geographical survey of the Himalaya to the Royal Asiatic Society. The diary of Messrs. Gerard commenced in the month of June at *Rol*, a small district in Chúárá, one of the larger divisions of Basehar, 9350 feet above the level of the sea, and the highest inhabited land *without* the Himalaya Mountains. Crops,—wheat, barley and peas. Road to *Buchkalghat* 11,800 feet, through fine woods of oak, yew, pine, rhododendron, horse-chesnut, juniper and long thin bamboos;—flowers abundant, particularly cowslips and thyme; soil, a rich moist black turf not unlike peat. Crossed the *Shátúl* pass (15,556 feet) rocks, mica slate and gneis—huge granite blocks, vast angular fragments of quartz, felspar, &c. jumbled together in the wildest confusion, the route over which was fraught at every step with considerable danger. Upon the snow (two of Mr. Gerard's servants were frozen to death at mid-day in September the previous year when crossing this pass) at Shátúl were many insects like musquitoes, which revived as the sun rose; some birds were seen resembling ravens,—mosses were found on a few rocks; the British travellers rested for the night under shelter of a large rock, (13,400 feet above the sea) where the steep ascent above them of 2200 feet higher seemed appalling; here and there a rock projected its black head; all else was a dreary solitude of unfathomable snow, aching to the sight and without trace of a path; when the snow was melted, plenty of lovely flowers were found but no bushes. The snow was soft at mid-day and affording good footing, but the suffering caused by the elevation as it affected the breathing and head was very great. On the 9th of June, the temperature did not rise above 41° at noon, it was 24° and 26° at sunrise,—in the evening it snowed. On the 11th of June our adventurous countrymen began their descent on the opposite side of the pass, along the dell of the *Andreti*, (a branch of the Pabar river) rising near Shátúl, and halted on the bank of a rivulet named *Dingrú,* just above the forest limit. The *lowest* point in the dell was 11,000 feet; leeks were gathered at 12,000 feet; the ground was a rich sward cut up in grooves by a large kind of field rat without a tail (*Mus Typhlus*). Mr. Colebrooke here observes that the Himalaya glens run for the most part perpendicular to the range, or from north-north-east to south-south-west and south-west; the north-west face being invariably rugged and the opposite one facing the south-east shelving. The roads to the most frequented passes lie upon the gentle acclivity; the difference in the elevation of the forest is very remarkable, in some instances exceeding 1,000 feet. The general height of the forest on the south face of the Himalaya is about 11,800 to 12,000 feet above the sea; oaks and pines reach that elevation, birches reach a few feet higher, and juniper was observed at 13,300 feet. At *Tagno* village, (8,800 feet) abundance of strawberries, thyme, nettles and other European plants were noticed, and the houses were shaded by apricot, walnut and horse-chesnut trees. The ascent of the Yúsú pass, (15,877 feet) at the head of the Sapan river, was performed with the greatest difficulty; the glen through which the *Sapan* forces its passage becomes more and more contracted, until it is at last bounded by mural rocks of granite, between which the river flows in impenetrable obscurity under immense heaps of indestructible ice, running in lofty ridges and studded with gigantic mounds of snow. The source of the *Pabar* is in a lake called *Charámái,* (15,000 feet high) above a mile in circuit, whence the river rushes forth over a perpendicular rock, forming a fine cascade, the appearance of which is heightened by the enormous banks of snow, 100 feet high, above it, some of which have cracked and fallen outwards into the lake. The dreary solitude of the place was now and then broken by the tremendous crashing sounds of falling rocks or mountain avalanches. Messrs. Gerard descended into the romantic valley of the noble *Baspa* river by sliding down the snowy declivities seated on a blanket (a mode invariably practised by the mountaineers where there are no rocks or precipices). *Rakham* village in the *Baspa* valley, (11,400 feet high) is situate in the western corner of the glen, here three furlongs wide, half of which is laid out in thriving crops of wheat and barley, and the rest occupied by sand-beds or small islands, with the Baspa river winding among them. Just above the village, high steeples of black mica rock rise abruptly 9,000 feet!

The *Kimliá* pass was attempted, but only 15,500 feet could be attained when the snow became impassable. Here the *Rusu* river, at 13,300 feet, foams along in dreadful turbulence and rapidity, the noise of the torrent being astounding. Deep blue lakes were passed, along the precipices skirting which notches had to be cut with a hatchet to enable the travellers to wend their weary, dangerous route. Vast fields of snow at 7,000 feet elevation, and heavy rain and sleet, prevented their further progress in the direction of the *Kimliá* pass; but the *Cháráng* pass was crossed, at 7,348 feet elevation, to the valley of the *Nangalti* river. The snow passed was often of a *reddish* colour, eighty feet thick, with terrific fissures, and the descent for half a mile, often at an angle of from 33° to 37° over gravel and snow, with here and there a sharp pointed rock projecting through it. At *Kiukúche*, on the banks of the *Nangalti* (12,400 feet high), there was an enclosure for cattle, and there were a few cross-bred between the *Yak* (Tartar bull) and common cow, feeding in the glen on a few hundred yards of grassy slope of odoriferous herbs and juniper bushes, surrounded by craggy cliffs of horrid forms.

The *Tidung* at its junction with the *Nangalti*, when visited, presented a furious rapid stream of great declivity, for six or seven miles the fall being 300 feet per mile, and in some places double: huge rocks were whirled along with frightful velocity, nothing visible but an entire sheet of foam and spray, thrown up and showered upon the surrounding rocks with loud concussion. and re-echoed from bank to bank with the noise of the loudest thunder; around the blue slate mountains tower 18,000 feet in sharp detached groups or pinnacles, covered neither with vegetation nor with snow, and exhibiting decay and barrenness in its most frightful aspect. (A Tartar village was found here called *Húns*). Where the dell was narrowest, there was so little space for the river that the road continued but for a small distance on the same side, and over this frightful torrent the English travellers had repeatedly to cross on ropes, or *sangas*, loosely hung from rock to rock on either side; one of these sangas was inclined at an angle of 15°. Messrs. Gerard one while picked their way upon *smooth* surfaces of granite *sloping* to the raging torrent; at another time the route led among huge masses and angular blocks of rock, forming spacious caves, where sixty persons might rest; *here* the bank was composed of rough gravel steeply inclined to the river,—*there* the path was narrow with precipices of 500 or 600 feet below, whilst the naked towering peaks and mural rocks rent in every direction threatened the passenger with ruin from above. In some parts of the roads there were flights of steps, in others frame work or rude staircases opening to the gulph below. In one instance, the passage consisted of six posts driven horizontally into clefts of the rocks about twenty feet distant from each other and secured by wedges. Upon this giddy frame a staircase of fir spars was erected of the rudest nature; twigs and slabs of stone only connected them together,—no support on the outer side, which was deep and overhung the terrific torrent of the *Tidung;* the rapid rolling noise of which was enough to shake the stoutest nerves. Some of these kind of passages were swept away and new ones had to be prepared for the British adventurers [1].

[1] A dangerous mode of crossing rivers prevails in the Alpine districts of Northern India. " Over a very rapid but narrow part of the river (Alacananda) was thrown a substitute for a bridge, called in the language of the country, *tùn*. It consists simply of two or three strong ropes, fixed by stakes into the ground on each bank, and elevated about eight or ten feet above the water. On these a person conveys himself across,

From the confluence of the *Tidung* with the Sutledj, the town of *Ribé* or Ridáing has a charming ap-

by clinging to them with his hands and feet, while a small hoop, suspended from the ropes, serves as a rest for the back, and is a trifling, though it must be allowed, a very frail security should the person quit his hold. This passage is not calculated for all descriptions of travellers; the water rolls below with such foaming violence and stunning roar, that it requires no small degree of resolution to make the attempt; however, where the inconvenience is without remedy, the hands and feet of the person are tied above the ropes, his eyes blindfolded, to prevent his seeing the danger, and he is drawn across by a cord passed round the waist *." On other parts of the river they substitute for the hoop a small bedstead, in which the traveller is placed, and drawn across by a rope †.

"There are," says Captain Raper, "several kinds of bridges constructed for the passage of strong currents or rivers, but the most common are the *sangha* and *jhula*. The former consists of one or two fir spars, thrown from bank to bank, or from one large rock to another; but where the extent is too great to be covered in this mode, they substitute the *jhula* or rope-bridge, which is made in the following manner: a couple of strong posts are driven into the ground, about three feet asunder, with a cross bar in the form of a gallows. One of these is erected on each bank of the river, and twelve or fourteen thick ropes, divided equally to both sides, leaving a space of about one foot in the centre, are stretched over the scaffold, and fixed into the ground by means of large wooden piles. These ropes form the support of the bridge, which describes a cantenary curve, with the lower part or periphery, at a greater or less elevation from the water, according to the height of the bank. About two

* Survey of the Ganges. A. R. vol. xi. p. 513.
† Survey, &c. vol. xi. p. 492.

pearance: yellow fields, extensive vineyards, groves of apricot, and large well-built stone houses contrast with the neighbouring gigantic mountains. Nature thus carefully adapts vegetation to this extraordinary country, for did it extend no higher than on the *southern* face of the Himalaya Mountains, Tartary would be uninhabitable by either man or beast [1]. On the southern slope of the range, the extreme height

feet below them a rope-ladder is thrown horizontally across, and laced with cords to the upper ropes, which form the parapet when the bridge is completed. The first passage of so unsteady a machine is very apt to produce a sensation of giddiness. The motion of the passengers causes it to swing from one side to the other, while the current (of the Bhagîrat'hî), flowing with immense rapidity below, apparently increases the effect. The steps are composed of small twigs, about two and a half, and sometimes three feet asunder, and are frequently so slender as to give an idea of weakness, which naturally induces a person to place his chief dependence on the supporting ropes or parapets, by keeping them steady under his arms. The passage, however, is so narrow, that if a person is coming from the opposite quarter, it is necessary that one should draw himself entirely to one side to allow the other to pass; a situation very distressing to a novice *."

[1] All the British travellers who have visited these lofty regions have expressed deep regret at returning again to the plains, notwithstanding the hardships endured and the rudeness of the climate; it is to be hoped we may soon be enabled to open a trade with Tartary through these passes, which will lead to new commercial intercourse.

---

* I have crossed torrents in Ceylon on similar bridges, and the remembrance of the danger incurred is even still fearful.— R. M. Martin.

of cultivation is 10,000 feet, and even there green crops are frequently cut; the highest habitation is 9,500 feet; 11,800 may be reckoned the upper limit of forest, and 12,000 that of bushes; and in some sheltered ravines dwarf bushes are found at 13,000 feet high. Mark the contrast on the *northern* side, in the valley of the *Baspa* river: there is a village 11,400 feet; cultivation reaches the same level; but advancing yet further, villages are found at 13,000 feet! cultivation at 13,600, fine birch trees at 14,000, and *támá* bushes (which furnish excellent firewood) at 17,000 feet above the level of the sea. To the eastward, towards Lake Mánassarówar, according to Tartar accounts, crops, forests, and bushes thrive at a still greater height. At Zinchin (*sixteen thousand one hundred and thirty-six feet above the sea*), where our travellers were stopped by the Chinese guards, about 200 wild horses were seen galloping about and feeding on the very tops of the heights; kites and eagles were soaring into the deep blue æther, large flocks of small birds like linnets flying about, and beautiful locusts jumping among the bushes. At times the sun shone like an orb of fire without the least haze, the stars and planets with a brilliancy only to be seen from such an elevation, and the part of the horizon where the moon was expected to rise could scarcely be distinguished before the limb touched it; the atmosphere sometimes exhibiting that remarkable dark appearance witnessed in polar latitudes. With a transit telescope of thirty inches, and a power of thirty, stars of the *fifth* magnitude were distinct in broad day. Thermometer 60° in the shade, at sunset 42°, and before sunrise 30° in July.

As every thing important relating to these gigantic mountains will doubtless be acceptable to the readers of this history, and probably at no very distant period advantageous in a mercantile point of view, no apology will be requisite for giving the elevations,—latitude and longitude of the principal peaks and river sources in the Himalaya mountains, between latitude 30° 33′ 10″ and 30° 18′ 30″ north, longitude 77° 34′ 40″ and 79° 57′ 22″ east, as surveyed by Captain Hodgson and Lieutenant Herbert, and which I believe has never been published in Europe [1].

[1] The Asiatic Society of Bengal printed the whole survey in their valuable 'Transactions' in Calcutta.

GEOGRAPHICAL POSITION OF THE HIMALAYA PEAKS, RIVERS, &c.

Station or Peak.	Height above the sea, feet.	Lat. N.	Long. E.	District or State.	Observations.
Saharunpoor ...	1013	29 57 10	77 32 12	Doab	Starting point of Survey.
Chandra Radani	7661	30 18 03	78 36 27	Rimola.........	Peak of ridge separating the Alacananda and Bhagirathi valleys. top clay slate, and bare of trees.
Surkananda	9271	23 24 28	78 16 33	Ditto...........	Ditto between the Jumna and Bhagirathi, overlooks the Dhoon, 15 miles direct from Dheera; summit, of a dull greyish stone, having a conchoidal fracture, semi-hard. Abundance of golden pheasants.
Bairat	7599	30 34 51	77 55 26	Jaunswar......	Fort between the Jumna and Tons, clay slate and quartz.
Jeytek	4854	30 35 25	77 19 10	Sirmoor	Ditto, extremely steep, yet heavy cannon were dragged up by the British in 1814 for its attack. Clay slate.
Chur	11689	30 50 36	77 28 30	Ditto & Jubal	Peak, highest central point in lowest range of mountains, ridges, spurs, and ramifications, visible all round, granite, firewood abundant, water procurable from snow; Juniper and red currant found on it, and its N. E. face shaded by forests of the cedar pine, S. W. face steep and rocky, with few trees.
Ditto Peak	12149	30 52 00	77 28 03	Ditto...........	
Uchalaru	14302	30 54 04	78 35 22	Gherwal	Separating ridge of Jumna and Bhagirathi, about 2500 feet above the forest limit, which is 11800 feet above the sea-level, only a patch of snow left in September.
Kedar Kauta ...	12689	31 01 08	78 09 33	Ditto	Ditto Tons and Jumna, Gneis, lost all snow in August.
Changshill	12871	31 09 10	77 56 10	Bissaher	Ditto between Russin and Pabar, gneis and white quartz, no granite above forest limit, highest productions black currant and juniper.
Whartu (fort) ...	10672	31 14 25	77 29 19	Ditto...........	Peak of Tungru range, connected with the Chur ridge; horseshoe form, throwing off on the concave side the Ghiri and other streams, on the convex feeds the Setlej, &c. Gneis and much red and white quartz, wooded to the very summit, where the wild strawberry grows. Ghoorka forts or watch-towers of unhewn stones.
1 Peak	**23531**	**30 18 30**	**79 45 54**	Jawahir ...	**These peaks are far to the East; so far as we know, No. 2 is the highest mountain on this globe.**
2 ditto	**25749**	**30 22 19**	**79 57 22**		
3 ditto	**23317**	**30 30 42**	**79 51 33**		
Sri Kanta.........	**20296**	**30 57 12**	**78 47 33**	Gherwal	**The Bhagirathi winds round the western foot of this peak, where it breaks through the base of the Himalaya chain, changing its course from W. N. W. to S. S. W.**
Various Peaks	**16982 to 19512**	**31 14 13 to 31 26 02**	**78 23 55 to 77 53 49**	**Bissaher...**	**S. or hither Himalaya shutting in to the N. the Baspa and Sutledj. giving rise on the S. to branches of the Russin, Pabar, &c. Various passes over the ridge from 15 to 16000 feet high.**

POINTS ON SOME OF THE RIVERS, INCLUDING THEIR SOURCES, CONFLUENCES, AND THE PLACES WHERE THEY ENTER THE PLAIN.

Bhagirathi	**13800**	**30 54 54**	**79 04** 00	Gherwal	Point where the Bhagirathi first emerges from the last snow bed or glacier, measuring 27 feet wide, and but 18 inches deep. Valley 500 feet wide, and 1 mile long.
Sukhi	**8869**	**33 59 55**	**78 41** 13	Ditto	The Ganges may be here said to break through the Himalaya proper: the river bed was found 1261 feet below Sukhi, or above the sea 7608 feet.
Hurdwar	**1024**	**29 56 16**	**78 09** 40	Doab	Ganges enters Hindostan plains.
Jumnautri	**10849**	**30 59 18**	**78 26** 07	Gherwal	Source of the river Jumna; a place of pilgrimage, boiling springs, temperature of the water 194.7 which for *the elevation* here given is nearly the heat at which water is converted into *steam!*
Berai Ganga ...	**12489**	**30 57 15**	**78 31** 36	Ditto	Supposed source, but even here a large stream, crossed on a *natural bridge of frozen snow!* the real source about 3 miles higher from the S. W. foot of the great snowy peak Bonderpuch.
Tons or Lupin...	**12784**	**31 02 48**	**78 28** 56	Ditto	First exit from snow bed, 31 feet wide, and knee deep: for several miles nothing but snow perceptible; origin from the N. face of the same cluster of peaks as the Jumna.
Lari on the Spiti	**11071**	**32 04 32**	**78 23** 40	Ladao	A village here; climate so dry that the houses are built of bricks *baked in the sun*: the houses being *flat* roofed shows that no great quantity of snow falls. Shawl goats abundant.

MINOR STATIONS OF SURVEY.

Simla	**7486**	**31 06 12**	**77 09** 20	Kyonthal	Now a delightful British station; view of the snowy range from thence highly interesting.
Sabbathoo	4456	30 58 12	76 58 37	Bareilli	British cantonment, romantically situate.
Ramghur Fort...	4054	31 05 08	76 46 59	Indus	Strong fort captured from Ghoorkas.
Jaka Station	8120	31 05 56	77 10 06	Kyonthal	High peak of Simla range, top clay slate, bare of trees to the S. well clothed with pine forests on the N. side.
Shalli..............	**9623**	**31 11 16**	**76 41** 17	Bagi	Connected with the Chur range, very inaccessible on account of peculiar shape, wooden temple on summit, where human sacrifices were (and are said to be so still) offered to the Hindoo goddess Cali.
Malown...........	**4448**	**31 12 39**	**79 41** 36		A steep ridge with strong fortress, captured by the British 1815.

PASSES.

Station or Peak.	Height above the sea, feet.	Lat. N.	Long. E.	District or State.	Observations.
Gunass Pass ...	15459	31 21 07	78 08 22	Bissaher	Pass over the outer ridge of the Himalaya, leading from the valley of the Rupin into that of the Baspa. Crossed 30 Sept. 1819, 6 miles of road over snow, very soft in some places, of which the general depth was from 3 to 6 feet, but on the summit of the pass not fathomable with sticks 9 feet long. Ther. at sunset 33° F, water boiled at 187. No granite on the ridge, nothing but gneis.
Buranda ditto ...	15296	31 23 28	78 06 22	Ditto	Pass from the valley of the Pabar into that of the Sutledj.
Childing Kona...	12860	31 37 16	78 27 27	Ditto	Pass above Muring to Nissang.
Sri Gerh	8424	31 24 17	78 25 10	Kullu	Fort on the right bank of the Sutledj.
Chuasi Fort	10744	31 24 56	78 28 47	Suk-hot........	Ditto ditto, there are other forts equally high.
Puari Village ...	6168	31 32 57	78 16 44	Bissaher	Good village on Sutledj, 300 feet above the river, excellent grapes to be had here.
Kanum ditto ...	8998	31 40 26	78 26 17	Ditto	Substantial village on ditto, 500 feet above the river, delicious apples, and grapes in abundance.
Hangarang Pass	14710	31 47 34	78 30 50	Ditto	Between Hang and Sungnam; summit composed entirely of limestone; no snow in October, though a few hundred feet above it laid in patches.
Majang La	17700	31 48 29	79 06 54	Chinese Tartary	Ridge crossed on the road from Shipki to Garu; a few traces of snow in October.
Nako	11975	31 52 34	78 36 31	Bissaher	Tartar village in Hangarang on the left bank of the Spiti; barley grows some hundred feet higher than the village, osiers and poplars are visible near the village.
Skalker Fort......	10272	32 00 02	78 32 18	Ditto	Fort, border of Bishar, right bank of Spiti.
Lasscha Pass ...	13628	32 02 56	78 32 06	Ditto	Pass from Skalkerfort to Surma village; no snow in October, but ink froze at 10 A. M.!

Of the other mountains a brief description will suffice.

The Ghauts (passages or gates, as they are expressively termed) commence in the plains about Coimbatore, in the southern portion of the Dekkan, and, diverging east and west, form, like the shores, the two sides of a triangle, the apex of which points towards Cape Comorin. The eastern Ghauts extend in a north-easterly direction seventy miles beyond Madras, and are only intersected by narrow defiles well lined with fortresses. The northern portion of this chain divides the Circars from the province of Berar, and is exceedingly rugged, precipitous, and difficult of access. Formed of naked granite, the summit of this ridge presents to the adventurous traveller the most dreary and desolate picture that can be imagined. In the rainy season, torrents of fearful volume and rapidity, dashing down through the dark and barren abysses of the mountains, sweep away every thing before them; but in that portion of the year, which in these countries may be termed summer, the sun glares in unmitigated brightness upon the rocks, washed as clean as the steps of a temple by the monsoon rains, and renders them painful to be looked upon. It was this dazzling appearance which led the natives to bestow upon the range the name of Ellacooda, or the White Mountains[1]. 'We are not informed,' says Hamilton, 'of the exact height of this ridge, but its general elevation is known to be considerably less than that

[1] Malte-Brun, tom. iv. p. 9.

of the western Ghauts. About the latitude of Madras, which is the highest part, it is estimated at three thousand feet; and the table-land of Bangalore, towards Ooscottah, which is within the chain, is more than three thousand feet above the level of the sea. As the rivers which have their sources in the upper table-land universally decline to the east, it proves the superior elevation of the western Ghauts, and they are by far the most abrupt in their ascent. The chief component part of these mountains is a granite, consisting of white feldspar and quartz, with dark green mica in a small proportion to the other two ingredients; the particles are angular, and of a moderate size. The rocks appear stratified, but the strata are very much broken and confused[1].'

The western Ghauts, of greater elevation and more picturesque appearance than the eastern, extend northward along the Malabar coast, at a short distance from the sea, and traversing Canara and Bejapore, and passing near Goa, enter the Mahratta country, where they branch off into numerous small ridges. Differing almost entirely from the eastern chain, these mountains are intersected by numerous deep ravines, through which many streams of water descend to the plains, while thick forests of the magnificent trees of the tropics clothe the summits and acclivities with a deep covering of verdure. At the feet of this amphitheatrical sweep of mountains the numerous towns and villages of Malabar glitter in the sun, and overlook the broad blue expanse of

[1] Hamilton, vol. ii. p. 249.

the Indian Ocean. Between these two chains of the Ghauts lies the plateau or table-land of the Dekkan, which breaks rapidly off in the western, and slopes down gradually in the eastern Ghauts, and extends in the north beyond the Nerbudda, where the Vindhya mountains mark its furthest projection towards the plains of Hindostan.

CHAPTER VIII.

GEOLOGY, SOIL, AND CLIMATE OF BRITISH INDIA.

It cannot of course be expected that much accurate information should be extant relative to the geological structure of the Hindostan peninsula. The crust of the territory has in several isolated places been explored, but it will require years of extensive scientific research to form a just idea of the nature of the rocks and soil; my duty, therefore, in this, as in other sections, is to register facts as far as they have been noticed, so that in time the materials for a connected view may be obtained. Primitive formations in which granitic rocks bear the principal proportions, occupy, it is thought, not only the great Himalaya northern chain, but also three-fourths of the entire peninsula, from the valley of the Ganges below Patna to Cape Comorin; although these rocks are frequently overaid by a thin crust of laterite, a ferruginous clay considered as associated with the trap formation. The transition formations have not as yet been clearly distinguished; the secondary formations described are—

I. The *carboniferous group*. Coal occurs extensively in the grits bounding the southern slope of the Himalaya, but it has been questioned whether this formation is the older coal or only lignite associated with nagelflue, as on the slope of the Alps; it has been particularly described, however, where the river Tista issues from this chain, (88° 35′ east longitude,) and there, undoubtedly, bears all the characters of the older formation; its strata are highly inclined, whereas the tertiary beds and even most of the secondary in this part of India are horizontal. The coal district on the river Damúda (100 miles north-west of Calcutta) extends on the banks of the river sixty miles, and appears from its fossil lycopodia to be undoubtedly the older coal; it reposes apparently on the surrounding primitive rocks, but it is not improbable that it extends across the delta of the Ganges to Sylhet, 306 miles, at the eastern extremity of Bengal. Tertiary rocks prevail in Sylhet, and it is doubtful whether the Sylhet coal be not really modern lignite. I believe no carboniferous limestone has been discovered.

II. *Next to coal is a great sandstone formation*, which, beginning at the Ganges on the east, first shews itself supporting basalt on the Raj-Mahal hills; it again prevails throughout the interval between the confluence of the river Soane, and of the Jumna with the Ganges, and then stretches across the west-south-west through the Bundlecund district to the banks of the Nerbudda, (which flows into the Gulf of Cambay as far as 79° east longitude,) where it is overlaid by the extremity of the great basaltic district of north-western India, near Sagâr, the red sandstone shews itself again emerging from beneath the north-west edge of this basaltic district, at Neemuch, near the west source of the Chumbul, and at Bang, in the valley of the Nerbudda.

In both places, as also along the central portion of the platform before described, stretching through Malwa, it is frequently covered with a thin crust of grey argillacekus limestone, supposed to represent English lias, but nearly destitute of organic remains, the general absence of which in the secondary rocks of India is remarkable. A primitive range extending from near Delhi to the head of the Gulf of Cambay separates the secondary rocks of Malwa from those of the great basin of the Indus; but on the west border of this ridge, through Ajmeer, the redstone again shows itself, containing rock-salt and gypsum. The diamond mines of Panna, in Bundlecund, and of the Golconda district, are situate in this formation, the matrix being a conglomerate bed with quartzose pebbles.

III. *Tertiary rocks* are found at the foot of the first rise of the primitive rocks of the Himalaya, in the north-west of Bengal, where the Brahmaputra issues from them at the passes of the Garrow hills. *Cerithiæ turritelli*, remains of crocodiles, sharks, lobsters, &c. are here found, and further east *nummulite* limestone[1] prevails at Sylhet.

[1] The soil throughout Bengal is often occupied by deposits of clay, containing concretionary lumps of limestone, called

The great basaltic district of the north-west of India extends from Nagpúr, in the very centre of India, to the west coasts, between Goa and Bombay, occupying the whole of that coast to its termination at the Gulf of Cambay, thence penetrating northward as far as the twenty-fourth parallel of north latitude.

So far with regard to the general view of the peninsula; I subjoin, however, some detached observations made in different parts of the country, beginning with Bengal, where, in the neighbourhood of Calcutta, we have ascertained the alluvial strata in consequence of a series of boring experiments which have been at intervals carried on between 1804 and 1833, for the purposes of obtaining water. The results of those experiments are thus summed up in the report of the committee appointed by Government.

'After penetrating through the artificial soil of the surface, a light blue or grey-coloured sandy clay occurs, becoming gradually darker as we descend, from impregnation with decayed vegetable matter, until it passes into a stratum of black peat, about two feet in thickness, at a depth, in Fort William, of fifty feet below the surface. This peat stratum has all the appearance of having been formed by the debris of Sundurban vegetation, once on the surface of the Delta, but gradually lowered by the compression of the sandy strata below. Assuming that the salt-water lake is five feet above the average height

kankar, probably of very recent origin; it affords the principal supply of lime in India.

of the ocean, the peat stratum is about as much more below the present level of the sea. In the grey or black clay above and immediately below the peat, logs and branches of a red[1] and of a yellow[2] wood are found imbedded, in a more or less decayed state. In only one instance have bones been met with (at twenty-eight feet), and they appear, from the report of the workmen, to belong to deer, though they were unfortunately lost before examination. A stratum of sand occurs generally above the peat clay, at from fifteen to thirty feet deep, from which the wells in the town are chiefly supplied with brackish water.

'Under the blue clays, at from fifty to seventy feet deep, the nodular limestone concretions, known by the name of *kankar*, occur sometimes in small grains (called *bajri* in Upper India), with the appearance of small land-shells; sometimes in thin strata of great hardness, and sometimes in the usual nodular shape. At seventy feet occurs a second seam of loose reddish sand, which yields water plentifully. It was reached also in the perforation under the lock-gates at Chitpore, and there, as Mr. Jones had previously asserted from his own experiment across the river, the supply of water was proved to be derived direct from the river. From 75 to 125 feet, beds of yellow clay predominate, frequently stiff and pure, like potters' clay, but generally mixed with sand and mica. Horizontal seams of kankar also run through it, re-

[1] The common sûndri of the Sundurbans.

[2] The root of some climbing tree, resembling the *briedelia*. N. Wallich.

sembling exactly those of Midnapur, or of the Gangetic basin. Below 128 feet, a more sandy yellow clay prevails, which gradually changes to a grey loose sand, extending to the lowest depth yet penetrated, and becoming coarser in quality, until, at 170 or 176 feet, it may rather be termed a quartzy gravel, containing angular fragments of quartz and feldspar, larger than peas, such as are met with near the foot of a granitic range of hills. This stratum has hitherto arrested the progress of the auger; the greatest depth attained by Dr. Strong, near St. Peter's Church, being 176 feet.'

On leaving the low and level delta of the Ganges, and approaching the Rajemhal hills in the neighbourhood of Boglipoor, we find primitive mountains composed of black whinstone in large masses. The hills at the foot of the mountains produce flint, nodules, iron ore, beautiful agates of various descriptions, quartz, crystallizations, and hard bolderstones fit for paving. The Curracknore hills are mostly composed of quartz, from which issue many hot springs, which constantly retain their heat in all seasons of the year. About Monghyr the rocks are quartz, except a few which are composed of a slaty stone of a bluish colour; the hills in Ghidore, near Mallypore, produce good limestone; and at Milkee, the quartz is so pure, that it might profitably be manufactured into glass. The Rev. Mr. Everest, in a journey from Calcutta to Ghazeepore, thus describes the geology of a part of the country he passed through:—'The isolated appearance of the hills on the new road, with the flat plains of sand, or disintegrated granite between them, forcibly suggest that, at one time, the former were islets in an ocean, in which were precipitated beds of their debris, and subsequently of the vegetables which grew upon them. The coal beds on the Dhammoodu abound with impressions of a reed which is not found in Europe, and may be deemed characteristic of the Indian coal. Between Bancoora and the Soane there are observable not less than four protrusions of trap, not cutting through like dykes, but pushed and spread from between the strata of sandstone and gneis, as if forced upwards under enormous pressure. The evanescent gradations between the primitive rocks, granite, gneis, greenstone, basalt, and sandstone, suggest the idea of their having been kept long in contact together while in a state of igneous fusion: the direction also of the trap protrusions, which at first dip to the north, then are vertical, and, towards Kutcumsandy, dip to the south, render it probable that they have all a common focus under the earth, and that the whole granitic plateau of Hazareebagh, and perhaps the whole range of the Vindhya mountains, has been upheaved by their instrumentality. The granite in the neighbourhood of the trap evinces, by its crumbling state, the extensive 'maladie,' as the French call it, to which it has been subjected.'

The same series of rocks occurs on both sides of the central plateau, extending in opposite directions, both to the vale of the Ganges and to the alluvium of Bengal. Coal is found on both sides, as is proved at Palamoo and Boglipore. The sandstones above the line are, however, more consolidated and useful. Mr.

Everest supposes the hot springs, so frequent in occurrence, to be indicative of gradual combustion of the coal strata, of which there is further evidence in the loads of cinders and burnt shale met with in the mines at Ranigunj. The reverend gentleman ascribes the kankur formation to the action of calcareous springs. As the Ganges is ascended towards Ghazeepore, the soil becomes more granitic, and is then succeeded by a gravel of burnt clay, argite, and cinders, resembling what is seen in other basaltic countries.

Let us now examine the western part of the peninsula. The elevated table-land of the Deccan is[1] exclusively composed of rocks belonging to the flat trap formation; the hills which rise on the west Ghauts as a base have conical or tabular forms, and are sometimes distributed in long ridges or terraces, which run east-north-east. Passing from the lower land of the Conkan into the higher part of the Deccan, these tabular forms are grand and beautiful; they are generally triangular-shaped, and insulated from each other by broad and deep ravines, of which the perpendicular descent cannot be less than 1200 or 1500 feet: the tables are a compact basalt of a black colour, in which hornblende predominates. About Poonah, and further south-east, the rocks are generally amygdaloidal, and become lighter in colour the farther they are removed from the western entrance. This amygdaloid is in no respect different from the sandstone of extra tropical climates; it shows embedded masses of calcedony, zoolites, and green earth, and in the neigh-

[1] According to Surgeon Bird.

bourhood of water courses, at the depth of twenty-five or thirty feet below the surface, contains drusy cavities of chrystallized quartz, the appearance of which in digging wells indicates that water is near; a clayey iron ore of a dark brown colour is found at this depth, and is sometimes penetrated by circular canals which have been pervious to water; the amygdaloid rock accompanying the iron ore is similarly penetrated, but its canals are filled up by spiral pieces of white calcedony. Calcareous carbonate, denominated chunam, abounds on the banks of the water courses, and is seen occasionally in alternate strata with an impure bole, called by the natives '*geru.*' Chunam is also found in the form of calc-tuft in the beds of the nullas (ravines), and is seen venegenous in the basaltic and amygdaloid rocks at the village of Lonud, where calc-spar is also found in veins. Greenstone, heliotrope, agate, and horn-stones are also met with, as is also rock crystal, immediately on the surface of amygdaloid, or below the soil. The amygdaloid runs through the Deccan east and west, corresponding with the hills of quartz rock met with in Pádshápúr. The basalt of the Deccan occurs both in columnar and globular forms, and varies in colour from a bluish grey to a deep black, the latter capable of receiving a high degree of polish, and employed by the Hindoos for the decoration of the interior of their temples. A porphyritic aggregated rock of a grey colour is found in beds. On the north bank of the Ghatpurba there are entire hills having some likeness to sandstone, but in fact they are aggregated quartz rock, the structure of which is extremely hard, varying from a secondary sandstone to that of a pure quartz. This structure extends to Belgaum, from whence to Kittoor numerous pieces of iron ore (some bubbled as if suddenly cooled while in a state of fusion) are found scattered over the country, indiscriminately huddled together with quartz and basalt. In Kittoor vicinity the structure of the rocks is coarse slate, composed of alternate layers of quartz and iron ore, varying in thickness up to an inch, and giving a striped appearance to the rock, which is highly magnetic when cut into a parallelogrammical figure.

The geology of the country between the Kistnah and Godavery is distinguished from most other countries of a similar extent by the existence of only two formations, differing very widely in their characters, viz. *granite* and *flœtz-trap*, both of which give a striking and separate character to the scenery, cultivation, and vegetable productions[1]. After quitting the limestone on the banks of the Kistnah, granite alone is the base of the country, even to the Godavery; the principal characteristics, as seen at Hydrabad[2] (1800

[1] See Journal of Asiatic Society of Bengal, No. 18, for June, 1833, for Dr. Voysey's Geological Report of Hydrabad.

[2] Captain Ousley, the resident at Housungabad, has, after various unsuccessful attempts, at last succeeded in discovering some very valuable beds of coal in the rich mineral district in which he is stationed. For some time past, it is stated, this officer had been induced to believe, from a variety of circumstances, that large deposits of that substance were to be found in the valley of the Nerbudda; but until recently small quantities of it only were obtained, and these, generally speaking, were of an indifferent quality. Information, however, was brought to him, that large masses of a black mineral were to

feet above the level of the sea), Maidak, Banchapilly, Koulas, &c., are, 1st, The great irregularity of extent, and direction of the ranges; 2nd, The narrow but lengthened veins or dykes of trap with which it is intersected, all running nearly in the same direction, and the masses of micaceous and sienitic granite with which it is intermixed; 3rd, The predominance of the red colour arising from the red feldspar, which is frequently in large crystals, giving the granite a porphyritic appearance; 4th, The concentric lamellar and distinct concrete structure, the greater facility of decomposition, and the rounded appearance of decomposed masses, logging-stones, and tors; 5th, The numerous lakes or tanks spread all over the country, some of which are of very large dimensions. Within twenty miles radius from the station of Suldapúr, on a misty morning, thirty-three lakes were counted,

be found on the banks of a small stream, called the Seta Reiva, one of the tributaries of the Nerbudda, which, on examination, proved to be beds of coal, of a superior kind. The discovery of this treasure in India would at any time be an interesting event, but at this period, when every exertion is making to bring steam communication between the distant places of India into use, it is of the utmost importance, as the greatest obstacle to the establishment of steam-vessels on the rivers was the difficulty of procuring a sufficient supply of coal without incurring an expense which the proceeds would not warrant. The locality of the newly-discovered mines is also advantageous, from the ready manner in which supplies can be received from the banks of the Nerbudda. The masses in which it has been found vary from ten to fifteen feet in thickness, and their extent horizontally appears, it is stated, to be very considerable.

most of them of considerable dimensions; they are partly natural, partly artificial, and used for irrigating the surrounding lower grounds.

The other geological divisions of the country, consisting of *basaltic trap*, are interesting, 1st, From its appearance on the upper half or summit only of some of the granite hills; 2nd, Its transition from a highly chrystalline compound of feldspar and horneblende (the greenstone of Werner) to coarse and fine basalt, to wacken, and to iron clay; 3rd, The direction and peculiar form of the ranges, the waving form of the land in some instances, and in others its flatness and conical peaks; 4th, Its intermixture of carbonate of lime with the wacken, the basalt, and even with some of the granite in the neighbourhood of the trap; 5th, Black cotton soil, arising generally from the decomposition of the basaltic trap forming the banks of rivers, and covering their neighbouring plains. This soil is rich, and peculiarly adapted to the cultivation of dry grains, such as maize, zea, different species of panicum, &c.

The rock in which the caves of Ellora are excavated is said to be a *basaltic trap*, which, from its green tinge and its different stages from hardness to disintegration, is supposed by natives to be full of vegetable matter, in a greater or less advance to petrifaction: the crumbling rock affords a natural green colour, which is ground up and employed by the natives in painting on wet chunam.

The vast Himalaya mountains are at a considerable angle: the dip of the strata is to the east of north, and their abutment to the west of south. The formations are primary; the first towards the plains consists of vast strata of limestone lying on clay slate, crowned by slate, grey wacken, or sandstone. Beyond the limestone tract gneis, clay slate, and other schistose rocks occur. Granite, I believe, has not been found in the outer ridges; it occurs in the mountains near the snowy range. The igneous rocks which have been concerned in the upheavement of the outer tracts are of the greenstone trap series, and are very generally dykes intersecting and rising through the regular strata. The formation of the Himalaya has a remarkable feature; the strata are in all directions fractured or comminuted; the slaty rocks are broken into small fragments as if they had been crushed, and the limestone rocks are vesicular or cavernous, and broken into masses. The soil is principally accumulated on the north sides, and that lying under the vegetable mould is clayey and calcareous, or limestone gravel, and from the humidity of the climate vegetation is exuberant.

Captain Gerard in crossing the Charang Pass, (17,348 feet high,) describes the neighbouring mountains to be all of blue slate, naked to their tops, and exhibiting decay and barrenness in their most frightful form; in other parts the mountains are of granite, with a great mixture of white quartz both in the veins and nodules; gneis however is the only extensive rock to characterise the Himalaya formation; various mineral productions, including iron, gold, plumbago, copper, lead, antimony, sulphur, &c. have been found.

That volcanoes exist in the regions of perpetual

snow is in some measure proved by the earthquake which recently occurred, as described at page 151; but it is remarkable that over so vast an extent of territory as Hindostan there should be so very few indications of the effects of subterranean fires;—on the contrary, traces of a universal deluge are most striking, not merely in the appearance of the land, its waving outline, and stupendous water courses, but in the fossil remains now being daily discovered, and the extensive beds of shells found on the highest grounds.

Dr. Gerard, in a letter to the Asiatic Society, describes some extensive tracts of shell formations, discovered by him in the Himalaya range at 15,000 feet above the sea. The principal shells comprised cockles, muscles, and pearl fish, univalves, and long cylindrical productions which are most singular objects. He found them lying upon the high land at 15,500 feet elevation, in a bed of granite and pulverized slate; the adjacent rocks being at the same time of shell limestone. All the shells were turned into carbonate of lime, and many were crystallized like marble; the larger blocks, composed of a multitude of shells of different sizes, imbedded in a matrix of calcareous tufa, was broken off from a solid mass of 150 cubic feet, apparently all of the same structure: four classes of shell formation were distinguished; in particular a *fresh water* bivalve, resembling the unio, which exists in great abundance at the foot of the lower hills and throughout the plains of the Doab.

In the Neermal hills, lying north of the Godaveri river, on the road from Hydrabad to Nâghpûr, many very perfect fossil shells, mostly bivalves, and evidently marine, have been recently discovered imbedded in a volcanic rock, together with the head and vertebræ of a fish. The formations rest everywhere on granite, and have the usual characters of this class of hills. A series of hot springs occur holding lime in solution. The Neermal Hills belong to *Sehsa* range, extending from south-east to north-west several hundred miles. The *Lunar* lake is forty miles from Saulna, and is a vast crater, 500 feet deep and from four to five miles round the margin; its waters are green and bitter, supersaturated with alkaline carbonate, and containing silex in solution, as well as some iron. The mud is black, and abounding in sulphuretted hydrogen; nevertheless the water is pure, and without smell.

At a meeting of the Geological Society, held the 9th of March, 1836, a memoir was read, 'On the Remains of Mammalia[1] found in a range of Mountains at the Southern Foot of the Himalayas, between the Sutlej and the Burhampooter,' by Captain Cautley, F.G.S.

As these mountains are not known to the inhabitants or geographers by a distinct name, Captain Cautley, to avoid the confusion arising from the terms, 'Lower hills,' 'Sub-Himalayas,' and many similar, has adopted the word "Sewalik," which was formerly applied to that portion of the chain lying between the Ganges and the Jumna.

The range is, in some places, connected with the Himalayas by a succession of low mountains: but, in

[1] Some gigantic fossil bones have been, I hear, sent to Mr. Mantel's valuable museum at Brighton.—R. M. M.

others, is separated from them by valleys varying in breadth from three to ten miles. The average height of the chain is about 2000, or 2500 feet, the loftiest peaks not exceeding 3000 feet above the level of the sea, or 1500 above that of the adjacent plains.

The formations of which the mountains are composed, consist of marls, sandstones, and conglomerates inclined at angles varying from 15° to 35°, and generally to the north, but the sections on the banks of the rivers sometimes present an anteclinal axis, where the strata dip both to the north and the south.

The conglomerates are composed of pebbles of granite, gneis, mica slate, quartz, and other rocks, derived apparently from the Himalayas; and Captain Cautley observes, that the beds of the existing rivers contain, in great abundance, exactly similar pebbles. The sandstones consist of grains of quartz cemented by oxide of iron, or carbonate of lime, and are sometimes quarried for architectural purposes. They generally contain carbonaceous matter, either as distinct fragments exhibiting vegetable structure, or as minute, disseminated particles; and in the Kalowala Pass, one of the entrances to the valley of Deyra, the author found elliptical masses of sandstone thinly coated with coal.

In the hills between the Jumna and the Ganges, the remains of mammalia had been noticed only in the marl, and in those to the westward of the Jumna only in the sandstone. In the former district the distribution of the organic remains obtained by Captain Cautley, was as follows :—

Conglomerate—Lignite, scarce.

Sandstone—Trunks of dicotyledonous trees in great abundance, lignite, and remains of reptiles.

Marl—Remains of a species of anthracotherium bear, caston, deer, horse, gavial crocodile, tortoises, fishes, and fresh-water shells.

The sandstones west of the Jumna have yielded a still greater number of mammalian remains, those hitherto determined belonging to the mastodon, elephant, rhinoceros, hippopotamus, hog, horse, deer, carnivora (canine and feline), crocodile, gavial tortoise, and fishes.

The *Soils* of Hindostan vary of course with the geological characters of the country—in the deltas of rivers, consisting of a rich alluvium—and in countries of a trap formation, a stiff clayey and tenacious surface, highly fertile when irrigated, prevails. In Lower Bengal the fertility of the soil seems to be inexhaustible, owing perhaps to its saline qualities; for several centuries it has been in unceasing cultivation as the granary of India, rudely tilled, without the application of scientific principles to agriculture, and yet there seems to be no diminution in its fertility; as we ascend the Ganges the quality of the earth of course varies.

The following is an analysis of three specimens of soil from sugar cane fields; the *first* was from a village on the Sarju, ten miles north of the Ganges, at Buxar; the other two from the south of the Ganges near the same place. Numbers one and two require irrigation, three was sufficiently retentive of moisture to render it unnecessary; there is a substratum of

Kankur throughout the whole of that part of the country, and to some mixture of this earthy limestone with the surface of the soil the fertility of the latter is ascribed ; the sugar cane grown yielded a rich juice.

	No. 1.	No. 2.	No. 3.
Hygrometric moisture on drying at 212°	2.5	2.1	3.6
Carbonaceous and vegetable matter on calcination	1.8	2.1	4.0
Carb. lime from digestion in nitric acid and precipitation, by carb. pot. (No. 3 alone effervesced)	1.6	0.6	3.9
Alkaline salt dissolved	1.0	1.1	0.3
Silex and alumina........................	94.1	24.1	88.2
	100	100	100

The earths were not farther examined, but the two first consisted chiefly of sand ; the third somewhat argillaceous. All were of a soft, fine ground alluvium, without pebbles, the analysis confirmed the quantities ascribed to each specimen.

Taking another country of different formation as a specimen, I close this section. The soils vary of the Hydrabad district, with the facility with which the rock of which they are formed decomposes ; it is generally silicious. The analysis of a garden soil at the cantonment of Secundarabad which had not received much manure, shewed specific gravity 1.70. Four hundred and eighty grains contained water of absorption, 10 grains ; stones consisting of quartz and felspar, 255 grains; vegetable fibre, 2; silicious sand, 154=431 grains. Of minutely divided matter separated by infiltration, viz. carbonate of lime, 7 ; vegetable matter, 7 ; oxide of iron, 2.5. ; salt, 4;

silica, 20; alumina, 8; loss, 10.5. Total, 480. The richest soil in this district, and the most spontaneously productive is that arising from the decomposition of the clay slate.

The soil of Bengal is extremely shallow, and a compound of saltish mud and sand, the former derived from the inundations of the rivers washing down the richest particles of the surface in the upper provinces, and the sand probably being the reliquie of the ocean which is here retreating from the land. The Regur or cotton ground, which extends over the greatest part of central India, is supposed to be a disintegration of trap rocks; it requires neither manure nor rest, slowly absorbs moisture, and retains it long, and it has produced the most exhausting crops in yearly succession for centuries. The saltpetre or nitrous soil is general in Bahar. All the soils of India have in general a powerful absorbing quality; hence, their fertile properties.

Climate.—The temperature of so wide an extent of country as British India, and of such different degrees of elevation is, of course, very varied; for its exposition I shall, therefore, adopt the division pursued in the preceding sections.

Bengal Proper.—No tract of country inhabited by man possesses a more damp climate than this flat province, where nearly one half the year it rains incessantly, and during the other half the dews are most penetrating. (*For its effects see Population Chapter*). Mr. Hamilton thinks the dampness of the climate cannot be ascribed to any inherent moisture of the earth, but that it must originate from the want of a general system of drainage, from luxuriant vegetation and deficient ventilation; but I think it evident that the saline quality of the earth and of the plants which grow in it peculiarly fit it for the retention of the vast quantity of rain, (amounting to seventy or eighty inches) which falls in the rainy season, coming in with June and continuing to the middle or end of October. During this humid period, the range of the thermometer affords no indication of the climate, or more properly speaking oppressiveness, of the weather; it may ascend to 88° or 90° F., or descend to 79° or even 72°, but the exhaustion of the European bodily frame still remains unchanged. I have felt more sinking—more prostration of strength in Bengal, lying on a couch beneath a *punka* with the thermometer at 77° or 80°, than in riding through the forests of New Holland during the blowing of a hot wind, with the thermometer at 110° F. The reason was, that in the former the atmosphere was saturated with the moisture, and in the latter almost painfully constrictive with dryness. To judge, therefore, of the effects of heat on the animal frame merely by referring to the height of the mercury in Fahrenheit's bulb, is exceedingly fallacious.

I give the following table as illustrative of the facts adduced in reference to the same subject in the southern hemisphere. (See Vol. II. Colonial Library.)

Influence of the moon in producing rain (Calcutta) in each year.

	First 4 months in each year.		For each year.	
	Inches of rain within 7 days of new moon.	Inches of rain beyond that period.	No. of rainy days within 7 days of new moon.	No. of rainy days beyond that period.
1825	1.82	0.58	8	4
1827	1.62	1.00	5	3
1828	0.16	1.82	1	5
1829	1.72	0.00	3	0
1830	6.48	0.74	9	3
1831	5.55	1.85	8	4
1832	4.86	2.25	6	2
1833	3.10	1.00	5	2
Total	25.31	9.24	45	23

From these observations, as well as others, made by the Rev. R. Everest, it appears that rain fell most abundantly on the 2nd, 5th, 6th, and 7th days before the new moon, and the 6th day after it.

The *rainy* season in Bengal is succeeded by what is termed the *cold* season, which lasts from November to the middle of February, when the *hot* season begins and continues to the middle of June. During the cold season the air is clear, sharp and bracing in some degrees. Thermometer 65° to 84° mean 72°; barometer medium 29° to 96°.

The commencement of the *hot* season in the lower parts of the province is almost intolerable even to a native of the country; men and beasts have been known to fall dead in the streets of Calcutta in April and May: the sun's fervid rays, so advantageous to the farmer and shepherd, seem to penetrate to the very marrow, while not a cloud appears in the heavens to check his burning beams. When the monsoon is on the eve of changing, the very air feels as it were thick, respiration is laborious, and all animated nature languishes, the oppressiveness of the night being nearly as great as that of the day. Observations were made by Mr. Goldingham at Madras; Major Burney at Ava; Benares Oriental Magazine,

1827; Captain Hodgson, and Dr. Royle, at Saharunpore, of the monthly deviations of the barometer and thermometer from their annual mean height.

Month.	Barometer at 32° Fahr.					Thermometer.			
	Ava, 1830.	Calcutta, for 8 years, 1829-30-31.	Benares, 4 years' observations, 1822—1826*.	Saharunpore,† 1826, 1827.	Madras, mean of 21 years' observations max. and min.	Ava, 1830, sunrise and 4 P.M.	Calcutta, 3 years' observations max. and min.	Benares, 4 years' observations max. and min.	Saharunpore, 1826, 1827.
	Inches.	Inches.	Inches	Inches.	Degrees.	Degrees.	Degrees.	Degrees.	Degrees.
Jan.	+ .229	+ .208	+ .273	+ .274	— 6.5	— 13.7	— 11.6	— 17.0	— 21.8
Feb.	+ .115	+ .172	+ .175	+ .219	— 4.5	— 4.9	— 6.0	— 11.5	— 20.9
March	+ .051	+ .095	+ .107	+ .151	— 1.8	— 2.8	+ 1.0	— 1.5	+ 0.1
April	— .028	— .030	— .043	+ .061	+ 9.7	+ 7.8	+ 5.1	+ 9.5	+ 6.1
May	— .105	— .152	— .136	— .060	+ 5.2	+ 5.6	+ 7.5	+ 13.9	+ 11.6
June	— .156	— .248	— .289	— .217	+ 7.4	+ 7.1	+ 5.5	+ 13.1	+ 17.5
July	— .176	— .218	— .308	— .398	+ 3.9	+ 4.4	+ 4.6	+ 6.9	+ 12.8
August	— .126	— .194	— .203	— .278	+ 3.0	+ 4.1	+ 3.6	+ 6.4	+ 10.0
Sept.	— .098	— .115	— .098	— .158	+ 2.1	+ 4.3	+ 3.7	+ 5.8	+ 9.5
Oct.	— .010	+ .020	+ .074	— .047	+ 0.1	+ 2.2	+ 2.5	+ 1.3	— 0.8
Nov.	+ .102	+ .161	+ .181	+ .209	— 3.1	— 4.2	— 5.4	— 9.7	— 10.8
Dec.	+ .201	+ .258	+ .279	+ .245	— 4.9	— 10.1	— 11.5	— 17.6	— 13.8
Annual Mean	29.573	29.764	29.464	23.766	81.69	78.39	78.13	77.81	73.5
	.405	.506	.587	.672	13.9	.21	19.1	31.5	.3

* Benares is about 300 feet above the level of the sea.

† Saharunpore is about 1000 feet above the sea-level.

The range of variation in atmosphere increases with the latitude, even up to the foot of the Himalaya mountains; and is accompanied by a corresponding increase in the range of the thermometer.

August is the most damp month of the year to the sense; but June is the month in which the atmosphere is really loaded with the greatest weight of aqueous vapour. January is in every respect the driest season of the year, but the drought at Calcutta naturally falls far short of what is experienced at Benares and Saharunpore, where the depression of the moistened thermometer sometimes exceeds thirty-five degrees.

Depression of the wet bulb thermometer, and deduced tension of vapour in the atmosphere at Calcutta, 1829, 30, 31.

Month.	Sunrise.		9.40 A. M.		Noon.		2. 50. P. M.		4 P. M.		Sunset.	
	Dep.	Ten.	Dep.	Ten.	Dep.	Ten.	Dep.	Ten.	Dep.	Ten.	Dep.	Ten.
	°		°		°		°		°		°	
Jan.	2.3	.82	8.4	.51	13.1	.37	15.9	.31	14.4	.32	9.3	.50
Feb.	1.6	.87	8.5	.56	12.4	.44	14.4	.38	13.9	.39	11.1	.47
March	1.9	.89	8.7	.59	12.6	.47	14.2	.41	14.1	.41	10.7	.51
April	1.4	.94	8.1	.66	11.7	.53	13.9	.46	12.7	.50	8.1	.64
May	1.8	.92	7.3	.69	9.8	.62	10.8	.58	9.7	.61	6.0	.73
June	1.6	.92	4.4	.78	6.6	.71	6.6	.73	5.2	.76	0.5	.83
July	1.9	.90	4.6	.79	5.5	.75	5.5	.74	5.0	.77	3.5	.83
Aug.	1.6	.93	4.4	.80	5.4	.77	4.9	.77	4.8	.78	3.1	.85
Sept.	1.7	.91	5.3	.76	6.5	.71	5.8	.73	5.2	.76	3.8	.81
Oct.	1.5	.92	6.1	.71	8.0	.65	8.6	.63	7.4	.66	4.3	.79
Nov.	2.8	.85	9.0	.55	12.3	.44	13.9	.40	12.6	.43	8.1	.59
Dec.	2.4	.83	7.4	.59	10.8	.47	12.5	.43	11.3	.44	6.9	.61
Mean Tension	...	.892		.665		.577		.547		.570		.680

The average fall of rain at Calcutta for three recent years, was inches 59-83.

A Meteorological Register for Calcutta during the Year 1833 (Assay Office).

	Barometer, reduced to 32 F.				Temperature of air in an open Viranda.				Hair Hygrometer.		Rain.	Wind.	Weather.
	5 A. M.	10 A. M.	4 P. M.	10½ P. M.	Minimum, 5 P. M.	10 A. M.	Regulated Maximum.	10½ P. M.	10 A. M.	4 P. M.	Inches.		
	°	°	°	°	°	°	°	°	°	°			
January ...	30.036	.095	.979	.056	61.1	68.0	81.3	66.4	85	78	0.05	Northerly.	Clear & dry.
February ...	.925	.969	.844	.951	67.5	74.0	83.5	71.5	86	78	0.48	Light airs.	Generally fine.
March	29.788	.880	.757	.829	75.0	82.3	91.7	77.8	90	80	1.77	S. (monsoon)	Squally.
April	.692	.765	.650	.699	78.8	87.5	97.2	80.8	92	83	3 52	Ditto.	Stormy.
May	.565	.617	.545	.593	80.8	87.5	94.0	83	95	90	12.86	Variable.	Heat
June	29.511	.569	.485	.550	84.3	90.5	95.8	85.1	92.5	88.2	3.04	Ditto.	Cool, rain.
July	.484	.533	.454	.522	81.3	86.3	91.8	83	95.4	94.0	12.44	Do. & calm.	Moderately rainy.
August	29.548	.599	.520	.582	81.0	85.0	90.2	80.5	96.0	93.0	8.15	Ditto.	Ditto.
September	29.593	.652	.548	.612	81.1	86.3	93.5	82.6	95	92	8.19	S. and E.	Squally.
October......	.790	.860	.751	.819	78.8	85.2	93.5	80.7	91	87	3.68	Calm.	Fine.
November .	29.953	30.029	.926	.978	70.3	79.0	89.2	74.7	88	74	0.06	Light breezes	Ditto.
December ..	29.927	.014	.906	.957	63.0	71.7	82.3	66.7	89.4	85.7	2.57	Ditto.	Cold.

On the north-east frontier of Bengal, where the country begins to be elevated above the level of the sea, the climate, when the land is cleared, is described to be very fine : indeed a sanatarium has been established at Churra Poonjee in the Kossya hills, situated about four marches distant from Sylhet, and the same north from Assam ; a detachment of sick artillery sent thither speedily recovered health, and the station has the advantage of being an important military position as well as a delightful sanatarium : two spots are described as exceedingly eligible for cantonments. One a fine plain, extending from the hill Chillingdes eastward to Nongkreem, and presenting a surface of about four or five square miles, unbroken by any undulation which could not be easily rendered practicable for wheeled carriages. The altitude is probably about 6800 feet, and the climate so moderate, that in May woollen clothes are worn by all the Europeans from choice. In winter there are frosts, but it does not appear that snow ever falls. The second spot is the plain, about three miles south of Nogundee, crossed by the road between that place and Sunareem. This possesses all the advantages of the former, but is probably a little lower, though not so much so as to be perceptibly warmer; and the access from this spot to Pundua is easier, besides enjoying obvious advantages of health and comfort, as corps in either of these positions would be prepared on emergency to afford a speedy and effectual support to any part of the north-east frontier.

Nuncklow station in the Kossya hills (the climate of which is now so much appreciated) is in north latitude 25° 40′ 30″, east longitude 91° 30′, and 4,550 feet above the level of the sea; it is described to be one of the loveliest spots in the world—more like a gentleman's demesne in England than what India is so erroneously supposed to be—all swamps or sand. The thermometer in May ranges from 67° to 75°, in June from 68° to 72° and frost and ice exist in winter.

Arracan.—The prevailing winds are two monsoons as in Bengal, but owing to local circumstances the south-west blows more frequently from the south, and the north-east more to the west of north. The *changes* of the moonsoon are also not so distinctly marked; the south-west is of the longest duration, beginning in April and ending in November. Our troops suffered much in Arracan during the Burmese war, but there is no doubt that as cultivation extends, the climate of Arracan will be found far superior to that of Lower Bengal. The principal rainy months are May, June, and July—seventy inches fall in June and fifty-nine in July.

Bahar.—The climate is divided into three seasons as in Bengal, but the intensity of the heat and moisture is considerably mitigated; from its elevation above the level of the sea, the cold season is more extended in duration and more frigid.

Tirhoot, a district of Bahar, between 27° and 28° north latitude extending in a south-east direction 160 miles, and bounded to the north by a lofty chain of mountains separating it from the alpine kingdoms of Nepaul, is placed in a happy medium free from the fogs of Bengal and the dry parching winds of the north-west provinces. The soil is luxuriantly fertile, and almost every European fruit and vegetable is produced in perfection and in abundance in Tirhoot. The following shows the—

Barometrical pressure and temperature at Tirhoot.

Months.	Barometer, at 32°, (inches.)			Thermometer (degrees.)				Wind.
	Average Monthly Altitude.	Monthly deviation from Annual Mean.	Mean Monthly diurnal Oscillation.	Average height in the house.	Mean of daily extremes in open air.	Monthly deviation from Annual Mean.	Mean diurnal ran. e.	
January	29.698	+.308	.111	60.6	60.4	—17.6	19.0	E. & W.
February ...	.575	+.165	.101	66.4	66.7	—11.3	23.2	W.
March	.479	+.089	.087	76.3	76.1	— 1.9	23.9	W.
April.........	.369	—.021	.089	81.6	85.2	+ 7.2	24.1	W. & E.
May	.522	—.138	.071	85.3	89.2	+ 7.3	19.5	E.
June	.146	—.244	.068	86.0	86.7	+11.2	19.1	E.
July	.125	—.265	.069	84.6	84.5	+ 8.7	12.3	E.
August	.173	—.217	.070	83.2	85.0	+ 6.5	9.8	E.
September	.237	—.153	.085	84.3	81.5	+ 7.0	10.5	E.
October	.445	+.055	.093	81.5	73.8	+ 3.5	14.7	E.
November	.570	+.080	.090	78.4	...	— 4.2	21.9	E.
December	.614	+.224	.080	63.6	61.6	—16.4	17.7	W.
Mean......	29.390	range .573	.084	77.5	78.0	range 28.8	17.9	

The climate of Benares is pretty similar to that of Tirhoot.

The *western provinces* under the Bengal Presidency, viz. Allahabad [1], Agra, Delhi, &c. are temperate, but

[1] A correspondent of the *Asiatic Journal* of Bengal gives the following particulars of a fall of fish, which happened on the 17th of May last, in the neighbourhood of Allahabad :—" The zemindars of the village have furnished the following particulars, which are confirmed by other accounts. About noon,

hot winds blow during a part of the warm season, when the wealthier natives sometimes resort to underground habitations to escape their torrifying effects.

The climate of central India is mild, and approaches much to that of the south parts of Europe, or to the table land of Spain; although the mercury may rise to 100, during the day, the nights are bland and invigorating.

The English dominions among the hills and along the Kumaon province are blessed with a delicious climate, the rigours of the winter solstice being moderated by great solar radiation, while the summer heats are tempered by the contiguous eternal snow-topped Himalaya. Indeed, during the summer season, the vicinity of the frozen region causes a continued current of atmosphere, which sets in daily as regularly as a sea breeze on a tropical shore, and with a nearly similar invigorating freshness. At Saharun-

the wind being from the west, and a few distant clouds visible, a blast of high wind, accompanied with much dust, which changed the atmosphere to a reddish yellow hue, came on; the blast appeared to extend in breadth about 400 yards, chappers were carried off, and trees blown down. When the storm had passed over, they found the ground, south of the village, to the extent of two bigahs, strewed with fish, in number not less than 3000 or 4000. The fish were all of the Chalwa species (Clopea Cultrata, Shakspeare's Dictionary), a span or less in length, and from one and a half to half a seer in weight. When found, they were all dead and dry. Chalwa fish are found in the tanks and rivers in the neighbourhood. The nearest tank in which there is water is about half a mile south of the village. The Jumna runs about three miles south of the village, the Ganges fourteen miles north by east. The fish were not eaten; it *is said* that in the pan they turned into blood!"

poor, in 30° latitude, and 1000 feet above the sea, the climate is similar to the southern parts of Europe; the mean temperature throughout the year is about 73°, and monthly mean temperature at Seharunpoor (1000 feet above the sea).

Jan.	Feb.	March	April	May	June	July	Aug.	Sept.	Oct.	Nov.	Dec.
52°	55°	67°	78°	85°	90°	85°	88°	79°	74°	64°	55°
At Mussoorri (7000 feet high).											
39	40	52	60	72	73	66	65	61	60	52	40

Mr. Trail thus describes the climate of the Bhot mehals (districts) of the Kumaon territory.—'During full half the year, the surface is wholly covered with snow, beginning to fall about the end of September, and continuing to accumulate to the beginning of April. In open and level situations, where the bed of snow is in some years twelve feet deep, it is dissipated early in June; in the hollows not till the middle of July. During the five months of absence of snow, the thermometer ranges at sun-rise from 40° to 55°, and at mid-day from 65° to 75° in the shade, and from 90° to 110° in the sun. At *Hawil Bagh* in Kumaon, 3887 feet above the sea, the range of the thermometer during the year was

	7 A.M.	2 P.M.		7 A.M.	2 P.M.		7 A.M.	2 P.M.		7 A.M.	2 P.M.
Jan.	35°	47°	April	54°	66°	July	72°	78°	Oct.	55°	69°
Feb.	37	55	May	57	73	Aug.	72	79	Nov.	42	60
March	46	61	June	73	76	Sep.	65	67	Dec.	34	52

'The heat of course diminishes as the height increases, and at Almora town in 29° 30′ (5400 feet high) the difference is 2° or 3° less than the above average. During the cold season, on the contrary, from the greater evaporation, the thermometer before sunrise is always lowest in the valleys, and the frost more intense than on the hills of moderate height (that is below 7000 feet) while at noon the sun is more powerful. The extremes in twenty-four hours have been known 18° and 51°. The snow does not fall equally every year; the natives fix on every third year as one of heavy snow, but in general it does not lie long, except on the mountain tops and ridges. On the Ghagar range between Almora and the plains, snow remains so late as the month of May. At Masuri, 6 to 7000 feet high, the mean animal heat is only 57° F.; indeed at 4000 feet elevation the hot winds cease, and vegetation assumes a European character. The quantity of rain falling at Almora is from forty to fifty inches per annum.'

Of the British territories in Berar we know, as I have before said, little or nothing certain; dense jungles and foaming cataracts impede the steps of the meteorological inquirer.

Orissa, or more properly speaking Cuttack, enjoys in the neighbourhood of the sea a refreshing breeze. Pooree, on the coast, is considered by Dr. Brander the Montpellier of Bengal, the climate being less moist, and a refreshing sea-breeze blowing continually from March to July; it is thus also with the Ultra Gangetic territories, viz. Assam, Tavoy, Ye, Tenasserim, &c., where the high lands are cool and not unsuited even to European constitutions, when the jungle has been cleared. The Cachar territory recently acquired is much praised by Captain Fisher, who says—'It is as sweet a country as I can well imagine, and it exceeds in fertility almost any country in India, although enjoying the very great advantage of being above inundations; it is therefore not only adapted to a rice crop, but to almost all other species of produce, and I should specify *sugar* as the one best adapted to the soil and climate. I have traversed the greater part of the cultivated grounds, or rather seen portions of the cultivation in all parts, and I cannot speak too highly of the standing rice crop, which is luxuriant and heavy, standing in most parts *five feet* above the ground, which is perfectly dry. Any one possessed of half a dozen thousand rupees, would here acquire for himself a princely domain, and before long would secure for his family a very handsome income. I have been out the greater part of every day, and find the climate very delightful; the heat is bearable, and the cold never intolerable. I am persuaded that, with good sense and better culture, these hills would yield an abundant crop of cotton; and it is here, if any where, that the coffee would succeed, as there are neither hot winds nor inundation. I have procured the Naga receipt for rice-beer, which is regularly malted; the Nagas speak of the beer as both meat and drink. The mountains are favourable to the growth, not only of cotton, but of various plants and grains. Perhaps no country in Asia presents greater variety of vegetable productions; from the oak and vine to the rattan and strawberry. Such, indeed, is the fertility of the soil at every altitude, that it seems likely every plant, whether of European or Asiatic origin, could be successfully raised on the Cachar hills.'

SOUTHERN INDIA.—The climate is influenced by

the north-east and south-west monsoons, and by the elevation of the country, the low lands being extremely hot, with dense exhalations, and the upper dry, cool and healthy, as on the Mysore table land. The thermometer ranges in the Carnatic higher than in Bengal (to 100° and 106° F.), but the moisture or evaporation not being so great, the heat is less severely felt; but on the other hand, the cold season is of very short duration.

THE SETTING IN OF THE MONSOON AT MADRAS has been often described. On the 15th of October, the flag-staff is struck, as a signal for all vessels to leave the roads, lest they should be overtaken by the monsoon. The premonitory symptoms of the approaching "war of elements" are small fleecy clouds appearing, at intervals, to rise from the horizon, and to dissipate, in a thin and almost imperceptible vapour, over the deep blue of the still bright sky. A slight haze upon the distant waters, seems gradually to thicken, although not to a density sufficient to refract the rays of the sun, which still flood the broad sea, with one unvarying mass of glowing light. A sensation of suffocating heat in the atmosphere, oppresses the lungs and saddens the spirits. Towards the afternoon, the aspect of the sky begins to change; the horizon gathers blackness,—masses of heavy clouds appear to rise from the sea, black and portentous, accompanied by sudden gusts of wind, succeeded by an intense, death-like stillness, as if the air were in a state of utter stagnation, and its vital properties arrested. Meanwhile, the lower circle of the heavens are of a deep brassy red; from the partial reflection of the setting sunbeams upon the thick clouds, which every where overspread it. The atmosphere becomes condensed almost to the thickness of a mist —increased by the thin spray scattered over the land, from the sea, by the violence of the increasing gales. The rain now begins to fall in sheeted masses, and the wind to howl more continuously; which, mingling with the roaring of the surf, produces a tumultuous union of sounds, perfectly deafening. The pale lightning streaming from the clouds in broad sheets of flame, appears to encircle the heavens, as if every element had been converted into fire, and the world was on the eve of a general conflagration; whilst the thunder peal instantly following, is like the explosion of a gunpowder magazine, or the discharge of artillery in the gorge of a mountain, where the repercussion of surrounding hills multiplies, with terrific energy, its deep and astounding echoes. The heavens seem to be one vast reservoir of flame, propelled from its voluminous bed by some invisible but omnipotent agency, and threatening to fling its fiery ruin upon every thing around. In some parts, however, of the pitchy vapour by which the skies are completely overspread, the lightning is seen only occasionally to glimmer in faint streaks of light, as if struggling, but unable to escape from its prison, igniting, but too weak to burst, the impervious bosom of those capacious magazines, in which it was at once engendered and pent up. So heavy and continuous is the rain, that scarcely any thing, save those vivid bursts of light which nothing can arrest or resist, is perceptible through it. The surf, raised by the wind, and scattered by thin billows of foam, over the esplanade, extends several hundred yards from the beach. Fish upwards of three inches long, are found upon the flat roofs of houses in the town, during the prevalence of the monsoon—either blown from the sea, by the violence of the gales, or taken up in the water spouts, which are very prevalent in this tempestuous season. It is, however, by these violent conflicts of the aerial elements that a tropical atmosphere is purified, and rendered not merely respirable, but absolutely delicious when the storm has subsided.

In Travancore, owing to the proximity of the ocean, and the waters on either side of the peninsular promontory, the climate is moist but not oppressive, as the sea breeze blows from one quarter or another the whole year round.

The climate of the Neilgherry hills resembles in the higher parts that of the great intertropical plateaus of America, which have become the centres of civilization in the new hemisphere, with the additional advantage, that it is not subject to an inconvenience attending the latter, namely, the sudden changes, and cold piercing winds occasioned by the variety of lofty mountains. The mean temperature at *Ootocamund* is rather more than that of London, but the annual range is very small, and the heat never sufficient to bring the more delicate European fruits to perfection. At the height of that station Dr. Christie observes, the cultivation of corn and vegetables can alone be expected to succeed; but lower down, at an elevation of from 5000 to 6000 feet, the valleys enjoy the delicious climate of Italy. It may here be reckoned, as applicable to all India, that the climate of the eastern as well as of the western hemisphere, is undergoing a remarkable change, one of the proofs of which is the length of *twilight* now visible and increasing in India, where none was formerly observed. Indian twilights are, however, now nearly as distinct as the European interval between sunset and darkness.

At Coimbatore the temperature during the cold season is minimum 31° F. maximum 59° F.; in April 65° in May 64° (a fuller detail is given at page 133). There are no sultry nights, a blanket being agreeable at all seasons of the year. The Neilgherries are indeed remarkable, not merely for the mildness of the climate, but also for its equability; the air is at all times perfectly clear, being beyond the zone of clouds and mists, yet the influence of both monsoons is felt; the elasticity of the atmosphere is evidenced by the remarkable distance within which sound is heard, and the lightness and buoyancy of the animal spirits: indeed it is an ordinary custom with the natives, when any thing tickles their fancy, to retire to a sequestered spot, cast themselves on a verdant bank, and there yield to the delightful enjoyment of a long continued burst of laughter, which we sombre mortals would find it difficult to rival, even with Momus Matthews before us.

Bangalore (latitude 12° 57′ north longitude 77° 38′ east) is one of the healthiest and gayest stations in India, and remarkable for the wholesomeness of its atmosphere. The thermometer seldom rises above 82° or falls below 56° F. The vine and cyprus grow luxuriantly; apple and peach trees yield delicious fruit, and strawberries are raised in the principal gardens. The monsoons, which sometimes deluge the Malabar and Coromandel coasts, have their force broken by the lofty Ghauts, and the *tableau* of Mysore (on which Bangalore is situate) is constantly refreshed by genial showers, which preserve the temperature of the air, and the lovely verdure of the fields throughout the entire year.

The Malabar and Canara coasts are not unhealthy (tropically speaking) except in the marshes beneath the Ghauts, where the miasm, as in all similarly situated places, is very deleterious.

In the Mahratta country, the north-western parts towards the Ghaut mountains, which attract the clouds from the Indian ocean, are visited with profuse rain, which sometimes continues three or four weeks without intermission, while to the south and east, perhaps not thirty miles distant, not a drop of rain has fallen during the same period.

As we proceed to the north and west peninsula, the climate approaches to that described under the western provinces of the Bengal Presidency, except in the neighbourhood of the sea. In Guzerat the westerly winds are burning hot in May, June, and July:—Candeish has a luxurious climate like Malwah; and Poonah, a central station in Upper India, 2500 feet above the level of the sea, 100 miles from Bombay[1] and 75 miles from the nearest sea

[1] The following data shews the improving climate of India, and which civilization will yet much further ameliorate.

His

coast, is delightfully situate within thirty miles of the Ghauts.

On the whole it may be said, that the climate of the British possessions on the continent of Asia, is essentially of a tropical nature, though varying in intensity, and sometimes verging into that of the temperate zone, either by reason of the peculiarities of the soil, or its elevation above the level of the sea. The following table affords a comparative view of the monthly and yearly mean temperature of the air of Calcutta, Madras, Bombay, and the Neilgherry mountains, (8000 feet high) compared with the temperature of the city of London, and the fall of rain in England.

His Majesty's troops serving in Bombay Presidency.

	Average Strength.	Died.	Invalid.
1826	3028	172	185
1827	3120	155	127
1828	3239	201	163
1829	3496	101	164
1830	3825	146	119
1831	3799	79	70
1832	3677	74	52

Comparative View of the monthly and yearly mean temperature of the air of Calcutta, Madras, Bombay, and the Neilgherry mountains, &c.

	Calcutta.		Bombay.		Madras.		Neilgherries.			London.		
	Mean Max.	Mean Min.	Mean Max.	Mean Min.	Mean Max.	Mean Min.	Monthly Means. 6 A.M.	Monthly Means. 3 P.M.	Average of rain for two years.	Mean Max.	Mean Min.	Average of rain for two years.
	3 P.M.	6 A.M.	4 P.M.	11 A.M.					Inches.			Inches.
January	75.1	63.	78	76	82.2	74.1	$45\frac{3}{4}$	$57\frac{1}{4}$	1.17	39.6	32.6	1.483
February	80.	67.	78	76	84.5	73.8	$45\frac{3}{4}$	$59\frac{1}{2}$	0	42.4	33.7	.746
March	88.1	68.	81	80	87.6	78.7	58	63	2.47	50.1	33.7	1.440
April	95.1	79.1	84	83	92.	84.1	58	$63\frac{3}{4}$	3.10	57.7	42.2	1.786
May	97.1	80.1	85	85	94.3	85.1	57	$63\frac{1}{4}$	5.21	62.9	45.1	1.853
June	88.	78.	86	85	90.5	84.2	$57\frac{1}{4}$	60	5.25	69.4	48.1	1.830
July	86.1	78.1	81	81	92.6	85.3	$52\frac{3}{4}$	$61\frac{3}{4}$	10.37	69.2	52.2	2.516
August	86.2	79.3	84	84	89.9	83.1	57	$60\frac{1}{4}$	11.77	70.1	52.9	1.453
September	86.	78.	80	79	89.7	83.3	$54\frac{1}{4}$	$60\frac{3}{4}$	2.40	65.6	50.1	2.193
October	89.2	76.1	85	84	87.8	82.4	$50\frac{1}{4}$	62	7.41	55.7	42.1	2.073
November	78.	65.2	85	84	84.3	80.1	$50\frac{1}{4}$	$61\frac{1}{4}$	10.86	47.5	38.3	2.400
December	75.	59.	81	80	80.2	76.	$46\frac{1}{4}$	60	3.87	42.2	35.4	2.426
Annual Means	85.3	73.4	82.4	81.5	87.9	80.8	$52\frac{3}{4}$	61	63.88	56.1	42.5	

CHAPTER IX.

VEGETABLE AND ANIMAL KINGDOMS—VARIETY OF TIMBER—GRAIN AND FRUITS, &c.—MINERAL KINGDOM—COAL, IRON, COPPER, &c.

VEGETATION partakes of the general features of a country, so varied in aspect as that just now described, and it is so extensive, beautiful, indeed magnificent, as to baffle attempts at a brief delineation. The sea coast border of our Indian territories, as in other parts of the tropical world, is covered with the graceful and almost indispensable cocoa palm, which fortunately for man, grows to luxuriance in sandy and barren spots, where scarcely any other valuable plant would thrive. The forest trees of India are not to be surpassed in any country, for superbness and number; their diversity and worth is as yet but little known in England, and they cover a great part of the country, from Cape Comorin to the Himalaya. Among them are oak, teak, pine, fir, walnut, jack, chesnut, cedar, ebony, sissoo, hornbeam, saul, yew, poon, mango, jarrool, &c. On the Kumaon range, the pine and arbor vitæ trees are not unfrequently seen with trunks of twenty-five feet in circumference, and 120 feet high, without a branch! The chief rice country in India is Bengal, which produces a surplus of this staple of life; but there are smaller quantities of rice cultivated in other parts (particularly in the western provinces) which are far superior in quality to that of Bengal. The Madras territories do not produce sufficient rice for home consumption, a great extent of waste land is now, however, being brought into cultivation, and the inferior sorts of grain are giving place to rice, of which there are twenty-seven varieties. The wheat grown in the northern and western provinces is of excellent quality, and a trade is now springing up between Liverpool and Calcutta, in the exportation of flour from the latter place, which is used and preferred in England for various manufactures [1]. The wheat of Bareilly is particularly fine, and the bread made therefrom, equal, if not superior to any met with in England. The seed was originally introduced (it is said), by Mr. Hawkins, and it is now generally cultivated. Wheat, the produce of the midland district of Kumaon, sells at Almora, at the rate of one rupee the twenty-five seirs, or *2s. for fifty pounds weight*. The barley of the north-west provinces is also good, and the Hindoos of the Himalaya range distil from it a spirit, not much inferior to Irish potheen.

The cultivation of potatoes (not the sweet potatoe found in almost every tropical country) is proceeding with unexampled rapidity; they are much liked by the natives, even small and watery as was their produce in Bengal until of late, when more care was adopted in the use of fresh European seed; and at no distant period, this wonderful root bids fair to effect a singular revolution in the cultivation of the soil of Hindostan.

[1] The quantity of wheat and wheat flour exported from India to England, in 1832, was 9853 quarters.

In the more eastern and southern provinces, the fruits are principally tropical; but in the north-west provinces, apples, pears, grapes, walnuts, strawberries, raspberries, and other fruits of temperate climates, are now being reared in abundance (the grapes of Malwa have long been celebrated); since the formation of agricultural societies at Calcutta, Bombay, Agra, &c. a marked improvement has taken place among the culinary vegetables; and turnips, parsnips, onions, carrots, peas, beans, brocoli, spinage, radishes, cabbage of every variety, cauliflowers, artichokes, cucumbers, &c., now crowd the bazaars during their respective seasons: a spirit of emulation has also grown up among the native gardeners, which promises much improvement. A witness before Parliament, in 1832, thus speaks of the desire of the native to improve and extend cultivation, when encouraged by the natural and wholesome stimulus of individual profit:—

'You have only to insure a profit to the cultivator, whatever may be the crop, and the cultivation will be undertaken; for instance, that of the potatoe, in which, extraordinary as it may appear, the first experiments by the Europeans failed, but those by the natives were successful. The cultivation of the potatoe is now in the district of Furrackabad, carried to an extent that is scarcely to be believed. I may state as an example in proof, that the fine class of cultivators alluded to, grow on the same land a crop of indigo, which they cut early in the rains, and then prepare the lands for potatoes, and that the two crops will give a return of about eighty-seven rupees per common begah of the country[1]. I think the men I now allude to would do anything possible in respect to cultivation. They will give any price for the manure from the stable: it is with the greatest difficulty that people in the town keep manure from them.'

On the Neilgheries, European plants and flowers, viz—the red and white honeysuckle, white and red jasmin, myrtle, violet, balsam, marygold, geranium, and daisy are in fine perfection; as are also red and white raspberries, strawberries, hill-gooseberries, and currants, &c. The indigenous fruits of the Kumaon country are pears, gooseberries, currants, (red and white), raspberries, and strawberries, none of which receive culture; on the Kossya, or Cossya Hills, in the neighbourhood of Sylhet, apples, pears, plums, straw, rasp, and blackberries abound; and the ever-verdant sod is carpeted with daisies—the whole country presenting the appearance of an undulating park of extremely beautiful scenery. In Kumaon, the apple, pear, apricot, cherry, walnut, pomegranate, mulberry, peach, mango, guava, orange, lemon, citron, plantain, vine, strawberry (tree and herb), rasp, black, barberry, currants, gooseberries, &c. &c., all arrive at perfection, as also all European vegetables and flowers.

The sugar cane grows luxuriantly in most parts, but the manufacture of sugar is principally confined

[1] A begah is about one-third of an acre, so that taking three times 87 rupees at 2s. the rupee, it would be a return of produce from one acre of ground to the amount of 26*l.* This simple fact shews how British India would prosper if encouragement were given to its agricultural products.

to Bengal and Benares: the grain of the latter sugar is large, bright, and sparkling, like the Mauritius sugar: that of Bengal has a whitish, sandy appearance, and a delicate, rather sickly, flavour, in consequence of the repeated fermentations which it undergoes in the tedious process of native manufacture; it is, however, preferred by the French confectioners in Europe, by reason of its possessing but little acidity. Coffee thrives best in a mild and moist temperature, in black, deep, arable ground, which retains the humidity well, and in the vicinity of forests and rivulets, rather shaded from the too intense heat of the sun. Cold and hard argillaceous earths, and also the sandy clay that lies on a bed of marl, does not suit the coffee plant, which requires a light and nourishing soil, free light and air, without too much exposure to the sun.

The coffee of the southern parts of the peninsula (lower Bengal is perhaps unsuited for it) is excellent, and it might be sent in the greatest abundance to England, but for the extra duties levied on it for the support of the West India interest; even the tobacco of Hindostan, which grows every where luxuriantly, and in many places has an exquisite aroma, is shut out from the home market by prohibitory duties. Opium forms one of the most valuable productions of Bengal, Behar and Malwa, and its yearly extending consumption in China (*vide Chapter on Commerce*), render it as valuable in a financial as in a mercantile or agricultural point of view. The following is the manner in which the poppy is cultivated. "The poppy (*papaver somniferum*) is plentifully cultivated both for making opium and on account of the seed, which is much used in the sweet cakes that are eaten by the higher ranks of the natives. In Aswaja (19th September to 18th October) dig the ground one cubit deep. In the following month smooth the ground, and divide it into small plots of three cubits square, separated from each other by small banks, like those of rice-fields, but neater and lower, and at the same time form channels winding through the plots, so that every one may have a channel running past one of its sides. By this method any quantity of water which the plant requires is very readily conveyed to the whole. When the channels and squares are formed, the garden is dunged, and the poppy-seed sown. Over this is sprinkled a little more dung. At every span's length, two seeds of the cossumba are then planted on the small mounds which separate the squares; or in place of cossumba, radishes are sometimes raised. Water is then given to every square, and once in four days this is repeated. After the plants have acquired strength, no preference is given to any particular time of the day for watering; but while they are very young, the morning is preferred. In six or seven days the poppies will be two inches high; and then the gardener with a shell removes those that are superfluous, so as to leave them four inches apart. In twenty days they are about six inches high; the weeds must then be removed with a small hoe, and a very little dung must be given. In two months and a half the poppy is ready for making opium, and in three months the seed is ripe. It is not injured by extracting the opium, which operation is performed by the gardeners who sell the produce to the drug-merchant. When the poppies are ripe, the fruit is scratched with a thorn, and the juice that exudes, after it has thickened by exposure to the air, is scraped off with a shell, and seems to be very good opium[1]." As it dries it is formed into lumps, which are wrapped up in coverings made of the flower-leaves of the poppy, joined together by placing them while fresh on a hot earthen pot. Some women earn a subsistence by preparing these coverings, which are sent to the factory ready joined. In the evening each capsule of the poppy, as it attains the proper degree of maturity, has a slight incision made in its whole length; and next morning what opium has exuded is collected. After two or three days, another incision is made at some distance from the first; and according to the size of the capsule it admits of being cut from three to five times; but the crop seasons last six weeks, as the capsules advance at different periods[2].

Indigo is only cultivated for manufacture to any extent in Bengal, Behar, and the north-west provinces, viz Oude, Allahabad, Agra, &c. The Bengal is the finest, probably not owing to any superior skill in the manufacture (for Europeans are employed in the upper as well as in the lower provinces), but to the superior richness, and perhaps saline quality of the soil in which the plant delights most to vegetate. The different parts of the country in which the plant is cultivated may be seen by the following

[1] Buchanan, i. 295: iii. 444. [2] Hamilton, vol. i. p. 242.

return of the indigo brought into Calcutta for the season of 1833:—From Furruckabad and Western Provinces, maunds, 3748; Allahabad, Mirzapore, and Benares, 2281; Juanpore, 463; Ghazeepore, 1875; Chupra and Tirhoot, 15264; Patna, Buxar, and Dinapoor, 3024; Purneah, 3741; Monghyr, and Boglipoor, 3181; Malda, 1919; Rajishye, Nattore, Dinajipore, 3930; Rungpore, 616; Mymensing, 296; Dacca and Jelapore, 1695; Jessore and Furridpore, 20449; Moorshedabad, 598; Nuddea and Kishnagur, 16426; Burdwan, Bancoorah, and Burbhom, 4788; Hooghly, and 24 Pergunnahs, 3348; Balasore, Midnapore and Cuttack, 156. Total 93,180 maunds.

The tobacco lands of Guzerat, are stated by English witnesses to be 'the cleanest and best farmed lands they ever saw.' Some sorts cultivated have a fine aroma.

Cotton, whether of the creeper, perennial or forest tree, (Bombax Ceiba) every where abounds, but sufficient care has not been bestowed on the growth, so as to render it a triennial instead of an annual, or in the picking and cleaning of it for exportation, although the natives sedulously attend to the same when preparing it for their own manufacture. East India cotton receives a brighter dye and retains it longer than American cotton; the Swiss and German cottons (so superior to the Lancashire cloths) are made from East India cotton chiefly. The Dacca cotton is unequalled, and the 'sea island cotton' from Saugur island at the mouth of the Hooghly, promises to be a valuable article of export. The mode of manufacturing very fine Dacca muslins is thus minutely described by Mr. Walters. 'The division of labour was carried to a great extent in the manufacture of fine muslins. In spinning the very fine thread, more especially, a great degree of skill was attained. It was spun with the fingers on a *tukwah*, or fine steel spindle, by young women, who could only work during the early part of the morning, while the dew was on the ground; for such was the extreme tenuity of the fibre, that it would not bear manipulation after the sun had risen. One ruttee of cotton could thus be spun into a thread eighty cubits long, which was sold by the spinners at one rupee eight annas per sicca weight. The *ruffooghurs*, or darners, were also particularly skilful. They could remove an entire thread from a piece of muslin, and replace it by one of a finer texture. The cotton used for the finest thread was grown in the immediate neighbourhood of Dacca; more especially about Sunergong. Its fibre is too short, however, to admit of its being worked up by any except that most wonderful of all machines—the human hand. The art of making the very fine muslin fabrics is now lost,—and pity it is that it should be so.'

The East India Company's Government have of late years made several attempts for the extensive introduction of the cotton plant into Guzerat, which seems well adapted for its culture. A farm has been established by the Company at the town of Broach, and the benefits resulting from improved cultivation, and greater care in the gathering and cleaning of the cotton, demonstrated to the people.

Roses are cultivated to an immense extent at Ghazeepore and other places, for the purpose of manufacturing rose-water, (a sovereign remedy for ills with the natives) and otto or attar of roses, which requires 200,000 roses to produce the weight of a single rupee in attar. The mode of extracting the essence of roses is said to have been accidentally discovered by the favourite sultana of Jehanghir. To please the voluptuous emperor, she caused the bath in the garden of the palace to be filled to the brim with rose-water, and the action of the sun concentrated the oily particles which were found floating upon the water. Supposing the water had become corrupt, the attendants carefully skimmed away the oily matter, in doing which they burst the little globules, and found that they emitted the most delicious odour. This suggested the idea of artificially procuring the essence by imitating the process of nature.

The result of the researches of the tea-deputation despatched to Assam under Dr. Wallich, respecting the tea-plant in that country. gives every reason to expect that tea will become in a short time a prime article of export from India. The plant has been found in extensive natural plantations, and the localities are such as to encourage the belief that it exists far more extensively than has been actually discovered, and to warrant the conclusion that Assam, and our northern frontier generally, will afford the most ample field for tea-cultivation of every variety.

Two of the localities in which the tea has been found are beyond Sudiya, in the tract of country occupied by the Singphos; and the natural presumption is, that it has migrated into that neighbourhood from the Chinese provinces to the eastward. If this be correct, there is every reason to expect that, on further investigation, it will be found to be plentifully diffused through the neighbouring mountains. The Singphos are tributaries, who acknowledge our paramount authority, and little difficulty need therefore be anticipated in extending the regular cultivation and manufacture of the tea into their country. At the same time, it is gratifying to know, that the tea produced on the adjoining frontier of China is very highly valued by the Chinese themselves. Other two localities of the tea are found in the Muttuck, or Mooamareea country, which extends on the south bank of the Bramhaputra, from the district of Sudiya to Upper Assam. The Mooamareeas are tributaries to us, like the Singphos, and more directly under our influence. Their country more nearly resembles the rest of the valley of Assam, which is immediately under our own government; and therefore the natural growth of the tea-plant in it affords the most gratifying assurance of the practicability of extending the cultivation through the province. The last tea locality examined lies amongst the Gabhroo Purbut group of small hills at the bottom of the Naga range, within a few miles of Jorhath, Raja Poorunder Singh's capital. As the Raja holds his territories by treaty from the British government, and expressly during good behaviour only, no difficulty can be experienced in extending the tea cultivation in them; and if any did occur, similar localities skirt on both sides the whole plain of Lower Assam, which is under the administration of our own officers. Over the Naga hills there is a line of communication between Upper Assam and Munipoor; and as Major Grant has brought to light the existence of the tea plant on the south side of the range, and it has now been found also on the Assam side, we may expect that it likewise occupies many intermediate spots. The mountaineers of this tract consist of a variety of tribes, of considerable extent of population, and rather wealthy and powerful.

The researches of the deputation have not been limited to the tea plant; the botanical and geological features of the country have been noted; and Dr. Wallich states that he has never seen or heard of so rich a *Flora* as that of Assam.

Mr. Forbes Royle in the interesting and valuable botanical Indian work which he is now preparing justly observes,—'In the peninsula of India and in the neighbouring island of Ceylon, we have a climate capable of producing cinnamon, cassia, pepper, and cardamoms. The coffee grown on the Malabar coast is of so superior a quality as to be taken to Arabia and re-exported as Mocha coffee. The Tinnivelly senna brings the highest price in the London market, and there is little doubt that many other valuable products of tropical countries may be acclimated, particularly as several are already in a flourishing condition in the botanic garden at Calcutta, such as the cocoa and nutmeg, as well as the camphor, pimento, cajeput, and cashew nut trees. In the Neilgheries a favourite site might, without doubt, be found for the *cinchona* (Peruvian bark) as well as for the different kinds of *ipecacuanha*, and as the potatoe has been introduced into almost every part of India, equal success and considerable benefit would probably result from introducing the several kinds of *arracacha*, so much prized for their roots as food by the natives of South America.

Along the coast of the Bay of Bengal the cocoa and areca nut palms flourish and abound, and the continent every where produces indigo, cotton, tobacco, sugar, and opium. The first hardly of any note as an Indian product thirty years ago, is now imported in the largest quantities into England; the cotton is indigenous to India, many provinces seem peculiarly adapted for its culture, particularly Malwa and those to the north-west. The tobacco brought home by Dr. Wallich from Martaban, was pronounced by competent judges to be equal to the best from America: Patna opium is preferred in China, and that of Malwa bids fair to rival Turkey opium in the European Market. *The sugar cane is cultivated in every part of India*, but very inferior sugar has hitherto been produced: lately, however, a manufactory has been established near Calna, (Burdwan) a new mine opened in the Burdwan coal formation, and very superior specimens of sugar sent home. Here the occurrence of sugar at the surface of the soil, and coal only a few feet below it, in a country where labour is so cheap, ought to be attended with decidedly favourable results. If from these we turn our attention to other products we shall still see that there are great capabilities every where; we should at least expect them, for though India is generally looked upon as a rice country, *wheat* is imported into and sold at a profit in England, from the northern provinces, and *flour* for making starch, is now one of the annual exports from Calcutta. Of dyes, medicinal drugs, resins, and gums, and oils, there are great varieties, and more might be successfully introduced. A recent number of the Asiatic Journal contains the following notice of a new vegetable oil, which has appeared in the Calcutta market, and which promises to prove a valuable article of trade :—

'This oil is in general use among the natives for mixing with colours, and is chiefly imported from Chittagong ; but it would appear, on Major Burney's authority, to be still more abundantly produced in the Tavoy district, and at much less cost ; the bazaar price in Calcutta averaging about nine or ten rupees per maud (82 lbs.) ; whereas, at Tavoy, it may be procured at about one-fourth that price. Both in India and in England it has been found to be a good substitute for linseed oil for outside work, especially in light colours, being worth for this purpose about 12*l*. to 15*l*. per ton. Mr. Dowie, a currier of Edinburgh, read a paper before the Edinburgh Society of Arts, on the mode of applying this vegetable oil alone, or mixed with tallow, to the preparation of leather for shoes, and he considers it as preferable to fish oil. This application is quite new ; and at Mr. Swinton's suggestions, some similar trials have since been made in Calcutta, by Mackenzie and Macfarlan, with success. The leather absorbs a great deal of the oil, and the specimens presented to the Society appear to be very soft and tough.

'Major Burney describes the tree whence the *gargan* oil is extracted as forming large forests in Tavoy, growing to a great height and size; its native name is *kaniyen.* The flag-staff at Moulmein, ninety-two feet high, is formed of a single kaniyen tree. Mr. Maingy says, that the oil is much improved by boiling, which gives it drying properties; he has often used it for boots, and has found it excellent in preparing tarpauling. The inhabitants of Tavoy and Mergui do not burn earth oil like other Burmese, but torches made of this wood-oil and touch-wood. The imports into Calcutta for the last three years were as follow:—In 1829-30, Br. mds. 759, average price, 7 8. 1830-31, 914, 6 4. 1831-32, 1,708, 7 2.' Timber of every kind is every where abundant, the coasts producing teak, ebony, and many others; the interior saul, sissoo, bamboos, and rattans, while a great variety of plants yield excellent materials for cordage. The northern and hill provinces grow at one season European grains, and at another those which are peculiar to the tropics, and many perennials of both these climates succeed equally well in the north provinces. In the hill provinces the forests are formed of oaks and pines; the hill-men make their strongest ropes for crossing rivers with *hemp* which every where abounds, and is of the finest quality. Opium, rhubarb, and turpentine, form articles of commerce as well as musk, Thibet wool, and borax, from the other kingdoms of nature. Somewhere in the valleys at the foot of these hills, or at moderate elevations, the more generally useful productions of European countries might be successfully introduced, as the *olive* and *hop*, the latter would be particularly beneficial, as a brewery has been established in the hills, where the climate is excellent. Here also there is considerable prospect of success in the cultivation of the *tea-plant*.'

'In the cold seasons,' Mr. Royle continues, 'there are cultivated (about Saharumpore) of *gramina*, wheat, barley, oats, and millet; of the *leguminæ*, peas, beans, vetch, tares, chick and pigeon-peas; of *cruciferæ*, a species of *sinapis* (mustard) and allied genera cultivated for oil seeds, and of the *umbelliferæ*, the carrot, coriander, cummin, a species of *ptychotis* and *fænnicullium pannorium*, as well as of other tribes, tobacco, flax, saf-flower, and succory. Almost all the esculent vegetables of Europe succeed remarkably well in the cold season in India. In the rainy season, a totally different set of plants engage the agriculturist's attention, as rice, cotton, indigo, maize: *holcus sorghum*, species of *panicum*, *paspalum*, and *elusinæ*, of *leguminæ*, species of *phaseolus* and *dolichos*. Many of the *cucurbitaceæ* as well as *sepanum* and the species of *solanum* for their esculent fruit.' In another place this scientific Botanist observes, 'as we have seen with perennials of other kinds so is it with those yielding fruit of an edible nature; many, both of tropical and temperate climes, succeed nearly equally well in the northern parts of India; so that taking Saharunpoor garden (latitude 30° north longitude 77° 32′ elevation above the sea 1000 feet, and 1000 miles north-west of Calcutta) as an example, we have collected in one place and naturalized in the *open air* the various fruit trees of very different countries, as of India and China, Caubul, Europe, and America. Of those belonging to hot countries we have the plantain, custard apple, shaddock, orange, lemon, guava, mango, tamarind, and others, which are common to every part of India. Of Chinese fruits, the *lechee, loquat, longaro, wampee,* flat peach and digitated citron, are perfectly naturalized. Of fruit trees from more northern countries, as Caubul and Cashmere, and from the hills of Europe, there are the almond, peach, nectarine, and apricot, plum, pomegranate, grape-vine, apple, pear, quince, mulberry, fig, and walnut: of useful trees of cold countries which thrive in what is at some seasons so hot a climate; *pines, oak, maple, dog-wood, service tree, holly, juniper, and box.* Of American trees, besides those first enumerated, the *logwood, mahogany, parkinsonia aculeata,* and *acer negundo,* may be instanced as perfectly naturalized [1].

The vegetation of the Kumaon ridge of the Himalayan Mountains is of course very different from that of the plains of Hindostan; the agricultural products are—buck-wheat, barley, and wheat, and a species of amaranthus; the crop of the two latter being uncertain and in many seasons never reaching maturity: the only vegetables raised are turnips and leeks, but many useful herbs grow spontaneously, amongst

[1] See large edition of the "History of the Colonies," for a minute description of the principal forest trees of India.

which is rhubarb. The Bhot villages are all situated on the northern side of the great chain, and are in some degree subject to the influence of its snows and shade. By any unusual accumulation of snow on the summit, the inferior bed is forced down, and with it the influence of the line of perpetual congelation, if not the line itself, descends, and it sometimes requires the heat of more than one summer to throw back the snow to its former level. In the southern and least elevated part of the ghat, oaks and pines flourish; but with the increase of elevation a gradual change in the forests takes place, from these trees down to the birch, which is found on the very verge of perpetual snow: the bark of this tree is highly useful as a substitute for paper and other domestic purposes.

Indeed the British possessions in India are rich to overflowing with every product of vegetable life, which an allwise and ever beneficent Providence could bestow to gratify the sight, and contribute to the comfort and happiness of his creatures; that they are not used to the extent they ought, is the fault of perverse man, who would seem to take delight in thwarting the benignity of the unseen Being, whose most bounteous blessings are too often ungratefully spurned or mischievously used.

The Zoology of India is no less extensive than the vegetable kingdom; 'every beast of the earth after his kind, and cattle after their kind, and every thing that creepeth on the earth after its kind,' teems in abundance on the Asiatic plains: and the hunter and the hawker,—the fowler and the fisher, as well as the farmer and shepherd, all find ample scope for their respective pursuits. The gigantic and gregarious elephant usurps the dominion of the forests, while the lonely and ferocious tiger infests every jungle, from the *embouchures* of the sacred Ganges to the Himalaya mountains. During the last four years, about 1000 children have been devoured by wolves in the vicinity of the city of Agra. The natives can with great difficulty be induced to kill a wolf in Upper India, from a belief that if its blood be spilt, the common people would desert the village, which would be haunted by the ghosts of the children slain: when a wolf is caught, therefore, he is only punished by having a bell hung round his neck, for the purpose of giving warning to little children. Animated nature here luxuriates in all its primitive grandeur, whether we regard the magnitude, the multitude, or the beauty which every where fills and adorns the earth, air, and water: happily however for man, the Creator has wisely ordained that his creatures should prey on each other, were it not so, the present evergreen surface of India must soon become a desert. To particularize the animals of the country, would in a work of this nature be supererogatory, suffice it to say, that no where may the epicure or the gourmand have his palate gratified, or his taste satiated, at less expense, and with greater variety than in British India, where it must be admitted, the reputed (but erroneously entertained idea of the) Pythagoranism of the Hindoos is fully atoned for by the carnivorousness of the Europeans and their descendants.

The quadrupeds which appear to characterise more particularly the regions of Continental India are the following[1]. They are arranged under those divisions of the peninsula where naturalists inform us they are chiefly found :—

1. *Hindostan generally.*

Genetta fasciata. Banded genett.
Mus giganteus. Gigantic rat.
Cercocebus radiatus. Radiated monkey.
Papio apedia. Thumbless baboon.
Papio niger. Black baboon.
Rhinoceros indicus. Indian rhinoceros.
Pteropus palliatus. Mottled bat.
Ursus malayanus. Malay bear.
Ursus labiatus. Thick-lipped bear.
Mangusta mungos. Indian ichneumon.
Prionodon ? albifrons. White fronted P.
Leo asiaticus. *Swains.* Asiatic lion.
Felis tigris. Royal tiger.
Felis venatica. Maneless hunting leopard.
Cervus porcinus. Brown stag.
Raphicerus acuticornis. Sharp-horned antelope.
Antilope cervicapra. Common antelope.
Raphicerus subulata. Awl-horned antelope.
Gerbillus indicus. Indian gerbil.
Hystrix fasciculata. Pencil-tailed porcupine.
Hystrix macroura. Long-tailed Indian porcupine.
Tetracerus Chicara (*H. Smith*). Chicara antelope.
Tetracerus quadricornis. Four-horned antelope.
Nœmorhedus duvaucelii (*H. Smith*). Duvaucel's antelope.
Bos bubalus. Common buffalo.
Bos Gaurus. Gaur buffalo.
Bos Gaveus. Gayal buffalo.

[1] From Murray's Geography. Article Asia.

2. *Bengal.*

Cerocebus cynosurus. The malbrouck.
Nycticebus bengalensis. Slow lemur.
Nyctinomus bengalensis. Bengal bat.
Pteropus marginatus. Bordered bat.
Genetta bondar. Bondar genett.
Viverra prehensilis. Prehensile viverra.
Manis crassicaudata. Short-tailed manis.
Cervus hippelaphus. Great russa.
Cervus aristotellis. Black stag.

3. *Pondicherry.*

Pteropus leschenaultii. Spotted bat.
Sorex indicus. Indian shrew.
Lutra nair. Pondicherry otter.
Viverra typus. Common vivèrra.
Mus indicus. Indian rat.
Mus Perchal. Perchal rat.

Of reptiles there is probably no existing species but it is to be found in Hindostan. Every variety of snakes abound: some are tamed by jugglers, even the most noxious. 'It is generally imagined,' says Mr. Caunter, 'and by persons too who have been some time resident in India, that the cobra di capello, exhibited by the jugglers in this country, is perfectly harmless, in consequence of its fangs being extracted by these practised adepts in the art of legerdemain; but this altogether a mistake. The fangs are positively not extracted; and the creature is presented to the spectator, possessing all its natural powers of mischief unimpaired. The bite from a snake shown by any one of these itinerant conjurors, would as certainly prove fatal as from one encountered in the jungle. This will, perhaps, appear strange to those who have heard of these reptiles being constantly shown in the houses of the curious, and more especially, when they are told that this snake is frequently permitted to put its head against the cheeks of the children of those who show them.

'The dexterity of the jugglers in managing these dangerous reptiles is truly extraordinary. They easily excite them to the most desperate rage, and, by a certain circular motion of the arms, appease them as readily; then, without the least hesitation, they will take them in their hands, coil them round their necks, and put their fingers to their mouths, even while their jaws are furnished with the deadliest venom, and the slighest puncture from their fangs would produce not only certain but almost instant death.

'The power which these people exercise over this species of venomous snake remains no longer a mystery, when its habits are known. It is a remarkable peculiarity in the cobra di capello, and I believe, in most poisonous reptiles of this class, that they have an extreme reluctance to put into operation the deadly powers with which they are endowed. The cobra scarcely ever bites unless excited by actual injury or extreme provocation; and even then, before it darts upon its aggressor, it always gives him timely notice of its design not to be mistaken. It dilates the crest upon its neck, which is a large flexible membrane, having on the upper surface two black circular spots, like a pair of spectacles—waves its head to and fro with a gentle undulatory motion, the eye sparkling with intense lustre, and commences a hiss so loud as to be heard at a considerable distance; so that the juggler always has warning when it is perilous to approach his captive. The snake never bites while the hood is closed, and so long as this is not erected it may be approached and handled with impunity. Even when the hood is spread, while the creature continues silent there is no danger: its fearful hiss is at once the signal of aggression and of peril.

'Though the cobra is so deadly when under excitement, it is nevertheless astonishing to see how readily it is appeased even in the highest state of exasperation; and this merely by the droning music with which its exhibitors seem to charm it. It appears to be fascinated by the discordant sounds that issue from their pipes and tomtoms.'

Insects are innumerable in species and varieties: the most annoying are musquitoes, and the most destructive the termites or white ants. Forbes, in his Oriental Memoirs, truly says, 'In a few hours those formidable insects will demolish a large chest of books, papers, silk, or clothes, perforating them with a thousand holes. We dare not leave a box on the floor without placing it on glass bottles, which, if kept free from dust, they cannot ascend. This is trifling when compared with the serious mischief they sometimes occasion by penetrating the beams of a house, or destroying the timbers in a ship. These destructive animals advance by myriads to their work, under an arched incrustation of fine sand, tempered with a moisture from their body, which renders the covered way as hard as burnt clay, and effectually conceals them at their insidious employment. I could mention many curious instances of depredation by the termites. One happened to myself. I left Anjengo in the rainy season, to pass a few weeks with a chief at his country house at Eddova, in the rural and sheltered situation. On my departure I locked up a room containing books, drawings, and a few valuables. As I took the key with me, the servant could not enter to clean the furniture. The walls of the room were whitewashed, adorned with prints and drawings, in English frames and glasses. Returning home in the evening, and making a cursory view of my cottage by candle light, I found every thing apparently in the same order as I left it; but, on a nearer inspection the next morning, I observed a number of advanced works in various directions towards my pictures. The glasses appeared to be very dull, and the frames covered with dust. On attempting to wipe it off, I was astonished to find the glasses fixed to the wall, not suspended in a frame as I left them, but completely surrounded by an incrustation cemented by the white ants, who had actually eaten up the deal frames and back boards, and the greater part of the paper, and left the glasses upheld by the incrustation or covered way which they had formed during their depredation. From the flat Dutch bottles on which the drawers and boxes were placed not having been wiped during my absence, the ants had ascended the bottles by means of the dust, eaten through the bottom of a chest, and made some progress in perforating the books and linen. The chief's lady, with whom I had been staying at Eddova, on returning to her apartments in the fort, found, from the same cause, a large chest in which she had deposited shawls, muslins, and other articles, collected preparatory to her leaving India, entirely destroyed by those voracious insects.'

Among the birds of Hindostan, the eagle, the vulture, and the peacock are the principal. The vulture abounds wherever there are many dead bodies. When there is a scarcity of human flesh, which, owing to the intestine wars and superstitions of the natives, there has seldom been in India, the vulture repairs to the sea-shore, and there patiently watches all day the action of the waves, in the hope that some dead fishes may be thrown up on the sand[1]. When this resource fails it will visit graves and cemeteries, and, like the hyæna, disinter and devour the putrid corpse. It is sometimes joined on the field by wild dogs and jackalls, which have been observed feeding with it on the same carcass[2]. The finest hawks, for the amusement of falconry, are brought from Cashmere. Owls, cockatoos, parrots, bee-eaters, and other birds found between the tropics, are common. Vast flights of aquatic birds hover over the Sunderbunds, and in the moist tracts about Surat, among which the mute swan, the jabiree, or snail-

[1] Pennant's View of Hindostan, vol. ii. p. 36.

[2] This occurred after the attack of the nabob's camp, before the battle of Plassey. Pennant, vol. ii. p. 36. Speaking of the same bird, he adds, "I have been told that whenever an animal falls down dead, one or more vultures (unseen before) instantly appear; so quick is their scent of death." p. 37.

eater, the argali, or adjutant *(ardea argala)*, the white-headed ibis [1], and the violet heron are the most remarkable. The peacock is found in a state of nature in no country but India [2], where it ranks as the first of birds, and with its glorious colours enlivens the solitude of the woods. The huge bats of India, and the vampire, or flying cat, may come in here in the rear of the birds, between which and the terrestrial animals they in some measure form the connecting link. The most extraordinary of Indian fishes is that small species which appears after the rainy season in places previously dry. It is caught by the natives on the island of Bombay, on the tenth day after the first rains, and is a common dish at their tables. Naturalists have suggested many modes of accounting for this phenomenon; some imagine the spawn may have been brought inland by the water-fowl; others that it is caught up by the whirlwinds, which rage with tremendous force at the commencement of the rainy season, and afterwards showered down upon the land in the torrents which then escape from the clouds; others that these fishes were originally frogs, but transformed by some wondrous process of nature, as the chrysalis is trans-

[1] The pink-coloured feathers of the tail of this bird are used by the ladies of Calcutta as part of their head-dress. Pennant, vol. ii. p. 158.

[2] Bishop Heber observes that he saw a flock of wild peacocks at Bareilly, and tame ones in all the villages on the banks of the Jumna and in the neighbourhood of Bhurtpoor. vol. ii. p. 141, 365. These birds were so rare in Greece that a male and female were valued at Athens at a thousand drachmæ,

formed into the butterfly[1]. The mango-fish, of a brilliant orange colour, like a ripe mango, swims up the Ganges, as far as Calcutta, in the month of June, spawns and returns to the sea in six weeks. This is the most delicious of Indian fish. Swarms of other fish are found in the Ganges[2]; such as the carp, the chub, the *anjana*, and the *ophidium aculeatum*. On the coasts of Coromandel and Malabar fish is so abundant that pigs, dogs, and horses are fed upon it[3]. The fierce heat of the torrid zone calls into life innumerable insects, unknown in more northern regions; and crowds of locusts, scorpions, black and white ants, and butterflies, swarm over the face of

or 32*l.* 5*s.* 10*d.* sterling. The island of Samos, which was sacred to Juno, was celebrated for its peacocks. Aulus Gellius, lib. vii. c. 16.

[1] Pennant's View of Hindoostan, vol. i. p. 102, 103; Seba, vol. i. p. 125; and Merian's Surinam, p. 71. According to the rational conjecture of Buchanan, the fish's eggs, which are exceedingly tenacious of life, remain all the year in the dry mud, and are quickened on the return of the rains. Journey, &c. vol. ii. p. 66; vol. iii. p. 342. This happens also in the small lakes of Lower Egypt, near the Pyramids. Egypt and Mohammed Ali, vol. i. p. 228.

[2] Pliny had heard of eels three hundred feet long being found in this river! Duperron supposes that he must have meant alligators, which would mend the matter but little, as alligators are no more three hundred feet long than eels. Tieffenthaler, tom. ii. p. 269.

[3] Malte-Brun, vol. iii. p. 43. In this general outline of the country, and in the ensuing more minute description of the provinces, reference was constantly made to Mr. Arrowsmith's Map of India, which, though not certainly without errors, is a work of great value to the geographer.

the country. Silkworms are found in Bengal, and towards the north of Poonah, in the Dekkan[1].

MINERAL KINGDOM.—The British possessions in India abound with iron, copper, lead, antimony, plumbago, zinc, sulphur, silver, and gold, together with inexhaustible supplies of coal, in various parts of the country. Boglipoor district is peculiarly rich in iron; and about Pointy and Siccary Gully, very large mines have been worked in former times: the ore is nodular, and yields from twenty to twenty-five per cent. iron. The Sylhet hills produce in the greatest abundance fine granular iron ore like sand. At a meeting of the Bengal Asiatic Society, 20th February, 1833, specimens of copper ore from Nellore were presented on the part of Mr. Kerr. The mines appear to lie to the northward of the Pennar river, thirty-six miles north-north-west of Nellore, and thirty-seven west from the sea, near a village called Ganypenta in Arrowsmith's map. Coal (see Geology) is now raised in Burdwan in considerable quantities, and it is preferred for the steam vessels at Calcutta, to European or New South Wales Coal, in consequence of its not so soon filling the flues, owing to the pureness of the bitumen and the superior quality of the gas.

In Sylhet a fine coal mine has been found; the

[1] See Dr. Roxburgh's paper on the silkworms of Bengal, in the seventh volume of the Transactions of the Linnæan Society; and Colonel Syke's account of the Kolisurra silkworms in the Dekkan, Transactions of the Royal Asiatic Society, vol. iii. p. 541, &c.

coal mine now working at Chirra Poonjee produces a mineral, which does not leave one fourth as much ashes as the Burdwan coal; the strata are nearly horizontal, requiring no pumps or machinery for drainage; it is delivered at the Sanatarium at 400 lbs. weight for 1*s*. The coal now worked is of the slaty kind, specific gravity 1.447, containing volatile matter, 36; carbon, 41; and a copious white ash, 23=100; seams of a superior coal, from two to four feet thick, have been more recently discovered contiguous to abundance of excellent iron ore. Coal has been recently discovered at Fatephúr (Nerbudda) which showed near the surface; water separated on a sand heat, 3,5; volatile matter not inflammable, 10.5; charcoal fixed, 22; earthy residue, red 64=100. Specific gravity of coal worked at the mines on the Kosya or Cossyah hills, 1.275; composition volatile matter or gas, 38.5; carbon or coke, 60.7; earthy impurities, 0.8=100, (the ash is exceedingly small). The coal found near Hardwar in the Himalaya mountains, has a specific gravity of 1.968, composition volatile matter, 35.4; carbon 50; ferruginous ash, 14.6=100; coal found in Arracan, specific gravity, 1.308; gives out bitumen and gas on ignition; composition, volatile matter, much 66.4; carbon, 33; ash, 0.6=100.

Mr. Wildey, late paymaster of His Majesty's Fourth Light Dragoons, who was stationed in Cutch, thus describes the coal found there. The best coal of the mine contains charcoal 70 per cent, bitumen 20 per cent, sulphur 5 per cent, iron 3 per cent, and calcareous earths 2 per cent. The second sort, charcoal 60, bitumen 15, oxide of iron 9, earths 10, sulphur 4, hydrogen and carbon acids 2 per cent[1].

Rich iron ore is abundant in Cutch, and is gathered in baskets on the surface of the earth, and possesses 22 per cent. of iron, and is from 10 to 12 per cent. more than the common iron ore. The natives of Cutch make steel chain armour, sabres, pikes, and various sharp-edged tools; they are the best blacksmiths in Asia; their horse-shoes are particularly fine, the iron being more malleable and soft, and not so likely to break. The veterinary surgeon of the fourth Dragoons said they were the finest shoes he ever saw, and far preferable to those made in England. The iron ore found in the south of India is equally good. Mr. Heath is now producing excellent iron near Madras. The Himalaya mines supply, chiefly, varieties of red iron ore, affording from thirty to sixty per cent. of metal. Near Kalsi, on the Jumna, there is an extensive bed of specular iron ore; red hematite, associated with micaceous iron ore, occurs in a large bed in gneis at Dhaniakat. At Rhamghur, on the road from Bhamouri to Almorah, there are beds of the scaly red iron ore, also in gneis; compact red iron ore occurs in clay-slate, containing beds of limestone at Katsari, on the Rhamganga. In some places a brown ore of the hydadit species, containing manganese, and affording a superior steel, is found. Boglipoor district is pe-

[1] Some recent accounts state that Cutch does not possess any extensive coal mines; I give however Mr. Wildey's statement in order to induce further inquiry.

culiarly rich in iron, and about Pointy and Siccary Gully, very large iron mines have been worked in former times; the ore is nodular, and yields from twenty to twenty-five per cent. iron. The Sylhet hills produce in the greatest abundance fine granular iron ore like sand. Copper mines are worked at Dhanpur, Dhobri, Gangoli, Sira, Pokri, Khari, and Shor Gurang. The ore found in the Dhanpur mine is gray copper ore, which affords from thirty to fifty per cent. of copper; it is associated with malachite, or green carbonate of copper. The ores are contained in a compact red-coloured dolomite; hence mining operations can be carried on without the expense of wooden frame-work, or masonry. The Pokri mine, or mines, are situated in talc slate of a loose texture, and hence the working is more difficult. The ores are vitreous and purple copper, both of them rich in copper. The waters flowing from the mine are impregnated with sulphate of copper or blue vitriol. The Sira and Gangoli mines are situated in beds of indurated talc, which are enclosed in dolomite. Sometimes the one, sometimes the other rock, form the walls of the mine. The iron is yellow copper or copper pyrites, mixed with iron pyrites and smaller portions of gray copper ore. The Khari and Shor Gurang mines are similarly situated, the ores are grey copper, yellow copper, or copper pyrites, and carbonate of copper. Mines exist to the northward of the Pennar river, thirty-six miles north-north-west of Nellore, and thirty-seven west from the sea, near a village called Ganypenta in Arrowsmith's map. The copper ore prevails over a considerable tract of country; it consists of malachite, and of black anhydrous oxide of copper, with red and yellow ochre imbedded in micaceous schist. The ore differs from the English coppers essentially, in being free from iron pyrites and other deteriorating ingredients, as lead, antimony, sulphur, &c., which make that ore difficult to purify, whereas the Nellore ore becomes quite pure by simple smelting. A specimen of reduced metal sent with the ores to the Asiatic Society is of a very fine colour and highly malleable. On analyzing the ore, it was found to contain carbonic acid, 16-8; black oxide copper, 60-75; red oxide iron, 19-4; silica and loss, 3-05—100. Four different varieties examined by the secretary contained from thirteen to forty-seven per cent. of red oxide of iron and silex.—*Lead.* The most productive of these mines are situated on the river Tonse, near the Deyrah Doon; the ore (a fine granular galena) is found in clay-slate and clay-limestone. It would be tedious to particularize other productions; two have been recently discovered. A native sulphate of alumina obtained from the aluminous rocks of Nepál, used by the native doctors to cure green wounds or bruises, yielding, on analysis, sulphate of alumina, 95; peroxide of iron, 3; silex, 1; loss, 1—100; and a native sulphate of iron is procured from the hills of Behar, and used by the dyers of Patna, yielding sulphate of iron, 39; peroxide of iron, 36; magnesia, 23; loss, 2—100. These two minerals, the natural productions of Nepál and Behar, may be had in the largest quantities, and would be found extremely useful in the manufacture of Prussian blue, calico printing, and dyeing,

Common salt (muriat of soda).—Carbonate of soda and nitrate of potash occur in many districts, forming the salt, soda, and nitre soils. A salt lake, twenty miles long by one and a half broad, is situate near Samber at Rajpoot Town, in latitude 26° 53′, and longitude 74° 57′; it supplies a great portion of the neighbouring country with salt on the drying up of the lake after the rains. In Berar there is a salt lake, called Loonar, lying in a sort of cauldron of rocks; it contains in the 100 parts, muriat of soda 20; muriat of lime, 10; muriat of magnesia, 6. Natron and soda lakes are said to occur in the Himalaya range. Towards the sources of the Indus salt lakes were observed by Mr. Gerard at 16,000 feet elevation above the sea, and there is an extensive salt mine in the Punjaub.

The valuable diamonds and other precious stones found in Golconda, in Orissa, in Bundlecund, &c. require no detailed notice. Silver ore, of a rich quality, is obtained in different places. Gold is found in the beds of most rivers, particularly in Nielgherries; but it exists in abundance in the state of ore in Malabar. This precious metal has been discovered not only in Coimbatore, but throughout that tract of the country lying west and south of the Nielgherry mountains and Koondanad. It is found here in great quantities. The whole of the country west of the Nielgherry mountains, in the taloogs of Parakameetil, especially at Nelliala, Cherangote, Koonyote, Kotah, Nambolacota, Daraloor, &c. &c., also the adjoining Koondanad and Ghåut mountains, and all the rivers and cholas (watercourses) down as far west as Nellambore, and south-west as Caladicota, Karimpure, Aliparamba, &c., the whole tract, including the mountains, perhaps comprising 2000 square miles, is impregnated with gold. Even the very stones in the beds of rivers, when pounded, have been found to contain particles of that valuable metal. It is found in solid pieces, but generally it is in extremely small particles, obtained in washing the sand of all the rivers as far as Nellambore, Karimpure, &c., as well as in the soil. Gold dust is procured in considerable quantities in every river in the Bhot Mehals of Kumaon, and is abundant in the multitude of rivers and streams in Assam. According to native statements, there is a valuable gold mine called Pakerguri, at the junction of the Dousiri, or Dòuhiri river, with the Brahmaputra, about thirty-two miles from Gohati. In 1809, it was estimated that 1000 men were employed in collecting gold, and that the State annually received 1500 rupees weight in gold. There can be no doubt that when the riches of India begin to be appreciated in England, the precious metals will flow in abundance from the eastern to the western hemisphere [1].

[1] It would be very desirable to form a general mining company for British India: there can be little doubt that the various minerals of the east would yield a valuable profit to English speculators. If the money which was expended in South American mines had been spent in India, how different would have been the results!

CHAPTER X.

POPULATION OF BENGAL, MADRAS, AND BOMBAY BY DISTRICTS —HOUSES, VILLAGES, &c.—GREAT VARIETIES OF CHARACTER AND DISTINGUISHING FEATURES OF THE PEOPLE.

We have no census of British India previous to our occupation of the country, and little information since that that can be relied on for minute correctness; I have searched the various public offices in India and England, and now proceed to detail as connectedly as possible the result of my inquiries. The earliest document I have obtained relates to the Bengal Presidency, in 1789; I give it from the manuscript return, with its comments, and I do not know that it has ever before been printed, or any of the other censusses which follow it, until they were published in the large edition of this work.

Estimate of the Population of the Provinces of Bengal and Bahar; the Company's possessions in Orissa; and the Province of Benares, formed from Estimates transmitted by the Collectors of the three former, and Resident in the latter, in answer to a reference made to them by desire of Lord Cornwallis, in July 1789.

Districts.	Men.	Women.	Children.	Total.
Benares	1071852	919852	919852	2911556
Bahar	333334	333333	333333	1000000
Beerbhoom	400000	520000	520000	1370000
Bhaugulpoor, (including Rajemahl)	262840	280000	100000	642840
Burdwan	380800	435200	544000	1360000
Calcutta	133334	133333	133333	400000
Chittagong	139828	154260	181087	475175
Dacca	307144	310608	320960	938712
Dinagepore	357733	349824	175872	883429
Jessore	280000	285100	491009	1056109

(Continued.)

Districts.	Men.	Women.	Children.	Total.
Midnapore	240944	242080	218077	701101
Moorshedabad	386181	410787	223604	1020572
Mymensing	200000	200000	200000	600000
Nuddea	437088	454609	467471	1359168
Pergunnahs, 24	150332	158663	137070	446068
Pumea, (including Dhurumpore)	353600	373900	472500	1200000
Ramgur, (including Pachete and Jelda)	242000	196625	166375	605000
Rangamatty	4435	4115	2366	10916
Rajshahy	613321	512963	372039	1498323
Rungpore, (including Cooch Behar)	187743	179285	92484	459512
Salt Districts	137433	158684	68320	364437
Shahabad	375000	410000	315000	1100000
Sirkar Sarum	420000	380000	100000	900000
Silhet	188245	164381	140319	492945
Tipperah	120563	112920	75001	308484
Tirhool	668843	642100	533356	1844309
Total...	8392593	8252632	7303428	23948653

Remarks on the foregoing Estimate, from the letters of the Resident at Benares, and the several Collectors of Bengal, Bahar, and Orissa.

BENARES.—The estimate of this province, formed by Mr. Duncan, is stated to have been made "according to the grain produce, allowing nine maunds on an average for the consumption of each person, children included;" excepting, however, the city of Benares and its vicinity, the population of which was estimated by Aly Ibraham Khan to be one million, but the Resident, deducting two-fifths, computes it to be 607,000 only.

BAHAR.—The computation in this district was made conjecturally by Mr. Law, who supposes the number of inhabitants "to exceed rather than fall short of a million." Mr. Seton has endeavoured to obtain more accurate information, but has not yet been able to procure it, or to distribute the number computed by Mr. Low among the men, women, and children; this distribution is therefore stated in equal proportions, which is nearly corresponding with the general average.

BEERBHOOM.—The estimate of this district, formed by Mr. Keating for Beerbhoom, and Mr. Hesilrige for Bishenpoor, is stated to have been founded on calculations made by some of the principal inhabitants. The children in this instance are stated to be below ten years of age.

BHAUGULPOOR.—The estimate of this district, formed by Mr. Davis, is calculated on the number of villages, and houses, or families, allowing four persons to each family or house, and twenty houses to each village. He adds, that the hill people of the Jungleterry were numbered in Mr. Cleveland's time, and found to be about 9000. The children in this estimate are said to be below fifteen.

BURDWAN.—The calculations in this district, made by Mr. Mercer, is also founded on the number of villages, and houses, or families, allowing four persons to each house, but he divides the villages into three classes, and computes the first class to contain 200, the second 50, and the third 5 houses.

CALCUTTA.—The different gentlemen who have held the office of collector of this town, and the fifty-five villages adjacent to it, having been unable to furnish any estimate of the population, the number specified has been assumed at nearly the average of different estimates furnished by intelligent natives to the compiler of the foregoing general estimate, a few years since, when he held the office of collector of Calcutta.

CHITTAGONG.—The estimate of this district was furnished by Mr. Bird, but he does not explain on what grounds it was formed.

DACCA.—The same remark is applicable to the estimate of this district, furnished by Mr. W. Douglas.

DINAGEPORE.—Also to the estimate of this district, furnished by Mr. Hatch.

JESSORE.—Ditto to the estimate of this district, furnished by Mr. Hinckell, which is, however, detailed for each mehaul.

MIDNAPORE.—Ditto to the estimate of this district, furnished by Mr. Burrowes, and also detailed.

MOORSHEDABAD.—Ditto to this estimate, furnished by Mr. J. E. Harrington, also detailed.

MYMENSING.—The different collectors of this district having been unable to procure materials for any computation, the number specified is stated conjecturally, on a general consideration of the relative assessment and extent of this district.

NUDDEA.—The estimate of this district, furnished by Mr. Redfearn, appears founded on a calculation of the number of houses or families, and an average allowance of seven or eight persons to each house; the proportions varying in different mehauls.

PERGUNNAHS (24).—Mr. Champain, who gave the estimate of this district, states it to be conjectural; he also observes, that the children included are under sixteen years of age.

PUMEA.—Mr. Heatly states the estimate of this district to have been formed " on the average of an actual investigation of three small villages, multiplied by 5800, the number of villages in the district," which, he adds, is a very low scale, and that " the general opinion swells the amount to 1,500,000 inhabitants ;" he also observes, that the girls are considered adult at eleven or twelve years of age, and the boys at twenty.

RAMGHUR.—Mr. Leslie states this estimate to have been the result of inquiries made by him, but does not explain the mode of inquiry.

RANGAMATTY.—This estimate, which includes Bisny, Currubary, and Rangamatty only, was furnished by Mr. H. Baillie, and is stated to be founded on the reports of the oldest inhabitants of each village.

RAJSHAHY.—This estimate, which respects Zillah Rajshahy as it stood in the year 1792, previous to the late new arrangement, is taken from a purgunnah estimate furnished by the Zemindar, deducting a fourth for an apparent over rate, on comparison with other districts.

RUNGPORE.—Mr. Macdowall, who furnished the estimate of this district, does not explain on what grounds it is founded, but it is detailed for each pergunnah.

SALT DISTRICTS.—The estimate of these districts is taken from detailed estimates furnished by Messrs. Hewett and Dent, but they do not explain the grounds of their calculations.

SHAHABAD.—Mr. W. A. Brooke, who furnished the estimate of this district, does not state the grounds of it.

SIRKAR SARUM.—Mr. Montgomerie states his estimate of this district to be conjectural.

Silhet.—The estimate of this district, furnished by Messrs. Willes and Smyth, is founded on a calculation of the number of houses, and persons in each house, the proportion differing in different mehauls.

Tipperah.—This calculation, received from Mr. Macquire, is stated by him to have been furnished by the Zemindars of the different pergunnahs.

Tirhool.—This estimate is stated in detail by Mr. Bathurst, but without any specification of the grounds on which it has been formed.

The credit due to the census of 1789 may be judged of from the foregoing comments,—I rather think that the number of inhabitants is considerably understated. The next census embraces nearly the same division of districts; I obtained it in India from Dwarkanant Tagore, a Hindoo of an enlarged mind, a most generous disposition, and a truly British spirit. Dwarkanant Tagore was then at the head of the salt and opium department at Calcutta, and had perhaps the best means of judging as to its correctness of any man in India;—he considered it as a fair estimate for 1820 or 1822. The calculations are founded on the number of villages and houses in each district; these I subsequently obtained from the East India House, and they are printed in the large edition of this work, in order that every possible information may be given on a subject of the greatest importance in a political, social, and commercial point of view.

Provinces, Districts, square Miles, Villages, Houses, and Population of the permanently settled Provinces of Bengal, Bahar, and Orissa, in 1822.

Province.	Districts.	Square Miles.	Villages.	Houses.	Population.
Calcutta.	City	7	...	53005	300000
	Suburbs of ditto	1105	710	72172	366360
	24 Pergunnas	3610	2891	129919	639295
	Hoogley	2260	3987	267430	1540350
	Nuddea	3105	4648	254622	1364275
	Jessore	5180	6239	345796	1750406
	Cuttack	9040	10511	396924	1984620
	Midnapore	8260	8536	382812	1914060
	Burdwan	2000	6576	256310	1487263
	Junglemehauls	6990	6492	269948	1394740
Patna.	Ramghur	22430	12364	479563	2325632
	Behar	5235	6312	268121	1340610
	Tirhoot	7732	10976	352970	1968720
	Sarun	5760	6118	292815	1494179
	Shahabad	4650	4185	181770	908856
	Patna	667	1098	51141	265705
Moorshedabad.	Bhaugulpore	7270	3667	159558	797790
	Purneah	7460	5268	296472	1560284
	Dinagepore	5920	12240	498360	2625720
	Rungpoor	7856	4231	268070	1340350
	Rajeshahye	3950	9170	817431	4087155
	Beerbhoom	3870	5287	253413	1267665
	Moorshedabad	1870	2342	152538	762690
Dacca.	Mymensing	6988	7904	290934	1454670
	Sylhet	3532	5717	216744	1083720
	Tipperah	6830	7529	274452	1372260
	Chittagong	2980	1108	140160	790806
	Backergunge	2780	2454	137328	686640
	Dacca	1870	2569	102777	512385
	Ditto (Jellapore)	2585	2543	117675	583375
	Total	153792	154268	7781240	39957561

There has been (it is a shame to say so) no census of Calcutta for several years. Those who may consider that 1,000,000, or 1,500,000 mouths is an over estimate for Calcutta, should recollect that Calcutta, as London, may be said to embrace both sides of the river; the mere city of Calcutta (embraced within the limits of the Supreme Court) may be likened to the

City of London separate from Westminster;—yet even the *City* of Calcutta contains half a million of inhabitants, if not more.

North Western Provinces.—In the return of the population of India by districts, as laid before Parliament in 1831, there are no data for ascertaining the inhabitants of each district in the Upper or Western Provinces, under the Bengal Presidency: Mr. Ewing, in his Police Report in 1826, gives a rough calculation of 32,206,806 for the Benares and Bareilly Provinces, the area of which (excluding Delhi, which is not given,) is 66,510 square miles (*the reader will find the area of each province in the table prefixed to this chapter*) but besides this area, there are 29,800 square miles of ceded districts on the Nerbudda, and 55,900 square miles of districts ceded by the Rajah of Berar in 1826, making a total of 85,700 square miles, of the population of which there are no returns. From Assam I have just received the following data: territory, 400 miles long, and sixty-five broad at the broadest part; population, 830,000; revenue, S. R. 3,50,000.

I give the accompanying return, recently received from India, as a simple form, which the Court of Directors ought to require from every Collectorate in India; where more detail was practicable it might be adopted,—

Population of the City and District of Allahabad in 1831-32.

City.	Houses.	Mussulmans.					Hindoos.					Grand Total.
		Men.	Women.	Children.		Total.	Men.	Women.	Children.		Total.	
				Males.	Females.				Males.	Pemales.		
City	9219	5661	6158	2251	2518	16593	9850	9621	4061	4903	28433	45021
Suburbs	4747	1338	1446	660	637	4076	5355	5388	2187	2603	15593	19764
Total......	13966	6999	7604	2911	3155	20669	15203	15009	6298	7606	44116	64785

	Houses.	Mussulmans.		Total.	Hindoos.		Total.	Grand Total.
		Males.	Females.		Males.	Pemales.		
District of Allahabad, exclusive of the city	143737	90531	70678	161209	251789	302417	554206	780190

The proportion of Mussulmans to the Hindoos in Lower Bengal in the principal Mahomedan city and district is thus shewn—

Population of the City and District of Moorshedabad for 1829.

Division.	Number of Houses.			Number of Inhabitants.		
	Mussulman.	Hindoo.	Total.	Mussulman.	Hindoo.	Total.
City........	14281	25837	40118	56090	90086	146176
District .	70453	97658	168111	356726	465224	821950
Total...	84734	123495	208229	412816	555310	968126

Proportion of sexes in the City.

	Males.	Females.
Mussulmans	28442	27648
Hindoos	44438	45648

Do. in District.

	Males.	Females.
Mussulmans	188036	168696
Hindoos................	241710	223514

Ratio of inhabitants per house 4.73.

MADRAS PRESIDENCY. — The Population of the Madras presidency, is thus given in some returns furnished me from the India House: it is acknowledged that the census of some of the districts was not correctly ascertained when the first returns were made, owing to the unwillingness of the zemindars to afford any information to government :—

Population and Area* of the Provinces under the Madras Government.

Districts.	Extent N. to S. miles.	Extent E. to W. miles.	Area in Square Miles.	Total of A.D. 1822.	Total of A.D 1827.	Fusly, 1240, A.D. 1830-31.		
						Males.	Females.	Total.
Ganjam†	120	30	3700	332015	468047	222891	215283	438174
Vizagapatam	110	50	5600	772570	1008544	545674	501740	1047414
Rajahmundry	100	80	4690	738308	660906	367292	327724	695016
Masulipatam	100	68	4800	529849	519125	295182	249490	544672
Guntoor	—	—	—	455754	476787	271792	246526	518318
Nellore	140	75	7478	439467	730608	448176	398396	846572
Bellary	280	264	12703	927857	941612	590831	538008	1128839
Cuddapah	262	160	12752	1094460	1000957	558300	504864	1063164
Chingleput }	120	130	8002	363121	289828	171699	160122	331821
N. Division }				892292	730410	397855	375113	772968
S. ditto	106	90	8500	455020	549795	288277	265111	553388
Salem	134	80	7593	1075985	955480	424048	398059	822107
Tanjore	108	70	3872	901353	1065560	578112	550618	1128730
Trichinopoly	96	48	3169	481295	476720	274151	262546	536697
Madura, &c.‡	190	166	6932	601293 }	1122979	578379	557032	1135411
Shevagunga	54	49	1724	186903 }				
Tinnevelly	135	80	5590	564957	766746	430142	420749	850891
Coimbatore	162	86	8392	638199	854050	425170	429664	854834
Canara	230	46	7477	657594	665652	367691	339880	707571
Malabar	118	65	4900	907575	100366	561172	552325	1113497
Madras City	—	—	—	462051	(No returns since 1822.)			700000
Total	2559	11628	97864	14006918	14287272	7796834	7293250	15090084

* I give the area and population from separate manuscripts at the India House, which do not agree in the names of the districts.

† Ganjam is exclusive of the Zemindaries, Jaradah, Vizianagaram, and Daracote, in which no census appears to have been taken in that year, thus accounting for the apparent decrease.

‡ This includes Ramnad, 2500, and Dindigul, 2024 square miles.

The census of the Bombay Presidency is less to be depended on than the foregoing; combining Colonel Sykes's information with the scanty intelligence laid before Parliament, I make up the following return, as the nearest approximation to truth which is at present attainable.

Divisions.	Collectorates.	Square miles.	Villages.	Houses.	Population.	Remarks.
	Bombay isle	18	...	20786	230000	In the Deccan, which includes an area of 48,987 square miles, and a population of 3,285,985, the average number of mouths to the square mile is 6708, and the proportion of males to females, about 100 to 86; the Mussulmans form only from 6 to 8 per cent. of the whole population; the Mahrattas, from 60 to 70 per cent., the Brahmins from 5 to 10 per cent., Rajpoots, from 3 to 6 per cent. and outcasts, &c. from 9 to 10 per cent.
Deccan.	Poonah	8281	1897	114887	558313	
	Ahmednuggur	9910	2465	136273	666376	
	Khandeish	12527	2738	120822	478457	
	Dharwar	9122	2491	187222	838757	
	S. Jagheerdars ...	2978	917	...	778183	
	Sattara, Ditto	6169	1703	...	736284	
	Concan, S.	6770	2340	...	656857	
	Concan, N.	5500	...	...	387264	
	Surat, &c.	1449	655	108156	454431	
	Broach	1351	400	55549	239527	
	Ahmedabad	4072	728	175926	528073	
	Kaira	1827	579	127231	484735	
	Total...	68074	16912	1096852	6940277	

Census of the Population of the Islands of Bombay and Colabah, taken in the months of August, September, October, and November, 1826.

Number of Houses.		English.	Portuguese.	Parsees.	Jews.	Americans.	Moors.	Hindoos.	Malays.	Chinese.	Total.
1219	Fort	432	359	6303	70	39	1232	5029	142	5	13611
520	Colabah	175	412	124	...	...	303	1358	204	...	2576
5457	Dungaree	46	1294	1764	1200	...	12888	29654	513	...	47359
4311	Byculla	51	114	983	...	...	9226	19076	1633	...	31083
631	Malabar Hill, &c.	59	44	119	...	...	51	2180	29	10	2492
2359	Gurgaum	61	1448	1074	...	...	519	9898	7	33	13040
894	Mazagon	82	810	304	...	...	302	3056	142	...	4696
1309	Mahim East	24	1219	41	...	...	258	4773	99	...	6414
3595	Mahim West	8	2320	26	...	...	1141	7568	236	...	11299
20195	Total										132570
	Military } Estimated										10000
	Floating } Estimated										20000
	Grand Total	938	8020	10738	1270	39	25920	82592	3005	48	162570

It is difficult to say how near any of the foregoing returns, except those for Madras, approximate towards correctness; the estimated population of 422,990 square miles here given is 89,577,206, leaving 91,200 square miles of British territory, of the population of which no accounts can be traced; but if we allow the low rate of ninety mouths to the square mile, it will make the population of the British territories about *one hundred million!* Now to this vast number, we are to add the inhabitants of the protected and allied states; the area of which is greater than that of the British territory by 100,000 square miles; and allowing an equal amount of population to the British territories, it will give a grand total of TWO HUNDRED MILLION INHABITANTS, directly and indirectly under the sway of Great Britain, and subject to the government of the Honourable East India Company! The number of whites, or Europeans, does not, including all the military, amount to 100,000.

The following estimate has been made of the population of the allied and independeut states:—Hydrabad, 10,000,000; Oude, 6,000,000; Nagpoor, 3,000,000; Mysore, 3,000,000; Sattara, 1,500,000; Guickwar, 2,000,000: Travancore and Cochin, 1,000,000; Rajpootana and various minor principalities 16,500,000; Scindias territories, 4,000,000; the Seiks, 3,000,000; Nepál, 2,000,000; Cashmere, &c. 1,000,000; Sinde, 1,000,000; total, 51,000,000. This, of course, is but a rough estimate by Hamilton.

SLAVERY IN BRITISH INDIA.—For the last forty years the East India Company's government have been gradually, but safely abolishing slavery throughout their dominions; they began in 1789 with putting down the maritime traffic, by prosecuting any person caught in exporting or importing slaves by sea, long before the British government abolished that infernal commerce in the western world, and they have ever since sedulously sought the final extinction of that domestic servitude which had long existed throughout the east, as recognized by the Hindoo and Mahomedan law. In their despatches of 1798, it was termed an '*inhuman commerce and cruel traffic;*' French, Dutch, or Danish subjects captured within the limits of their dominions in the act of purchasing or conveying slaves, were imprisoned and heavily fined. and every encouragement was given to their civil and military servants to aid in protecting the first rights of humanity.

Mr. Robertson, in reference to Cawnpore observes:[1]—'Domestic slavery exists; but of an agricultural slave I do not recollect a single instance. When I speak of *domestic* slavery, I mean that *status* which I must call slavery for want of any more accurate designation. It does not, however, resemble that which is understood in Europe to be slavery: it is the mildest species of servitude. 'The domestic slaves are certain persons purchased in times of scarcity; children purchased from their parents: they grow up in the family, and are almost entirely employed in domestic offices in the house; not liable to be resold.

'There is a certain species of slavery in South Bahar, where a man mortgages his labour for a certain sum of money; and this species of slavery exists

[1] Lords' Evidence, 1687.

also in Arracan and Ava. It is for his life, or until he shall pay the sum, that he is obliged to labour for the person who lends him the money; and if he can repay the sum, he emancipates himself.

'Masters have no power of punishment recognized by our laws. Whatever may be the provision of the Mahomedan or Hindoo codes to that effect, it is a dead letter; for we would not recognize it. The master doubtless may sometimes inflict domestic punishment; but if he does, the slave rarely thinks of complaining of it. Were he to do so, his complaint would be received.' This, in fact, is the palladium of liberty in England.

In Malabar, according to the evidence of Mr. Baber, slavery as mentioned by Mr. Robertson also exists, and perhaps the same is the case in Guzerat and to the north; but the wonder is not that such is the case, but that it is so partial in extent, and fortunately so mild in character, approximating indeed so much towards the feudal state as to be almost beyond the reach as well as the necessity of laws which at present would be practically inoperative. The fact that of 100,000,000 British inhabitants, [or allowing five to a family, 20,000,000 families,] upwards of 16,000,000 are landed proprietors, shews to what a confined extent even domestic slavery exists. A commission has been appointed by the new charter to inquire into this important but delicate subject.

It does not fall within the province of a work, the object of which is to enable the British public to appreciate duly the vast importance and actual condition of the Colonies of this Empire,—it does not, I say, fall within the legitimate or advisable scope of such an undertaking to speculate on abstract questions, such, for instance, as the *origin* of the Hindoos, —whether the earth was primitively peopled from the Polar regions (as asserted by a French philosopher), or from the lofty table land of Hindostan (as contended for by many),—whether the Hindoos were originally migratory Scythian or Tartar colonists, or emigrants from Egypt, or *vice versa* [1], or whether they are a nation of 1,000 or 12,000 years' antiquity; all these disquisitions would be unsuited to a work of this description, and as until the last fifty years little or nothing had been known in Europe of peninsular Asia, probably more time will be requisite for the just development of important truths; I will, therefore, proceed to observe that a misconception has long prevailed that the inhabitants of British India, to the number of 100,000,000, are a primitive, simple people, usually termed Hindoos, who abstain from eating any thing that ever breathed the breath of life, and are invariably the disciples of Menu. It would be as absurd to speak of all the inhabitants of Europe as one race, because they wear hats, shave, and are (at least) professedly Christians, as it would be absurd to speak of the many millions who inhabit our possessions on the continent of Asia as one people, because they, generally, wear turbans, do not shave their faces [2], and are nominally the worshippers of Brahma. In fact, there is a greater diversity of cha-

[1] I have remarked a striking resemblance between the customs and appearance of the Ceylonese and Egyptians.

[2] The Hindoos shave the chin, cheeks, and part of the head, but not the upper lip, which is nearly the reverse of the Mahomedans.

racter and language among the natives of Hindostan than there is in all Europe.

Bishop Heber justly observed, ' it is a great mistake to suppose that all India is peopled by a single race, or that there is not as great a disparity between the inhabitants of Guzerat, Bengal, the Dûab, and the Deccan, both in language, manners, and physiognomy, as between any four nations of Europe;' and again, 'the inhabitants of the presidencics of Madras and Bombay, and of the Deccan, are as different from those nations I have seen, and from each other, as the French and Portuguese from the Greeks, Germans, and Poles.' Colonel Todd remarks that along the course of the River *Chumbul* (500 miles) may be found specimens of the various Indian races of *Soondees, Chunderawats, Seesoodias, Aaras Gore, Jadoon, Sikerwal Goojur, Jaût, Tuar, Chohan, Bhadoria, Kutchwaha, Sengar, Boondela,* &c., each in associations of various magnitudes, from the substantive state to the little republic communes between the *Chumbul* and *Cohari.* Mr. Crawford thinks that, ' in India there are at least thirty nations, speaking as many distinct languages;' and that, these Indian nations are unknown to each other; the Mahrattas being as much strangers to the people of Bengal, or to those of the Carnatic as we are; the Seiks are strangers to the Mahrattas, and some 15,000,000 Mahomedans differ from each other in nation, in sect, and often in language. Bengal, Assam, Arracan, Behar, the upper provinces Kumaon, the Sikh States, Rajpootana, and Bundlecund (to say nothing of southern or western India) contain respectively a people as different from each other as Holland, France, Spain, Portugal, England, Scotland, Germany, and Switzerland; Madras, Bombay, and central India contain a population as different from each other as the foregoing, and may be likened to the Greeks, Austrians, Prussians, Poles, and various Russian tribes.

The Mussulmans are divided into two chief sects—the Soonee and the Shea, as different from each other as Protestant and Catholic among the Christians; and there are numerous subdivisions (as various as those of the Reform faith) whose tenets have more or less effect on their conduct in the affairs of common life; there are also Jains, Parsees, Chinese, Malays, Armenians, Syrian, and Roman Catholic Christians, Portuguese descendants, and hundreds of other classes. But even among the disciples of Bramah there is a great diversity. The majority perhaps of the Hindoos of Bengal and Orissa do not eat meat, and it has been ascribed to a religious precept forbidding the destruction of animal life; but almost every Hindoo eats *fish*, several eat kid, and many birds: the abstinence from animal food was, in the first instance, owing to an interdict of the priests, in consequence of its scarcity or dearness. Many of the highest Rajpoots and Brahmins in northern and western India will eat goat's flesh, venison, and *wild* hog's flesh, while they abhor that of sheep, or *domestic* swine; some will eat the jungle cock (which is pretty similar to our game cock except in size) who would think the touch of a domestic fowl pollution; very many castes will eat some particular kind of food but refuse others: at Bickaneer, all the Hindoos profess an abhorrence of fish; at Kumaon they will eat the *short*-tailed sheep of the hills, but will not touch one with a *long* tail: many castes will eat bread baked by people who would lose caste if they were to touch boiled rice prepared by the same hands: an *earthen* pot is polluted past redemption by being touched by an inferior caste, a metal one suffers no such deterioration: some tribes allow a man to smoke, through his hands, from the bowl (chillum) which contains the tobacco, but would not allow the same person to touch that part of the hookah which contains the water. Instances such as these might be multiplied *ad infinitum*.

In points of greater importance there is as great a difference between the various tribes of Hindoos, as among the different sects of Christians; even the religious holidays observed in Bengal are different from those kept in the Upper Provinces, the barbarous ceremonies of Juggernaut's car, and the abominations of Churruk Poonjah (where men are swung in the air with hooks fastened through their loins) are utterly unknown in Northern and Western India: in some parts of Hindostan female infanticide is almost universal, in others it is held in just abhorrence; again, in some parts polygamy prevails, in others polyandria (as in the Himalaya districts, where one woman is married to all the brothers in a family, for the purpose of keeping property in the family); in some places the marriage of a daughter is a cause of great expense to her parents; in others the source of profit, as the husband pays a considerable sum for his wife, and has the power of selling her again, or even of mortgaging her for a certain time in security for a debt which he is unable to pay. Even the Indian Mussulmans have their castes, for which they are thoroughly despised by a Persian or Affghan. The number of Moslems throughout British India has been estimated at from ten to fifteen million; in some places they do not form one sixteenth of the population. The Deccan is the principal country of the Mahrattas: the total population of this division of Hindostan is about 3,285,985 souls, of whom about 70 per cent. are Mahrattas; the remainder, according to Lieutenant Colonel Sykes, consists of low caste Brahmins, Mussulmans, and Rajpoots. The clear evidence of this talented officer before Parliament thus displays the difference between the portion of the Hindoos called Mahrattas and those who are not; and he also draws a comparison between the Hindoos generally and the Mussulmans. 'The Mahrattas are a nation speaking a language peculiar to themselves. The nation comprises Mahratta Brahmins, Mahratta low castes, and other various castes of Hindoos; but the genuine Mahratta belongs to that great division of the Hindoos denominated Shoodrah, a division comprising an infinity of distinctive groupes or races, none of the members of which will eat or intermarry with Shoodrahs not belonging to their own group or race. There are certainly minute shades of difference amongst the Mahrattas, but no distinction of caste. There are local circumstances that probably prevent one family intermarrying with another; but still every Mahratta can eat with his neighbour Mahratta, unless the latter should have been expelled from his caste, an event of no unusual occurrence.'

Colonel Sykes thinks that the minds of the Mussulmans are superior to the Hindoos; the Mussulmans are men of greater elevation of sentiment, greater energy of purpose and dignity of character; they are more luxurious and dissipated, but they are decidedly more martial, manly and cultivated, as a people, than the Hindoos: they are, however, great bigots, which the Hindoos are not. They harmonize, however, very well with the Hindoos; the Hindoos even assist to celebrate some of their religious festivals; and it is very remarkable that all the butchers' meat consumed by the Hindoos (which is considerable), is prepared, as far as the slaughter and cutting up of the animal goes, by Mussulman butchers only.

The Parsees (of whom there are 10,738 in Bombay island) are one of the finest races of people that are any where to be found; although descendants of the Guebers, or fire worshippers, whose heroism is so well known, they are now generally engaged in traffic, in the details of which they display an honesty, intelligence, and nobleness which is no where surpassed.

The Jews are very numerous in India and in China, and many are to be found in the ranks of the Bombay army, where they have behaved bravely; the Asiatic Jews are distinguished from those of Europe by immense 'Roman' noses.

The Mughs, or natives of Arracan, are a short

muscular race, of a copper colour, with round, flat features. They possess more activity and natural courage than the Bengalees, but less than their late masters, the Burmese. Their food is chiefly fish and rice, but they object not to a dish of stewed rats, boiled snakes, or a fried section of the putrifying carcase of an elephant; nothing, in fact, from a maggot to a mammoth, comes amiss to a voracious Mugh. These ancient people form six-tenths of a population of 100,000 in Arracan; the Mussulmans three-tenths, and the Burmese the remaining one-tenth.

The population of Assam (400 miles long by 65 broad) is 830,000; the inhabitants in general are remarkable for their timid submission and apathetic character, and for their ordinary features, or it might be termed ugliness, not even excepting the women; there are a few hill tribes of a more manly character and appearance, and the Camroop women are spoken of as handsome. The Assamese are of the Brahminical faith, but separated into an almost infinite variety of sects.

Among the timid navigators of the east, the mariner of Cutch is truly adventurous; he voyages to Arabia, the Red Sea, and the coast of Zanguebar in Africa, bravely stretching out on the ocean after quitting his native shore. The 'moallim,' or pilot, determines his position by an altitude at noon, or by the stars at night, with a rude quadrant. Coarse charts depict to him the bearings of his destination, and, by long-tried seamanship, he weathers, in an undecked boat with a huge lateen sail, the dangers and tornadoes of the Indian Ocean. The use of the quadrant was first learned by a native of Cutch, who made a voyage to Holland in the middle of the last century, and returned, in a green old age, to enlighten his countrymen with the arts and sciences of Eusope. The most substantial advantages introduced by this improver of his country were the arts of navigation and naval architecture, in which the inhabitants of Cutch excel. For a trifling reward, a Cutch mariner will put to sea in the rainy season, and the adventurous feeling is encouraged by the Hindoo merchants of Mandavie, an enterprising and speculative body of men.

The Jâts originally migrated from the province of Mooltan, on the banks of the Indus, and subsisted partly by plunder and partly by commerce and agriculture. During the civil wars of Aurungzebe's successors, the Jâts secured a large portion of the country between the Ganges and Jumna, accumulated much treasure by pillage and spoil, and built several forts, one of which was Bhurtpore; the title of Rajah was then assumed by their chiefs, the principal of whom reigns in Bhurtpore, the total area of whose government is about 5000 square miles. The Jâts thus alluded to are descnded from a low *Sudra* caste, having subsequently assumed the title of *Khetri*, or military caste, and are distinct from the Jâts or old Mahomedan peasantry of the Punjab. The Indus tribe are, however, well entitled to assume the appellation of Khetri, as they are a brave independent race, and one of the most determined enemies which the British forces have engaged with on the battle field.

The Oorians inhabit Orissa, and so feminine are they in appearance, that it is difficult to distinguish them from women, both dressing exactly alike. They are timid, but exceedingly dissolute and obscene; they are more versed in low cunning, dissimulation and subterfuge, than perhaps any people in the east, and that is saying much for their character. Their honesty and industry are two remarkable features in contrast with the foregoing traits, with which Mr. Stirling depicted the Oorians.

The different nations, classes, and sects of Hindostan may be thus summarily distinguished, in order to mark their variety. Insidious, cruel, and talented Brahmins, war-like Khetries, industrious Shoodras, ambitious but sensual Moslems, war-like and cunning Mahrattas, peaceful money-changing Jains [1], feudatory and high-spirited Rajpoots, roving and thieving Batties and Catties [2], scrupulously honest Parsees, lynx-eyed Jews, heroic Goorkas, professionally murdering Thugs and Phasingars [3],

[1] The Jains are somewhat similar in features as well as in manners and religion, to the Budhists of Ceylon and Siam.

[2] These wandering outlaws worship the sun, and hold the moon in great veneration.

[3] The Phasingars of the south of India are professional murderers, like the Thugs; the latter, however, are composed of men of all castes, and it is remarkable that *Brahmins* are the most numerous and the chief directors of the horrid vocation of their sect.

mercantile Armenians [1], freebooting Pindaries, vindictive but grateful Nairs, sedate Nestorians [2], filthy Mughs, haughty Persians, actively commercial Chinese [3], mercenary Sindeans, martial Seiks [4], fanatical Roman Catholics [5], despotic Poligars, bigotted Gosseins, proscribed Sontals, piratical Concanese, turbulent Mhairs and Meenas, degraded Muniporeans, sanguinary and untameable Koolies, timid and apathetic Assamese, Quaker-like Kaits [6], wild Puharees [7],

[1] The Armenians in their manners and peaceful, honourable calling as merchants, bear no slight resemblance to the Parsees.

[2] The Nestorian Christians are very numerous in the south of India, and deservedly much admired for their peaceful, intelligent, and industrious habits.

[3] This extraordinary race are colonizing themselves fast in Calcutta, and by their superior skill as artizans, are engrossing to themselves the principal handicrafts of the city.

[4] The eagle eye, Roman nose, and flowing beard, give the Seik cavaliers a noble appearance; and in horsemanship they are perhaps not excelled by any other nation, European or Asiatic.

[5] The Roman Catholics (descendants from the Portuguese and French, or converts to their faith) amount, it is said, to 600,000; they are sunk in a state of idolatry not far removed from Hindooism. There are 50,000 Portuguese, or converts to their religion, assuming Portuguese names, in the territories under the Bombay Presidency.

[6] The Kaits, like the Quakers, support each other;—none are uneducated, they are never seen in a state of indigence or in a menial capacity; they differ from the 'Quakers' in not being of a strictly moral character.

[7] The Puharees inhabit the hilly country between Burdwan and Boglipoor, and appear to be the aborigines of Bengal; they have no castes, care nothing for the Hindoo faith, and do

pastoral Todawars[1], maritime Cutch, usurious Soucars and Shroffs[2], outcasts Pariars, ferocious Malays, innocent Karians, dissolute Moguls[3], peaceful Telingars, anomalous Grassias, grasping Jauts or Jats, effeminate Ooriens, keen-sighted Bunnias[4], mendicant Byragies, jesuitical Charuns and minstrel Bhâts, avaricious Mewatties, restless and depraved Soondies[5], well-trained fighting Arabs and Patans[6], commercial Bringaries and Loodanahs[7] aboriginal Gonds[8],

not worship idols; their language, features and manners are alike distinct from the people of the plains.

[1] This manly race, who in features and independent feelings strongly resemble the ancient Romans, inhabit the table land of Coimbatore.

[2] Bankers and money changers, a tribe spread all over India.

[3] The dingy white colour of the Moguls of the north-west provinces is as displeasing to the eye as their filthy licentiousness is to the mind.

[4] The retail and petty dealing in central India is in the hands of the Bunnias.

[5] Illegitimate descendants of the Rajpoots, looked on by other tribes with disgust for their numerous and habitual vices.

[6] The Arabs and Patans are mercenary soldiers, and, like their European Swiss brethren, ready to fight for those who pay them best.

[7] These people live in tents, have no home, and trade generally in grain, with which they travel from country to country, or follow the route of armies, who in their fiercest contests, consider these valuable attendants as neutrals: they preserve a marked separation and independence of other races, and their dress and usages are peculiar.

[8] The Gonds, who may be considered the aborigines of the south part of India, *and who bear a striking resemblance to the*

monkish Kapriyas[1] and in fine tribes of Sours, Baugeries, Moghies, Googurs, Gwarriahs[2], &c., too numerous and diversified to depict, and presenting, if not a similar number of languages, a corresponding diversity of dialects and a complete distinction in manners, customs, and occupations.

Nothing is more natural than to expect among so many millions of people spread over so varied a country a marked distinction of character; have we not endless variety in climates, in soils, in waters, in minerals, in vegetables, in fish, in insects, in birds, and quadrupeds, subject to certain defined laws of the Creator, and influenced by natural causes? Why should it be otherwise with the human race, who in colour, physiognomy, stature, speech, gesture, habits, and mental as well as physical peculiarities, present such an extraordinary diversity, that no two persons were ever found alike?

Even in the same family, we see no two individuals having similar characteristics; notwithstanding all the efforts of education we find a difference in moral qualities, as well as in mental capabilities; in handwriting even, in the intonation of the voice, in gait, in animal propensities,—and this distinction becomes the more marked, if we compare two brothers with the nation of which they form a part, while a wider

African negro, still continue to offer human sacrifices where they are not subject to our control.

[1] Similar in habits and rules to the Dominican friars.

[2] The Gwarriahs live by stealing women and children to sell.

line of demarcation is seen on comparing the people of a province with those of other and distant climes. That I may the better exemplify my assertion as to the variety of British subjects in India, I request a moment's attention to Italy, where the climate and soil is so varied. In that classic land, we have the descendants of a race of men as ancient in record as the Hindoos; but (as in Hindostan) the inhabitants of the north, are essentially different from those of the south, the former produces the best soldiers (Rajpoots) the latter the keenest politicians, (Bengalees) the people of the one are industrious, peaceful, of tamer manners, or if I may so express my meaning, *domesticated;* those of the other, of a wild and stormy temper, generous but revengeful, capable of the most heroic as well as the basest deeds, of an uncultivated genius, and impatient of discipline; whence then this marked contrast in Italy? (a country so small compared with Hindostan) the political institutes, the religion, the language is common to all, but the *climate and soil are essentially different.*

The north of Italy is a fertile, champagne country, intersected by numerous rivers, cultivated to an astonishing degree, covered with wide and level roads, never ending avenues, and thickly-populated towns and villages, with a highly luxuriant but dull and sleepy landscape; (this description might serve for lower Bengal) the south is crowned with purple tinged mountains and golden edged clouds, diversified with stupendous and sometimes inaccessible crags, foaming torrents, Cashmerian vales, wild but beautiful forests, and a scenery which presents the most splendid pictures at every step; (those who have visited many parts of the highlands of India will recognize the same features as in southern Italy). Is it to be wondered that the character of men inhabiting such different countries should be dissimilar? Hence in the low, hot, and damp swampy regions of India, we have a timid, pacific, commercial, phlegmatic, and even servile race; educated, but prone to superstition, tyrants over females, yet addicted to compliments, and extravagant in all the littleness attending on the ceremonials of behaviour; while in the elevated, dry, and cool regions of our possessions in Asia, the inhabitants are fearlessly brave, filled with martial ardour, chivalrous to women, courteous to strangers, glorying in deeds of heroism, sanguine in their achievements, desperate enemies and warm friends,—as individuals, serfs, yet proud, in the aggregate of national independence, at all times ready to reject the pen and the ploughshare for the sword and the war steed, and, as justly expressed by the noble bard,—

"Who for itself can seek th' approaching fight,
And turn what some deem danger to delight;
Who seek what cravens shun with more than zeal,
And where the feebler faint can only feel—
Feel to the rising bosom's inmost core,
Their hopes awaken and their spirits soar;
No dread of death if with them die their foes,
Save that it seems even duller than repose!"

Such in fact is the varied character of the nations of Hindostan; hence the discrepant testimony of various witnesses who have only judged of the portion of the people among whom their avocations may have located them for a number of years; one party extolling them to the skies as exhibiting patterns of every virtue which adorns man,—the other representing them as a slavish, lying, cruel, treacherous, unprincipled and ungrateful race. Truth in this, as in most other instances, lies between the extremes; the Hindoos (independent of the effects of climate, soil, and food [1]) display the terribly demoralizing results which centuries of despotism are so surely calculated to produce. 'Tis true they have not had iron fetters on their wrists and ankles like the slaves in the West Indies, but they have had for ages fetters on the mind far more efficacious for the debasement of the immortal spirit of man,—

> ———— " Is there no tyranny but that
> Of blood and chains? The despotism of vice—
> The weakness and wickedness of luxury—
> The negligence, the apathy, the evils
> Of sensual sloth, produce ten thousand tyrants,
> Whose delegated cruelty surpasses
> The worst acts of one energetic master,
> However hard and harsh in his own bearing."

But those who have studied minutely and extensively the characters of the Hindoos, will admit that they have prejudices to be humoured, affections to be won, passions to be dreaded, and virtues to be cherished and developed. Since the conquest of

[1] Those Hindoos who, though professing the religion of Menu, live in some degree on animal food, are a very different class of people from those who live principally on vegetables.

India by England, the British rulers have been carefully annihilating a chain of feudalism which ever marks an age of barbarism; society which heretofore consisted of only two classes, is now being levelled, by the removal of the slavish dependence of the low upon the higher castes, and millions of human beings are now for the first time learning to know their own worth, and to be conscious that by industry, talent, and integrity, they may elevate themselves to the foremost rank in society; human sacrifices have been abolished, infanticide materially checked, and the horrid rite of female cremation completely prohibited; those palladiums of liberty, the press and trial by jury, are being gradually extended; the natives sit on the judgment seat and fill the magisterial chair: and if common justice be done them in their commercial dealings with England, (and no insane attempt be made to interfere with their religious principles before couching them for the moral cataract which yet dims their mental vision,) the future may be looked forward to with glowing anticipations; but when we witness the powerful opposition that even yet exists to the abolition of the diabolical rite of widow burning among the Hindoo population (remembering that the proportion of Europeans to Asiatics in India, is as *one* to *five thousand!* and of Mahomedans to Hindoos as *one* to *ten*) let us beware not to proceed too fast, let us temper benevolence with prudence, principle with policy, and justice with expediency.

Sir Thomas Munro has placed on record a minute which has reference to the precipitancy of some of our measures in 1824, he says, 'Our experience is too short to judge what rules are best calculated for this purpose. It is only within the last thirty years that we have here begun to acquire any practical knowledge. A longer period must probably elapse before we can ascertain what is best. Such a period is as nothing in the existence of a people; but we act as if this were as limited as the life of an individual.' With regard to precipitation he has this observation: 'One great error in this country, during a long course of years, has been too much *precipitation* in attempting to *better* the *condition of the people,* with hardly any knowledge of the means by which it was to be accomplished, and indeed without seeming to think that any other than good intentions were necessary. It is a dangerous system of government, in a country of which our knowledge is very imperfect, to be constantly urged by the desire of settling every thing permanently, to do every thing *in a hurry*, and in *consequence* wrong: and in our zeal for permanency, to put the remedy out of our reach. The ruling vice of our government is innovation, and its innovation has been so little guided by a knowledge of the people, that although made after what was thought by us to be mature discussion, must appear to them as little better than the result of mere caprice. We have in our anxiety to make every thing as English as possible, in a country which resembles England in nothing, attempted to create at once, throughout extensive provinces, a kind of landed property which had never existed in them.' These, indeed, are profound truths.

CHAPTER XI.

VARIETIES OF LANGUAGE, THEIR FILIATION, &c.—APPEARANCE AND STATURE OF THE HINDOOS—PHRENOLOGICAL INDICATIONS—PERSONAL PROWESS, &c.

As may be expected among so great a variety of people, several languages are in use; the modern spoken dialects are thus enumerated,—Hindustany, Bengalcse, Cashmerian, Dogura, Ooch, Sindy, Cutch, Gugeratty, Concancese, Punjaby, Bicanere, Marwar, Jeypoor, Odeypoor, Harowty, Malwa, Broach, Bundlecundy, Mahratta, Magadha, Koshala, Maithala, Nepaulese, Orissa, Telinga, Carnata, and Tamul; but in fact (in the upper provinces of Bengal for instance) the languages of the body of the population are so little settled that it would be extremely difficult to translate the regulations of government into any language that would be understood by them, unless a separate translation were made for every district.

The celebrated Sanscrit is not enumerated in the foregoing list, it having long ceased to be a spoken tongue, from the extraordinary perfection to which it has been matured. That it is the parent of so many eastern tongues or dialects is not to be wondered at when we find that to all present appearance it is the *parent* of all the existing languages in the world, it being more readily decompounded—retraced to its roots, or reduced to simple elements, and from its possessing the unique feature of an absence of exotic terms. Colonel Vans Kennedy, of the Bombay army, in his elaborate work on the Origin and Affinity of the Languages of Asia and Europe, thus assigns the—

FILIATION OF LANGUAGES.

Babylonian or Sanscrit.

Language of Asia Minor.

- Latin.
  - French.
  - Italian.
  - Spanish, &c.
- Greek.
- Thracian, *extinct.*
  - Anglo-Saxon.
  - German.
  - Swedish, &c.

Syria and Arabia.

Parent *extinct.*

- Hebrew.
- Arabic.
- Syriac, &c.

Distinct Languages without Affinities.

Persian in Asia. Celtic in Europe.

India.

North of the River Krishna.

Parent *extinct.*

- Marat'tha.
- Guzjirate.
- Hindi.
- Bengali.
- Panjabi.

South of the River Krishna.

Parent *extinct.*

- Tamil.
- Malayalam.
- Telinga.
- Canara.
- Tulava.

The Sanscrit apparently forms the basis of most of the dialects now spoken in the northern parts of India, especially of the Bengali, the Hindoostani, the Mahratti, &c.; but it is entirely distinct from the Tamul, or *Tamil,* which occupies nearly as conspicuous a rank among the languages of the Deccan as the Sanscrit does among those of the northern provinces. The Tamul language, spoken by a population of more than four millions, in current is the southern portion of the peninsula of India, throughout the Jaghire, the districts of South Arcot, Salem, Coimbatoor, Combaconum, Tanjore, Trichinopoly, Madura, Dindigal, and Tinivelly, as well as in many parts of the extensive kingdom of Mysore. It is said not to be derived from any language at present in existence, being either itself the parent of the Teloogoo, Malayâlam, and Canarese languages, or, more probably, having its origin in common with these in some ancient tongue, which is now lost, or only partially preserved in its offspring. In its more primitive words, such as the names of natural objects, the verbs expressive of physical action or passion, the numerals, &c. it is quite unconnected with the Sanscrit; and what is thence so largely borrowed, when the Tamuls, by intercourse with the more enlightened people of the north, began to emerge from barbarity, has reference to the expression of moral sentiments and abstract metaphysical notions, and is chiefly to be found in the colloquial idiom. In this remarkable circumstance, and also in the construction of its alphabet, the Tamul differs much from other languages of the south, which are found to admit Sanscrit more largely in literary compositions than in conversation, and which adopt the arrangement of the Sanscrit alphabet with little variation.

Bengali is spoken by about 30,000,000 people in Lower Bengal, and the Hindostani under a variety of dialects by about 20,000,000 in North and West India.

The three principal languages of Southern India are the Teloogoo, the Tamul, and the Carnatica. The first is spoken in the provinces to the northward of Madras; the second to the southward; the third to the westward, or the table-land above the passes of the mountains; and also in some districts below the Ghauts, on the western side of the peninsula.

Efforts are now in progress in India, and in some instances adopted by Government, of representing in Roman characters the principal Asiatic characters; such as Bengalee, Persian, Nagrie, &c. The different classes of letters (gutturals, nasals, &c.) are discriminated by distinctions and marks. The English language (see Education chapter) is now being widely extended.

APPEARANCE AND STATURE OF THE HINDOOS[1].—The stature, complexion, and physiognomy of the Hindoos are so different, that no general picture can represent the various dissimilar races which compose the body of the people. Among the Rajpoots and mountaineers of the north are frequently found men of gigantic stature and Herculean proportions, who would be considered remarkable in any country in Europe for their size and muscular power. Colonel Tod says, 'Gokul Das, the last chief of Deoghur, was one of the finest men he ever beheld in feature and person. He was about six feet six, perfectly erect, and a Hercules in bulk. His father at twenty was

[1] An interesting popular little work, published by Mr. Knight, entitled the 'Hindoos,' has furnished me with several collected observations.

much larger, and must have been nearly seven feet high.' In general, the inhabitants of the plains are inferior in height, and of a more slender make; but both the latter and the former are in general of an agile, graceful form, and capable of enduring considerable fatigue. Few deformed persons are seen, but, from various causes, blindness is not uncommon. The complexion of the people, according to climate and circumstances, varies from a dark olive, approaching to black, to a light, transparent, beautiful brown, with an olive tinge, resembling that of the natives of northern Italy or Provence; but the mind being so well disciplined, the countenance seldom betrays the fiery passions which are at work within. The face of the Hindoo is oval; forehead moderately large and high; eyes and hair black; eyebrows finely turned, and nose and mouth of an European cast; the look is calm, placid, and prepossessing, with nothing of the sinister aspect of the Malay, or the impassioned expression of the Persian or Arab. The women, when not exposed to the air, or stunted by severe labour, are often possessed of extraordinary beauty, the form being delicate and graceful; limbs finely tapered and rounded; features mild; eyes dark and languishing; hair fine and long; and skins remarkably polished and soft. The Hindoo women of the Brahminical caste bear away the palm of loveliness, more particularly those of the Canara and Malabar coasts. The beauties of form attributed to their countrywomen in general are found in a still higher degree of perfection in them. The contour of the neck and shoulders is exceedingly lovely, the bosom beautifully formed;

the limbs slender, but exquisitely moulded; the feet and hands delicately small; their air and motions easy, graceful, and dignified. Nor are the beauties of the countenance inferior to those of the figure. The face is of the finest oval, like the Greek; the nose long and straight; the lips ruddy, and the upper one beautifully curved; the mouth rather small; the chin round, and, in most cases, dimpled *amoris digitulo*. The eyes, shaded by long dark lashes, and surmounted by finely arched slender eyebrows, are full, black, humid, sparkling with fire, yet neither wanton nor petulent[1]. No women can be more attentive, says Forbes, to cleanliness than the Hindoos, 'they take every method to render their persons delicate, soft, and attractive.' A writer in the Asiatic Journal thus truly describes the women of India:—'In spite of the disadvantages attendant upon the colour of the skin, perhaps no part of the world can present more perfect specimens of feminine beauty than are to be found in Hindostan. Travellers are struck with admiration at the appearance of many of the women, filling their waterpots at the ghauts and wells, or going about the towns and villages in the pursuit of their daily avocations. Their fine erect forms, set off by the graceful drapery, wound in so picturesque a manner around them, are highly attractive, even when the veil casts its shroud over the face, leaving 'half an eye to do its worst of witchery.' The custom of carrying light

[1] Bory de Saint-Vincent, Essai Zoologique sur le Genre Humain, tom. i. pp. 226—228.

burdens upon the head from childhood, gives great breadth to the chest, uprightness to the figure, and freedom to the movements; and the unfrequent use of shoes, or the substitution of an easy slipper for the tight ligatures worn in Europe, imparts a beauty which few, save oriental females, possess, that of a perfect foot. Though seldom much below the middle height, and occasionally tall, all the native females are delicately framed; their hands and feet are exquisite, and the latter, when not encumbered by ornaments, resemble those carved by the chisel of a Grecian sculptor. The beauty of feature, though not quite, is almost as common as that of figure; all have the splendid, dark, gazelle-like eyes, which form the characteristic mark of orientals. Not even the enthusiasm of poetical fervour can go beyond the truth in the description of those liquid, loving, melting eyes. In the whole population, the general expression is softness; excepting when inflamed by rage, very few are fierce, and there is an indescribable charm, a fascination, about their eyes, which in many instances is quite irresistible, and, with the exception of a few obstinately prejudiced persons, has the effect of interesting a stranger very strongly in favour of the people possessing them. The form of the face is usually very fine, boasting that beautiful curve, from the ear to the chin, which is always given to statues. Strangers in India have few opportunities of judging of the beauty of the women, except from specimens found amongst the lower orders. Some idea of the great superiority of the higher ranks may be formed by the appearance of the sepoys, a very handsome class of men, who are said to derive much of their personal attractions from their mothers Many of the nautch girls are lovely creatures, and, though personal beauty is not considered essential to their profession, when superadded to other accomplishments, it is of course highly prized, and some romantic stories are told of the extraordinary attachments inspired by females of this class in the breasts both of native and European admirers.

The complexion of Indian women varies from a pale yellow to a very dark bronze, the intermediate shades being numerous; fairness is considered a great advantage by the natives themselves, but has not the same attraction to European eyes, for it is almost always of a sallow and somewhat unearthly hue, far less agreeable than the warm browns, which are the prevailing tints. Natives are exceedingly anxious to be thought fair, and those whose skins nearly approach to black will not wear any thing which might tend to make them look darker. Servants have been known to object to livery turbans on this account, and in taking their portraits it is always necessary to give the sitter the advantage of a complexion a few shades lighter than the real. Sometimes, though rarely, skins may be seen of a clear olive tint, not darker than those of many Italians; but fairness is generally so totally without the transparency which Europeans have been accustomed to admire, that it cannot be at all pleasing to the eye.

The Indian ladies endeavour to heighten their beauty by the aid of art, but not always with effect, some being so injudicious as to blacken their teeth.

Naturally, the teeth of the natives of India are very beautiful, and the rows of even pearls revealed by the parting lips contrast finely with the dark hue of the skin. This charm is of course utterly destroyed by a process which is erroneously supposed to make the face appear fairer, but which seems quite as barbarous to European eyes as the custom of tattooing. This black dye is a preparation of antimony, called *missee*, and it is sometimes applied to the lips as well as the teeth. This sort of paint is also used to darken the eyebrows, and to improve the arch, which is as popular in the east as in the western world; a small portion sometimes appears beneath the eyelid, and, when skilfully put on, may be said to aid the dark languish of the orb. Rouge is not much in request amongst the Indian ladies; for, the cheeks never assuming any tint akin to the hue of the rose, it would seem out of place; nevertheless, it is occasionally employed, and a red dye produced from *mhendee* is much in request for beautifying the palms of the hands and the soles of the feet.

Though tight lacing is altogether unknown, the Indian ladies are not destitute of some support for the bust; a simple kind of corset, called the *ungeeah*, is the substitute for the stays worn in England: short tight sleeves are attached to this bodice, which is fastened at the back. No woman, however low in station, who prizes the symmetry of her figure, will discard this essential portion of her apparel, those by whom it is rejected speedily becoming shapeless and almost disgusting in their appearance. Wealthy persons have the *ungeeah* made of silver tissue, or, at the least, profusely embroidered with silver, and richly spangled. The Mussulmaunee women wear a short vest over it, called a *coorte,* usually made of some transparent material, edged with beautiful embroidery in silver or gold. This falls below the top of the *pyjamahs*, or trousers, which are fastened over the hips; there is, therefore, a portion of the body, between the waist and the bosom, which the *coorte* covers, but does not conceal. The *pyjamahs* are usually so exceedingly wide as to look like a petticoat; they are made of rich brocades, and are embroidered at the bottom. The veil, of a transparent silver gauze, richly bordered, completes a costume which is very becoming in itself, and set off by a profusion of jewels worn upon the neck and arms, the head and the feet. The ground work of the bordering of the ladies' dresses in India is sometimes of seed-pearls, a gem which enters profusely into their needlework, being also frequently employed as an edging of the gold and silver flowers introduced in rich patterns round the hems of the drapery. *Pyjamahs*, made of the finest Cashmere shawl, are thus embroidered at the feet, and a whole dress of this description has been valued in England at 400*l*. The slippers are equally rich, being frequently of gold tissue, worked with pearls; these are only worn in crossing the court-yards and gardens of the zenana: they somewhat resemble the shoes in fashion some centuries ago in Europe, the points being always curled over the front, and frequently rising very high.

It will be seen by this account of the toilet, that the Indian ladies neglect nothing which may increase the effect of their charms; those charms, however, generally speaking, are of a very short duration. A woman is getting old at five-and-twenty, and at forty too often becomes a perfect hag. That exquisite roundness of limb, which is a general characteristic —a beauty rare in other countries, but common throughout India, where no rawboned, clumsy, angular women are to be seen—is lost either in a skeleton-like meagreness or in an incumbrance of fat. It would be difficult to imagine any thing more hideous than a very old woman in any part of Hindostan. Some of the men, together with a venerable appearance, preserve the remains of former good looks; but the women are altogether frightful—impersonations of witches of the most withered and revolting description. A few, however, notwithstanding the loss of every outward attraction, retain a strong influence over the minds of the other sex. It is said by some persons, but with what truth it is difficult to judge, that the Hindoos, being by nature less sensitive and more apathetic than the fervid disciples of Mohammed, are not so feelingly alive to the decay of feminine charms. Indian women, perhaps, owe the greater portion of the power they have been known to possess of inspiring strong and lasting attachments, both in natives and Europeans, to their untiring and obsequious attendance upon their lords and masters. They willingly pay those attentions which women in many other countries expect to receive, rendering themselves slaves to the comfort of the husband or the lover. They will cook for him, wait upon him, soothe him under irritation or fatigue, by that gentle process of shampooing, in which Indian women are such adepts, fan him while he is sleeping, and, in short, render themselves essential to every idle habit in which he may delight to indulge.

The contempt which most, if not all, the different races in India manifest for the fear of death is very remarkable [1]. It may be said that fanaticism is the exciting cause; but it should be remembered that, wherever a British officer leads, his Sepoy troops will follow, and numerous instances have occurred where the Hindoo artillerymen have been cut down at their guns rather than desert them. The gallant manner in which the natives will, single-handed, and armed only with a long knife, attack the most furious tiger for a trifling reward, has been often described, and needs not recapitulation; but their agility and bravery in voluntarily encountering a formidable shark in his native element, for the sake of a few shillings, is not so well known. An illustration of this fact, as it occurred when I was in Calcutta, in 1830, may be here given:—The boat was on its progress down the Hooghly, when a huge shark was seen swimming

[1] In one city, that of Delhi, the instances of self-murder were as follows:—

Self-murder or attempts at such at Delhi during the year 1832.

	Died	Recd.	Total
By opium	44	6	50
— Arsenic	11	5	16
— Bang Ganga	0	9	9
— Leaping into wells	9	5	14
— Ditto from tops of houses	1	14	15
	65	39	104

round it,—a Hindoo prepared to attack it on receiving a small reward for his dexterity. Holding the rope, on which he had made a sort of running knot, in one hand, and stretching out the other arm, as if already in the act of swimming, he stood in an attitude truly picturesque, waiting the re-appearance of the shark. At about six or eight yards from the boat the animal rose near the surface, when the native instantly plunged into the water, a short distance from the very jaws of the monster. The shark immediately turned round, and swam slowly towards the man, who, in his turn, nothing daunted, struck out the arm that was at liberty, and approached his foe. When within a foot or two of the shark, the native dived beneath him—the animal going down almost at the same instant. The bold assailant in this frightful contest soon re-appeared on the opposite side of the shark, swimming fearlessly with the hand he had at liberty, and holding the rope behind his back with the other. The shark, which had also by this time made his appearance again, immediately swam towards him; and while the animal was apparently in the act of lifting himself over the lower part of the native's body, that he might seize upon his prey, the man making a strong effort, threw himself up perpendicularly, and went down with his feet foremost—the shark following him so simultaneously that we were fully impressed with the idea that they had gone down grappling together. As far as could be judged, they remained nearly twenty seconds out of sight, while we stood in breathless anxiety, and it may be added horror, waiting the result of this fearful encounter. Suddenly the native made his appearance, holding up both his hands over his head, and calling out with a voice that proclaimed the victory he had won, while underneath the wave,—'*tan—tan!*' The people in the boat were all prepared—the rope was instantly drawn tight, and the struggling victim, lashing the water in his wrath, was dragged to the shore and dispatched. This truly intrepid man received only a cut on the left arm, apparently from the fin of his formidable enemy.

The Rev. H. Caunter relates the following instance of physical courage to which he was an eye witness at an entertainment given by the Rajah of Coorg. 'A man entered the arena, armed only with a Coorg knife, and clothed in short trousers, which barely covered his hips, and extended half-way down the thighs. The instrument, which he wielded in his right hand, was a heavy blade, something like the coulter of a plough, about two feet long, and full three inches wide, gradually diminishing towards the handle, with which it formed a right angle. This knife is used with great dexterity by the Coorgs, being swung round in the hand before the blow is inflicted, and then brought into contact with the object intended to be struck, with a force and effect truly astounding. The champion who now presented himself before the rajah was about to be opposed to a tiger, which he volunteered to encounter almost naked, and armed only with the weapon I have just described. He was rather tall, with a slight figure; but his chest was deep, his arms long and muscular. His legs were thin; yet the action of the muscles was perceptible with every movement, whilst the freedom of his gait, and the few contortions he performed preparatory to the hazardous enterprise in which he was about to engage, showed that he possessed uncommon activity, combined with no ordinary degree of strength. The expression of his countenance was absolutely sublime when he gave the signal for the tiger to be let loose: it was the very concentration of moral energy—the index of a high and settled resolution. His body glistened with the oil which had been rubbed over it in order to promote the elasticity of his limbs. He raised his arm for several moments above his head when he made the motion to admit his enemy into the area. The bars of a large cage were instantly lifted from above; a huge royal tiger sprang forward and stood before the Coorg, waving his tail slowly backward and forward, erecting the hair upon it, and uttering a suppressed howl. The animal first looked at the man, then at the gallery where the rajah and his court were seated to see the sports, but did not appear at all easy in its present state of freedom: it was evidently confounded at the novelty of its position. After a short survey, it turned suddenly round, and bounded into its cage, from which the keepers, who stood above, beyond the reach of mischief, tried to force it, but in vain. The bars were then dropped, and several crackers fastened to its tail, which projected through one of the intervals. A lighted match was put into the hand of the Coorg; the bars were again raised, and the crackers ignited. The tiger now darted into the arena with a terrific yell; and while the crackers were exploding, it leaped, turned, and writhed as if in a state of frantic excitement. It at length crouched in a corner, gnarling as a cat does when alarmed. Meanwhile its retreat had been cut off by securing the cage. During the explosion of the crackers, the Coorg stood watching his enemy, and at length advanced towards it with a slow but firm step. The tiger roused itself and retreated, the fur on its back being erect, and its tail apparently dilated to twice the usual size. It was not at all disposed to commence hostilities; but its resolute foe was not to be evaded. Fixing his eyes intently upon the deadly creature, he advanced with the same measured step, the tiger retreating as before, but still presenting its front to its enemy. The Coorg now stopped suddenly; then moving slowly backward, the tiger raised itself to its full height, curved its back to the necessary segment for a spring, and lashed its tail, evidently meditating mischief. The man continued to retire; and as soon as he was at so great a distance that the fixed expression of his eye was no longer distinguishable, the ferocious brute made a sudden bound forward, crouched, and sprang with a short, sharp growl. Its adversary, fully prepared for this, leaped actively on one side, and as the tiger reached the ground, swung round his heavy knife, and brought it with irresistible force upon the animal's hind-leg just above the joint. The bone was instantly severed, and the tiger effectually prevented from making a second spring. The wounded beast roared; but turning suddenly on the Coorg, who had by this time retired several yards, advanced fiercely upon him, its wounded leg hanging loose in the skin, showing that it was broken. The tiger, now excited to a pitch of reckless rage, rushed forward upon its three legs towards its adversary, who stood with his heavy knife upraised, calmly awaiting the encounter. As soon as the savage creature was within his reach, he brought down the ponderous weapon upon its head with a force which nothing could resist, laid open the skull from ear to ear, and the vanquished foe fell dead at his feet. He then coolly wiped the knife on the animal's hide, made a dignified salaam to the rajah, and retired amid the loud acclamations of the spectators.'

The exploits of Indian jugglers have been seen in this country, and so often related, that it would seem impossible to recount any more wonderful than those already known. The following as seen and related by the Rev. H. Caunter, are certainly very extraordinary.

'One of the men taking a large earthen vessel, with a capacious mouth, filled it with water and turned it upside down, when all the water flowed out; but the moment it was placed with the mouth upwards, it always became full. He then emptied it, allowing any one to inspect it who chose. This being done, he desired that one of the party would fill it; his request was obeyed; still, when he reversed the jar, not a drop of water flowed, and upon turning it, to our astonishment it was empty. These and similar deceptions were several times repeated; and so skilfully were they managed that, although any of us who chose were allowed to upset the vessel when full, which I did many times, upon reversing it there was no water to be seen, and yet no appearance of any having escaped. I examined the jar carefully when empty, but detected nothing which could lead to a discovery of the mystery, I was allowed to retain and fill it myself, still, upon taking it up, all was void within; yet the ground around it was perfectly dry, so that how the water had disappeared, and where it had been conveyed, were problems which none of us were able to expound. The vessel employed by the juggler upon this occasion was the common earthenware of the country, very roughly made; and, in order to convince us that it had not been especially constructed for the purpose of aiding his clever deceptions, he permitted it to be broken in our presence: the fragments were then handed round for the inspection of his highness and the party present with him. The next thing done was still more extraordinary. A large basket was produced, under which was put a lean, hungry Pariah bitch; after the lapse of about a minute, the basket was removed, and she appeared with a litter of seven puppies. These were again covered, and upon raising the magic basket a goat was presented to our view; this was succeeded by a pig in the full vigour of existence, but which, after being covered for the usual time, appeared with its throat cut; it was, however, shortly restored to life under the mystical shade of the wicker covering. What rendered these sudden changes so extraordinary was, that no one stood near the basket but the juggler, who raised and covered the animals with it. When he concluded his exploits there was nothing to be seen under it; and what became of the different animals which had figured in this singular deception, was a question that puzzled all. A man now took a small bag full of brass balls, which he threw one by one into the air, to the number of thirty-five. None of them appeared to return. When he had discharged the last there was a pause of full a minute; he then made a variety of motions with his hands, at the same time grunting forth a kind of barbarous chant; in a few seconds, the balls were seen to fall, one by one, until the whole of them were replaced in the bag; this was repeated at least half-a dozen times. No one was allowed to come near him while this interesting juggle was performed. A gaunt-looking Hindoo next stepped forward, and declared he would swallow a snake. Opening a box he produced a Cobra di Capello not less than five feet long, and as big as an infant's wrist. He stood, however, apart, at some distance from us, and like his predecessor, would not allow any person to approach him, so that the deception became no longer equivocal. He then, as it appeared to us, took the snake, and putting its tail into his mouth gradually lowered it into his stomach, until nothing but the head appeared to project from between his lips, when, with a sudden gulp, he seemed to complete the disgusting process of deglutition, and to secure the odious reptile within his body. After the expiration of a few seconds he opened his mouth and gradually drew forth the snake, which he replaced in the box. The next thing that engaged our attention was a feat of dexterity altogether astonishing. An elderly woman, the upper part of whose body was entirely uncovered, presented herself to our notice, and taking a bamboo, twenty feet high, placed it upright upon a flat stone, and then, without any support, climbed to the top of it with surprising activity. Having done this she stood upon one leg on the point of the bamboo, balancing it all the while. Round her waist she had a girdle, to which was fastened an iron socket; springing from her upright position on the bamboo, she threw herself horizontally forward, with such exact precision, that the top of the pole entered the socket of her iron zone, and in this position she spun herself round with a velocity that made me giddy to look at, the bamboo appearing all the while as if it were supported by some supernatural agency. She turned her legs backward until the heels touched her shoulders, and grasping the ankles in her hands, continued her rotation so rapidly that the outline of her body was entirely lost to the eye, and she looked like a revolving ball. Having performed several other feats equally extraordinary, she slid down the elastic shaft, and raising it in the air, balanced it upon her chin, then upon her nose, and finally projected it to a distance from her, without the application of her hands. The next performer spread upon the ground a cloth about the size of a sheet; after a while it seemed to be gradually raised; upon taking it up there appeared three pine apples growing under it, which were cut and presented to the spectators. This is considered a common juggle, and yet it is perfectly inexplicable.'

Miss Roberts describes the feats of those jugglers who so far excel any of their European brethren. A man who in 1828, seated himself in the air without any apparent support, excited as much interest and curiosity as the automaton chess-player who astonished all Europe a few years ago; drawings were exhibited in all the India papers, and various conjectures formed respecting the secret of his art, but no very satisfactory discovery was made of the means by which he effected an apparent impossibility. The bodies of the Madras jugglers are so lithe and supple as to resemble those of serpents rather than men. An artist of this kind will place a ladder upright on the ground, and wind himself in and out through the rungs until he reaches the top, descending in the same manner, keeping the ladder, which has no support whatever, in a perpendicular position. Some of the most accomplished tumblers will spring over an enormous elephant, or five camels, placed abreast; and in rope-dancing they are not to be outdone by any of the wonders of Sadler's Wells. Swallowing the sword is a common operation, even by those who are not considered to be the most expert; and they have various other exploits with naked weapons of a most frightful nature. A woman—for females are quite equal to men in these kind of feats—will dip the point of a sword in some black pigment, the hilt is then fixed firmly in the ground, and after a few whirls in the air the artiste takes off a portion of the pigment with her eyelid. A sword and four daggers are placed in the ground, with their edges and points upwards, at such distance from each other as to admit of a man's head between them; the operator then plants a scymetar firmly in the ground, sits down behind it, and at a bound throws himself over the scymetar, pitching his head exactly in the centre, between the daggers; and, turning over, clears them and the sword. Walking over the naked edges of sabres seems to be perfectly easy; and some of these people will stick a sword in the ground, and step upon the point in crossing over it. A more agreeable display of the lightness and activity, which would enable the performers to tread over flowers without bending them, is shown upon a piece of thin linen cloth stretched out slightly in the hands of four persons, which is traversed without ruffling it, or forcing it from the grasp of the holders. The lifting of heavy weights with the eyelids is another very disgusting exhibition. Some of the optical deceptions are exceedingly curious, and inquirers are to this day puzzled to guess how plants and flowers can be instantaneously produced from seeds. I have witnessed juggling feats in Bengal and other parts of India, equally as extraordinary as the foregoing and equally difficult to account for.

While travelling in different countries, I made a collection of the skulls of different nations, a part of the collection I had the pleasure of presenting to the Asiatic Society Museum, at Calcutta, where they may now be seen, and it is exceedingly curious to observe, what a marked configuration the crania of diverse people exhibit, even among nations with scarcely a perceptible natural boundary between them. The most striking example noticed was the difference between the Bengalee and the Burmese; the skull of the former possesses a greater occipital protuberance than that of any people I have ever met; it is, in fact, semi-globular, and the whole skull extraordinarily small, divested of any angular or rugged projections, and of remarkably thin laminæ. These observations are founded on the examination of hundreds of the Bengalee skulls. The cranium of the latter (Burmese) possesses what I have never found in any other nation, a perfectly flat occipital bone; so much so, that a Burmese skull will rest on a broader and firmer base when placed with the face upwards, than in any other position. As if to compensate for the flatness of the occipital bone, the parietal or side walls of the skull bulge out in an extraordinary manner; the brain case (unlike the Hindoos) is very large, and the laminæ extraordinarily thick. Among my Burmese specimens were the mutilated skulls of Burmese soldiers, found near Rangoon, some of which were clove in twain by the prowess of British soldiers. On another occasion, I will trace the characters of nations, as exemplified in the mental shield. (For a measurement of the crania and skeletons of a male and female New Hollander, see vol. iv., New South Wales.)

Since the first edition of this volume went to press, that distinguished Brahmin (or rather Hindoo) Rajah Rammohun Roy, died near Bristol. I knew the Rajah well, having lived for some months with him at his garden house, near Calcutta. He had his faults (who has not?); but they were more than counterbalanced by his virtues. Immediately on his demise, a cast was taken of his head, (which was not only of a very unusual size for a Hindoo, but even for the generality of Englishmen,) for the purpose of promoting phrenological inquiry. I give the details (as I have the osteological measurements of the New Hollanders in my fourth volume), for the purpose of stimulating to further inquiry on so interesting a subject.

DIMENSIONS, IN INCHES, OF THE SKULL OF THE LATE RAMMOHUN ROY, FROM A CAST TAKEN WHILE THE BODY WAS YET WARM[1].

Greatest circumference of head, measuring horizontally over Individuality, Destructiveness, and Philo-progenitiveness, $24\frac{1}{4}$; from occipital spine to Individuality, over top of the head, 15; ear to ear, vertically over top of the head, measuring from upper margin of the meatus, $14\frac{3}{8}$; Philo-progenitiveness to Individuality, in a straight line, $8\frac{3}{8}$; Concentrativeness to Comparison, $7\frac{3}{4}$; ear to Philo-progenitiveness, $4\frac{3}{4}$; to Individuality, $5\frac{3}{4}$; to Benevolence, $6\frac{5}{8}$; to Veneration, $6\frac{3}{8}$; to Firmness, $6\frac{1}{2}$; Destructiveness to Destructiveness, $6\frac{1}{4}$; Secretiveness to Secretiveness, $6\frac{1}{4}$; Cautiousness to Cautiousness, $5\frac{1}{4}$; Ideality to Ideality, $4\frac{1}{2}$; Constructiveness to Constructiveness, $5\frac{3}{8}$; Mastoid process to Mastoid process, $5\frac{3}{4}$.

Developement.—(1.) Amativeness, very large; (2.) Philo-progenitiveness, rather large; (3.) Concentrativeness, full; (4.) Adhesiveness, large; (5.) Combativeness, large; (6.) Destructiveness, large; (7.) Secretiveness, large; (8.) Acquisitiveness, full; (9.) Constructiveness, rather full; (10.) Self-Esteem, very large; (11.) Love of Approbation, ditto; (12.) Cau-

[1] In stating the actual dimensions of the head, allowance has been made for the hair.

tiousness, large; (13.) Benevolence, ditto; (14.) Veneration, full; (15.) Firmness, very large; (16.) Conscientiousness, ditto; (17.) Hope, full; (18.) Wonder, rather full; (19.) Ideality, ditto; (20.) Wit or Mirthfulness, ditto; (21.) Imitation, rather large; (22.) Individuality, ditto; (23.) Form, full; (24.) Size, rather large; (25.) Weight, ditto; (26.) Colouring, full; (27.) Locality, rather large; (28.) Number, moderate; (29.) Order, rather full; (30.) Eventuality, full; (31.) Time, full; (32.) Tune, moderate; (33.) Language, rather large; (34.) Comparison, ditto; (35.) Causality, ditto.

Having had an intimate acquaintance with Rammohun Roy, and possessing, from his own lips and those of his confidents, a knowledge of circumstances which he did not think proper to reveal in the scanty materials of his life that he furnished, I may with confidence state that phrenological science is not in danger from the development of the animal portion of the brain; but in the mental development there are not only contradictions, but positive negatives. From No. 1. to 6. his passions were powerful, on occasion, in some instances, uncontrollable, and with difficulty subjected to his extraordinary masculine understanding; his Benevolence was not merely large, but very largely in activity; he had no Order in any domestic concern, and the only symptom of it observable was in the construction of his sentences in writing; Language is described as 'rather large;' in reality it was very remarkable; he understood a variety of tongues thoroughly, and acquired them with facility: Caution is described only as large; if a deep concealment of motives, not unfrequently degenerating into cunning, be Caution, no man possessed it more than Rammohun Roy, whose Veneration nevertheless for a Supreme Being was not merely full, but unbounded.

Costume of the Hindoos.—Their dress is peculiarly becoming; in the higher classes it consists of a long piece of silk or cotton, tied round the waist, afterwards brought over the body in negligent folds, and hanging in a graceful manner to the feet; under this they cover the bosom with a short waistcoat of silk or satin, but wear no linen. Their long black hair is adorned with jewels and wreaths of flowers; their ears are bored in many places, and loaded with pearls; a variety of gold chains, strings of pearl and precious stones fall from the neck over the bosom, and the arms are covered with bracelets from the wrists to the elbow; they have also gold and silver chains round the ancles, and abundance of rings on their fingers and toes; among the former is frequently a small mirror. Forbes thinks the richer the dress the less becoming it appears, a Hindoo woman of distinction always appearing to be overloaded with finery; while the village nymphs, with fewer ornaments, but in the same elegant drapery, are more captivating; although there are very few women, even of the lowest families, who have not some jewels at their marriage [1].

The same writer, describing the village of Harasar, celebrated for the sanctity of its temple and the beauty of its women, observes, that their jetty locks

[1] Oriental Memoirs, vol. i. p. 74.

were adorned with jewels, while their garment, which consisted of a long single piece of silk or muslin, put on in graceful folds, fell like the drapery of a Grecian statue [1]. Various fashions prevail, however, in different parts of India. In the kingdom of Attinga, on the Malabar coast, the women go uncovered from the waist upwards. It is thought indecent to do otherwise; and Grose tells a story, which was afterwards confirmed to Forbes on the spot, of a Malabar woman, who, living with an English lady at Anjengo, to please her mistress, dressed in the European fashion, but appearing afterwards in the queen of Attinga's presence with her breasts covered, the barbarous despot ordered them to be cut off, for what she was pleased to consider so signal a mark of disrespect [2]. It is not the inferior classes merely who dress thus sparingly; the greatest princesses are clothed in the same style, and only differ from their slaves by wearing a more transparent muslin and a greater profusion of jewels. Even where persons are accustomed, as they are in several of the southern provinces of the Peninsula, to wear clothing on the upper part of the body, the rules of politeness require, even in women, that they shall uncover the shoulders and breast when addressing any person whom they respect, whether male or female [3]. It was the breach

[1] Oriental Memoirs, vol. i. p. 190, 191.

[2] Grose, Voyage to the East Indies; Forbes, Oriental Memoirs, vol. i. p. 391.

[3] Dubois, Description of the Manners, &c. of the People of India, p. 211.

of this rule of good breeding by the Malabar woman, that roused the anger of the female despot of Attinga.

The kind of tissue which, in the south, forms the sole garment of the Brahmini women, is only used in female dress. It is usually from eight to ten yards in length, and about a yard broad, of every variety of quality and colour, with a border of different hue at each extremity. This is wrapped twice or three times round the body, and forms a kind of petticoat, which in front falls as low as the feet, but behind does not reach lower than the calf of the leg, and sometimes not so low. One end of this long web is fastened at the waist, the other, in many districts, passes over the head, shoulders, and breasts; but this is an innovation. The primitive fashion, throughout the peninsula, required the women always to appear naked to the girdle [1].

In Malabar the dress of the women is quite similar to that of the men. Their black, glossy hair, tied in a knot on the middle of the head, is copiously anointed with cocoa-nut oil, and perfumed with the essence of sandal, mogrees, and champahs; their ears, loaded with rings and heavy jewels, reach almost to their shoulders; this is esteemed a beauty. Instead of a small gold wire in the orifice, as is practised in other countries, the incision is filled with a filament from the cocoa-nut leaf, rolled round; the circles are increased until the orifice sometimes exceeds two inches in diameter, the ear is then healed, and being

[1] Dubois, Description of the Manners, &c. of the People of India, p. 220, 221.

stretched to the perfection of beauty, is filled with rings and massy ornaments. Round the waist they wear a loose piece of muslin, while the bosom is entirely exposed; this is the only drapery of the Malabar women: but they are adorned with a profusion of gold and silver chains for necklaces, mixed with strings of Venetian and other gold coins; they have also heavy bangles, or bracelets; a silver box, suspended by a chain on one side, forms a principal ornament, and contains the areca or betel-nut, with its appendages of chunam, spice, and betel-leaf. Their skin is softened by aromatic oils, especially among the Nairs and Tetees, who are peculiarly attentive to cleanliness in their persons[1].

The female Portuguese Christians in Calcutta wear a petticoat and loose body made of muslin and silk, trimmed with lace, while their long black hair is turned up *à la Grecque*, and fastened with gold ornaments. The Malay girls' costume is somewhat similar, with sometimes the addition of long, flowing, white veils.

In Northern India, where the power and example of the Mahomedans have operated so many other changes in the manners of the Hindoos, even the national costume has undergone various modifications. Here the dress of the women consists of a close jacket with sleeves, which, in some instances, reach no farther than the elbow, in others, cover even the tops of the fingers. This jacket, fitting tight to the shape, and showing to advantage the beauty of the form,

[1] Oriental Memoirs, vol. i. p. 390.

with women of rank is made of rich silk. Instead of drawers, some ladies, says Abul Fasel, wear a *lengha*, stitched on both sides, and fastened with a belt, which appears to be a short under-petticoat; no chemise. Over the lengha is worn the common shalice, or petticoat. Some ladies wear veils and long drawers[1].

The costume of a northern mountaineer, inhabiting those parts of the Himalaya where the manners of the Hindoos and Tatars appear to mingle and slide into each other, is of course different. 'An *Uniya* woman,' says Mr. Moorcroft, 'wife of one of the goatherds, very good-naturedly filled the water-vessels of those persons who came to the little well, and did not take up her own part till the different candidates for water received the quantity which they asked for. She had rather a pleasing countenance, was of middle stature, and about thirty-five years old. There was much of curiosity in her looks at seeing us, but nothing of fear or impertinence. Her dress was woollen, and of the same form with that of the men. Her boots were likewise woollen, and much diversified by patches of various hues. Her hair, which was of a deep black, was plaited in tresses from the forehead down to below the waist, where the plaits, to the number of fifty, after each being terminated by a cowrie shell, were assembled in a band of leather, which was tipped with a tassel of red worsted thread. Her head-lappet, if I may so name it, was of leather, and extended from the forehead

[1] Ayeen Akberry, vol. ii. p. 521.

down the back to the waist, but in the latter part gradually ended in a point; at the forehead it was bordered with silver, and from this rim hung seven rows of coral beads, each row consisting of five, which were terminated by seven silver *timáshás*, that played upon the forehead. The crown of the lappet was studded with small pearls, distributed in seven rows, and the lower part was decorated with green stones, something like turquoises, but marbled with coral beads, and many bands of silver and of a yellow metal, probably gold, about a finger's breadth. A stiff band of leather, something like a soldier's collar, was placed loosely round her neck, and ornamented with five rows of coral beads. The collar was secured with a button and clasp of silver. In her left ear was a coral bead set in silver, and in her right were two smaller beads in the same material. On her right thumb she wore a square gold ring, with characters engraved on the table [1].'

In Rajast'han, and throughout the north-western provinces, the costume varies in each district and tribe, though the materials of dress are every where the same; in summer, cotton, in winter, quilted chintz or broadcloth. The ladies have only three garments; the *ghagra*, or petticoat; the *kanchli*, or corset; and the *dopati*, or scarf, which is occasionally thrown over the head as a veil [2]. Tattooing, which may be regarded as a kind of substitute for dress, has not yet wholly disappeared in India. The Hindoo

[1] Asiatic Researches, vol. xii. p. 422, 423.

[2] Colonel Tod, Annals of Rajast'han, vol. ii. p. 651.

women, in many parts of the country, paint various figures, chiefly of flowers, on the arms, chin, and cheeks of their daughters. This is effected, as among the South Sea islanders, by making with the point of a needle, slight punctures in the skin, over which the juice of certain plants is then poured; and thus the figures become ineffaceable[1]. Many Brahmini women dye their whole bodies, or, at least, so much of them as is uncovered, with a saffron coloured infusion, which, instead of increasing their beauty, renders them frightful, at least, in the eyes of Europeans. The young and beautiful attempt to increase the dark lustre of their eyes by the use of *surmeh*, or powder of antimony, that famous collyrium which played so conspicuous a part in the toilette of the Grecian ladies. The ladies of Hindostan moreover paint with black the border of the eye-lids, and prolong the eye-lashes and eye-brows at the corners, while the hair is adorned with sweet-scented flowers, and ornaments of gold.

The ornaments of the Hindoo women are rich and numerous. Every toe has its particular ring, so broad above as frequently to conceal the whole toe. Their bracelets are sometimes large hollow rings of gold, more than an inch in diameter, while others wear them flat, and more than two inches in breadth. Round their necks are suspended several chains of gold or silver, or strings of gold, pearl, coral, or glass

[1] Dubois, Description, &c. p. 221. They likewise, as do also the Arabs, dye their fingers, the palms of their hands, and the soles of their feet with *henna*.

beads. Many ladies have collars of gold, an inch broad, set with rubies, topazes, emeralds, carbuncles, or diamonds; besides an ornament for the forehead set with jewels; earrings, of which there are no less than eighteen species; nose jewels; necklaces; strings of flowers or pearls; belts ornamented with little bells and jewels; and numerous other ornaments of the same costly kind [1].

The dress of the men, in which there are neither buttons, strings, nor pins, is admirably adapted to the climate, and produces a very graceful effect. It differs, however, but little, in many parts of the country, from that of the women. The shoes worn by the rich are embroidered with gold or silver thread, open at the heels, and curled up at the toes. Few persons wear stockings [2]. Turbans are sometimes worn by the Brahmins, and very commonly by all other persons of the superior classes. The head and beard are generally shaved, but mustachios are worn, and a small lock of hair is usually left upon the crown. A *jáma*, or long gown of white calico, confined round the waist with a fringed or embroidered sash, replaces the simple robe of the eastern provinces; and the princes and nobles adorn their persons with necklaces of pearl and golden chains, sustaining clusters of costly gems; while their turbans are crusted with diamonds, rubies, and emeralds. Their golden bracelets are likewise set thick with

[1] See Ayeen Akberry, vol. ii. p. 521, 522.

[2] Ward, View of the History, &c. of the Hindoos, vol. i. p. 186, 187.

gems. The shoes are of red leather, or English broadcloth. In the ears they wear, like the women, large gold rings, which pass through two pearls or rubies. Both sexes are greatly addicted to the use of *attar*, and other perfumes[1].

In Northern India another variety of costume is found. Here the garments of the men consist of trowsers of every shape and calibre, a tunic girded with a ceinture, and a scarf, form the wardrobe of every Rajpoot. The turban is the most important part of the dress, and is the unerring mark of the tribe; the form and fashion are various, and its decorations differ, according to time and circumstances. The *balabund*, or silken fillet, was once valued as the mark of the sovereign's favour, and was tantamount to the courtly 'orders' of Europe. The colour of the turban and tunic varies with the seasons; and the changes are rung upon crimson, saffron, and purple, though white is by far the most common. Their shoes are mere slippers, and sandals are worn by the common classes. Boots are used in hunting and war, made of chamois leather, of which material the warrior often has a doublet, being more commodious and less oppressive than armour. The dagger, or poniard is inseparable from the girdle[2]. At Calcutta, and the other presidencies, the inhabitants are approximating towards the dress of Europeans, with the exception of the hat.

The *paita*, or thread of investiture, supposed to be-

[1] Forbes, Oriental Memoirs, vol. i. p. 70, 71, 83.

[2] Colonel Tod, vol. ii. p. 652.

long to the three superior castes, is sometimes worn indiscriminately by all: this, therefore, being no distinction, the Brahmins resort to other means of making known their rank. Those of the north of the peninsula are distinguished by a perpendicular line, drawn with the paste of sandal-wood on the middle of the forehead; in the farming districts this line is drawn horizontally, and the Vishnuite Brahmins, who are exceedingly numerous in all the south of India, imprint on their forehead three perpendicular lines, joined at the base, and thus representing the figure of a trident. Of these three lines the middle one is red or yellow, while those on the side are white, and being drawn with a kind of clay, called *nama*, this has grown by degrees to be considered the name of the figure itself. The mark of the Sivaïtes is the Lingam, which they either wear stuck in the hair, or suspended to the arm, in a small golden or silver tube: it is also worn suspended by a ribbon from the neck, like the *bulla* of the Roman youth, which was frequently of the same form: or else it is enclosed in a silver box which hangs upon the bosom[1].

DWELLINGS.—The houses of the rich, in most parts of India, are built of brick, and, like a caravanserai, run round the four sides of a quadrangle. On the north (the sacred point of the Hindoos) stands the family chapel, which contains the household god. The other three sides are occupied by porticoes and apartments for the family. The windows of these apart-

[1] Dubois, Description, &c. p. 9, 48. 51, 57. Antiquitates Middletonianæ.

ments are mere air-holes, through which the women may be seen peeping as through the gratings of a gaol. During the great festivals, an awning is extended over the whole court, as is the fashion in Arabia and different parts of Africa; and here the common people are admitted, while those of superior rank occupy the verandahs. The dwellings of the middle classes are constructed in the same style, but with different materials; the walls being of mud, the roofs of bamboo and thatch. A low mud-built hut, containing but one room, is the usual dwelling of the poor in Bengal[1].

In the south of India, the poor build their huts of a reddish ferruginous clay, intermixed with small fragments of quartz, and other materials of decayed granite, forming walls, which, with ordinary care, will resist the rains for many years. In many towns and villages the houses have flat roofs terraced with this mud, which is laid on in the dry season, and turns the rain very well. The buildings erected with this clay have a very tolerable appearance, the surface of the walls being neatly smoothed, and, like the houses of the ancient cities of Italy and France, painted with alternate vertical stripes of red and white. These huts are in the form of a parallelogram, without chimneys or windows. The rich, instead of enlarging the house, merely erect several huts in the same style[2]. In many cases the rooms are white-washed within, and the houses roofed with tiles. They are in general clean, and, had they any windows, would be

[1] Ward, View of the History, &c. vol. i. p. 192.

[2] Journey through the Mysore, &c. vol. i. pp. 33—38.

comfortable. In Malabar, the huts, called *chera*, are like bee-hives, and consist of a circular mud wall about three feet high, which is covered with a long conical roof of thatch. Contrary to what might have been expected in a hot climate, but agreeable to the custom of almost all Hindoos, one small door is the only outlet for smoke, and the only inlet for air and light. Each family has a hut for sleeping, another for cooking, and a third for a storehouse. Wealthy men add more huts to their premises; but seldom attempt at any innovation in the architecture of the country[1].

The *agrarums*, or *grámas*, villages occupied by the *Puttar* Brahmins in Malabar, are remarkable for their taste. The houses are built contiguous, in straight streets; and they are among the neatest and cleanest villages to be seen in India. The beauty, cleanliness, and elegant dress of the girls of the Brahmins add much to the look of these places. Their greatest defect is, that the houses are thatched with palm-leaves, which never can be made to lie close, and which render them very liable to fires. The houses of the Namburis, Nairs, and other wealthy persons are much better than those usually met with in the villages of India. They are built of mud, so as generally to occupy two sides of a square area, that is a little raised, and kept smooth, clean, and free from grass. The mud is of an excellent quality, and in general is neatly smoothed, and either whitewashed or painted.

[1] Journey through the Mysore, &c. vol. ii. p. 192.

In other parts of Malabar the houses are two stories high, built with stone, and thatched with cocoa-nut leaves. Windows also, though very diminutive ones, are more common on this coast than in any other parts of India[1]. The kitchen is always situated in the part of the house least accessible to strangers, whose very look, according to the prejudices of the natives, would pollute their earthen vessels, and compel them to break them. The position of the hearth is generally on the south-west side of the dwelling, because, in their opinion, the dwelling of the god of fire is in that quarter: a peculiar divinity presides over each of the eight points of the compass. It not being customary for men, unless they happen to be near relations, to visit the female part of the family, to avoid the necessity of introducing strangers into the apartments where they are usually occupied with household affairs, verandahs or alcoves are constructed both within and without the principal gate of entrance; in these the men assemble, and, sitting cross-legged on the floor, converse on business, religion, politics, receive visitors, "or pass their time in empty talk[2]."

Somerset-house, the British Museum, the Louvre, and many other places and houses both in England and France, represent exactly, in point of form, the common dwellings of the wealthy Hindoos, whether they be erected of stone or of mud. Even in Rajpootana the same style prevails. The mansions of the

[1] Buchanan, Journey, vol. iii. p. 99.

[2] Dubois, *ubi supra*.

Rajpoots, Colonel Tod observes, are quadrangular piles, with an open paved area, the suites of apartments carried round the sides, with latticed or open corridors extending parallel to each suite. The residence of the Rana of Oodipoor might not, perhaps, lose greatly by a comparison with Windsor Castle; and is very much superior, both in taste and magnificence, to the Chateau of the Tuileries. 'The palace is a most imposing pile, of a regular form, built of granite and marble, rising at least a hundred feet from the ground, and flanked with octagonal towers, crowned with cupolas. Although built at various periods, uniformity of design has been very well preserved; nor is there in the east a more striking or more majestic spectacle. It stands on the very crest of a ridge running parallel to, but considerably elevated above, the margin of the lake. The terrace, which is at the east end and chief front of the palace, extends throughout its length, and is supported by a triple row of arches from the declivity of the ridge. The height of this arcaded wall is full fifty feet; and although all is hollow beneath, yet so admirably is it constructed, that an entire range of stables is built on the extreme verge of the terrace, on which the whole personal force of the Rana, elephants, horse, and foot, are often assembled. From this terrace the city and the valley lie before the spectator, whose vision is bounded only by the hills shutting out the plains, while from the summit of the palace nothing obstructs its range over lake and mountain[1].'

[1] Annals of Rajast'han, vol. i. pp. 474, 475.

In several districts of Rajpootana the houses are built with a red sandstone, and, wood being scarce and dear, they have likewise roofs of stone, which are supported by numerous slender pillars. The façade, in many instances, is coated with marble chunam, and the whole surrounded by a flower-garden, intersected by neat stone channels, through which the water is conducted, for irrigation, from a tank. Bishop Heber, describing one of these gardens, observes, 'Some of the trees were of great size and beauty, and the whole place, though evidently uninhabited, was kept in substantial repair, and not the less beautiful in my eyes because the orange-trees had somewhat broken their bounds; the shade of the flowering plants assumed a ranker luxuriance, and the scarlet blossoms of the pomegranate trailed more widely across our path than was consistent with the rules of exact gardening. At the farther end of the garden we found ourselves on the edge of a broad moat, with some little water still in it, surrounding an old stone-built castle with round towers and high ramparts of stone[1].'

Rajpoot villages are frequently situated on the slopes of hills, or rocky eminences, and surrounded by groves or numerous scattered trees. Here, through the soft fleecy mists of the morning, large herds of deer may often be seen grazing, while the branches of the fruit-tree groves swarm with wild peacocks. In Marwar the construction of the villages differs entirely from any thing elsewhere seen in India, and approaches, in physiognomy, the wigwams of the

[1] Narrative of a Journey, &c. vol. ii. p. 372.

western world. Each commune is surrounded by a circumvallation of thorns, which, with the stacks of chaff rising above it at intervals, has the appearance of a respectable fortification. These stacks of chaff, intended to supply the cattle with provender in scanty rainy seasons, are erected to the height of twenty or thirty feet, and are coated with a cement of earth and cow-dung, with a sprinkling of thorns, which are added to keep away the birds from roosting in them. If fresh coated occasionally, they will endure ten years, and when necessity requires them to be eaten, the 'kine may be said to devour the village walls.' These villages, picturesquely scattered through the plain, break very agreeably the monotony incidental to a level surface. Near the banks of rivers the houses are sometimes thatched with bulrushes, which grow to the height of ten feet[1].

In the country above the Ghauts, the villages are fortified in a different style. Every collection of houses, however small, is defended by a round wall, or rather tower, of stone, sometimes forty feet in diameter, and six feet high. This is surmounted by a parapet of mud, in which there is a door that can be approached only by a ladder. Into this tower the inhabitants were wont on the appearance of a plundering party to retire with their families and most valuable effects; and having drawn up the ladder, defended themselves by hurling down stones on the

[1] Colonel Tod, Annals of Rajast'han, vol. i. pp. 700—773; Bishop Heber's Narrative, vol. ii. pp. 351—357—368—372—374.

assailants, in which they were vigorously aided by their women. More populous villages have square forts, flanked by round towers, which may, in some cases, deserve the name of a citadel. A circumvallation of mud is likewise thrown up around the villages. In many places the villages are defended, as in Ajmere, by hedges, which rise very high and thick, so as almost entirely to conceal the mud wall. These hedges greatly contribute to enliven the prospect, which is further adorned by the mangoes and other fruit-trees that usually grow around a village.

In Guzerat the villages are open, and the inhabitants more at their ease. 'The villages in the Dhuboy Pergunnah,' says Forbes, 'generally consist of thatched cottages, built of mud, and a few brick houses with tiled roofs; a small dewal, a mosque, and sometimes a choultrie, are the only public buildings. Near the large villages there is generally a tank or lake, where the rain is collected for the use of the cattle in the dry season, when, for the space of eight months, not a single shower falls, and no water is to be met with except in these reservoirs; they are often enclosed with strong masonry, and their banks adorned by banian, mango, and tamarind trees, to shade the weary traveller, and lessen evaporation. The tanks are constructed at the expense of Government, or by an assessment on the villages; they also contribute to the masonry of a good well and cistern for cattle, when the large reservoirs fail. Sometimes these useful works are private acts of charity, from a rich individual, as instanced in the noble works of Govindsett, in the Concan. Large wells with a grand flight of steps down to the water are not uncommon in remote situations, where travellers, merchants, and caravans are obliged to pass, far from other supplies.' After expatiating on the value of these blessings in the torrid zone, he continues, 'Hospitality to travellers prevails throughout Guzerat; a person of any consideration passing through the province is presented, at the entrance of a village, with fruit, milk, butter, firewood, and earthen pots for cookery: the women and children offer him wreaths of flowers. Small bowers are constructed on convenient spots, at a distance from a well or lake, where a person is maintained, by the nearest villages, to take care of the water-jars, and supply all travellers gratis. There are particular villages where the inhabitants compel all travellers to accept of one day's provision; whether they be many or few, rich or poor, European or native, they must not refuse the offered bounty[1].'

The villages on the banks of the Ganges, though merely a collection of mud-walled, thatched cottages, covered, however, in many instances, with a creeping plant bearing a beautiful broad leaf, of the gourd species, being embosomed in groves of cocoa-palms, banyan, and other trees, have a highly picturesque and rural appearance. A little graceful temple, generally of Siva, in a style almost Gothic, considerably increases the beauty of the scene. In one of these villages, Bishop Heber, on his first sailing up the Ganges, describes the appearance of an Indian farm-yard and homestead: 'In front,' he says, 'was a

[1] Forbes, Oriental Memoirs, vol. ii. pp. 413—415.

small mud building, with a thatched verandah looking towards the village, and behind was a court filled with cocoa-nut husks, and a little rice straw; in the centre of this was a round thatched building, raised on bamboos about a foot from the ground, which they said was a *goliah*, or granary; round it were small mud cottages, each to all appearance an apartment in the dwelling. In one corner was a little mill, something like a crab-mill, to be worked by a man, for separating the rice from the husk. By all which we could see through the open doors, the floor of the apartments was of clay, devoid of furniture and light, except what the door admitted[1].'

The furniture of the Hindoo is exceedingly simple: their ordinary plates and dishes are formed from the leaf of the plantain-tree, or of the nymphæa lotus, that beautiful lily which abounds in every lake. These are neatly sown together with some grassy fibre; but, however neatly fashioned, are never used a second time. Even in the houses of the Nairs, which are neater and better kept than ordinary, you find little beyond a few mats, earthen pots, grindstones, and utensils for cleaning the rice, with a swing for the amusement of the family. A few earthen pots, and two jars, the one for the water, the other for oil, comprise the whole stock for a villager. The cooking utensils are sometimes of brass, or copper, as are likewise their drinking vessels, which are made with a spout, that they may pour out the water in a small stream, as in drinking it is thought indelicate to touch

[1] Narrative, &c. vol. i. p. 18.

the vessel with their lips. In the superb dwellings of the Rajpoot nobles, where the painted and gilded ceiling is supported by columns of serpentine, and the walls are lined with mirrors, marble, or china, no costly furniture, no hangings, no chairs, tables, beds, couches, or candelabra are to be seen. The floors are covered with soft rich carpets, over which, to preserve their glowing freshness, a white cloth is spread, and here the Rajpoot sits and sleeps. However, we find that on the coast of Malabar a different fashion sometimes prevails. The hall in the Zamorin's palace, into which Vasco de Gama and his companions were conducted on their first arrival, was set round with seats, rising one above another, like those of an amphitheatre; the floor was covered with a rich carpet: the walls were hung with silk tapestry interwoven with gold; and there were sofas for the prince and his guests. Neat little bedsteads of cane, manufactured by the hill tribes, are in use in many parts of India, as are likewise chairs and tables. In the wealthier habitations silver utensils assume the place of earthen, and now that riches can be exhibited without fear of confiscation, there is evidently, in the large cities, an adoption of many articles of European household furniture.

Diet of the Hindoos.—The Hindoos in general, whether of high or low caste, do not, as has been erroneously supposed, subsist upon rice, or abstain from animal food. Even among the Brahmins no such pious abstinence from every thing which has had the principle of life exists, or ever did exist. Persons of this sacred caste eat animal food like their neighbours; and if certain individuals, or certain sects among them, abstain, it is simply as a matter of taste, and not from any religious motive; for both by their laws and their scriptures the flesh of animals is expressly permitted to be eaten [1]. There are Hindoos, however, both Brahmins and others, who restrict themselves to a vegetable diet.

The sect of Vishnu composes, in Hindostan, a very numerous body, and contains individuals of every caste, from the highest to the lowest. These sectarians, according to the Abbé Dubois, belong to the carnivorous part of mankind, of whom they by no means constitute the most abstemious members. They eat publicly all sorts of meat, excepting that of the cow, and drink toddy, arrack, and all other liquors that the country supplies, without shame or restraint [2].

The Brahmins, in general, according to Dubois, add to their other numerous vices that of gluttony. When an opportunity occurs of satiating their appetite, they exceed all bounds of temperance; and such occasions, it is added, are frequent [3].

Intoxication is still more common among the Brahmins than the use of interdicted food. A large quantity of wine and brandy imported into Calcutta is drunk by the Brahmins and other classes of Hindoos; to say nothing of the Mussulmans.

The Kshatriyas, or Rajpoots, are eminently carnivorous. When not engaged in war they usually, at

[1] See Institutes of Menu, chap. v. ver. 36, 56, &c.

[2] Description, &c. p. 53. [3] Ibid. p. 161.

the proper season of the year, devote a large portion of their time to the pleasures of the chase. Among the larger game, the most common is the wild boar. Of the flesh of this animal they appear to be particularly fond; and they pursue it with their utmost ardour. But the covers afforded by the nature of their country, especially the fields of maize, which there grows to the height of ten or twelve feet, not unfrequently affords the boar a chance of escape. In the barren plains of Marwar maize porridge is the common fare; but in Mewar, the paradise of the Rajpoot, the luxury of wheaten bread is well understood. Maize and Indian corn, gathered in an unripe state, are tied into bundles, roasted in the ear, and eaten with a little salt. For the introduction of melons and grapes, which at present form the principal dessert of the Hindoos, India is indebted to the emperor Baber, the most ingenuous and chivalrous of eastern conquerors. Tobacco was introduced by his grandson Jehângîr. When or by whom the use of opium was made known to the Rajpoots is not known; but 'this pernicious plant,' says an acute observer, 'has robbed the Rajpoot of half his virtues.' Under the influence of opium his natural bravery often degenerates into ferocity, while his countenance, when he is not thus excited, has an air of drowsy imbecility.

From the earliest ages the soldiers of Hindostan, like those of most other countries, have been addicted to intoxicating drinks; but these, though still in favour, are secondary in importance to the opiate. 'To eat opium together is the most inviolable pledge, and an agreement ratified by this ceremony is stronger than any adjuration. If a Rajpoot pays a visit, the first question is, Umul kya? 'have you had your opiate?'—Umul kao, 'take your opiate.' On a birthday, when all the chiefs convene to congratulate their brother on another knot to his years, the large cup is brought forth, a lump of opium put therein, upon which water is poured, and by the aid of a stick a solution is made, to which each helps his neighbour, not with a glass, but with the hollow of his hand held to his mouth. To judge from the wry faces on the occasion, none can like it, and to get rid of the nauseous taste comfit-balls are handed round. It is curious to observe the animation it inspires; a Rajpoot is fit for nothing without his *umul*, and Col. Tod often dismissed their men of business to refresh their intellects by a dose, for when its effects are dissipating they become mere logs. Opium to the Rajpoot is more necessary than food [1].

Scarcely any kind of animal food is rejected by the Rajpoot, excepting such as by all civilized nations has been accounted unclean. His game consists of the hare, the deer, the boar, the elk, the buffalo and of the wild-dog, the hyæna, the wolf, and the tiger; of which the latter class are destroyed as noxious. The votaries of *Canïya*, who have taken refuge in his sanctuary at Nât'hdwârâ, confine themselves, in penance, to a vegetable diet, which consists of dried fruits, spices, and curd, which however, in these degenerate days, are seasoned with rose-water,

[1] Annals of Rajast'han, vol. i. p. 644, 645.

amber, and all the aromatics of the East. When entertaining Europeans, the Rajpoots, fearful that their dishes may not be suited to the palates of their guests, sometimes request them to bring along with them their *cuisine*. An example of this occurred to Colonel Tod at Júdpoor. Having been invited to dinner by the Rajah, the prince added to the invitation the above curious request, as he feared that the fare of the dessert might prove unpalatable. 'But this,' says the traveller, 'I had often seen done in Scindia's camp, where joints of mutton, fowls, and fricassees, would diversify the provender of the Mahratta. I intimated that we had no apprehension that we should not do justice to the gastronomy of Júdpoor; however we sent our tables, and some claret to drink long life to the king of Maroodes. Having paid our respects to our host, he dismissed us, with the complimentary wish that appetite might wait upon us, and preceded by a host of gold and silver sticks, we were ushered into a hall, where we found the table literally covered with curries, pillaws, and ragouts of every kind, in which was not forgotten, the *hari moong Mundore ra*, 'the green pulse of Mundore,' the favourite dish next to *rabri*, or maize porridge, of the simple Rahtore. Here, however, we saw displayed the dishes of both the Hindoo and Mussulman, and nearly all were served in silver. The curries were excellent, especially those of the vegetable tribes made of the pulses, the kakris or cucumbers, and of a miniature melon, not larger than an egg, which grows spontaneously in these regions, and is transported by kasids or runners, as presents, for many hundred miles round [1]

Fruit, as might be expected from its plenty and cheapness, enters largely into the food of the Hindoos. Their groves and gardens supply an abundance of guavas, plantains, bananas, custard-apples, tamarinds, oranges, limes, citrons, grapes, pine-apples, and pomegranates. But of all the fruits of India the best as well as the most plentiful is the mango, which is found in all parts of the country, even in the forests. The superior kinds of mango are extremely delicious, being not unlike the large yellow Venice peach, heightened by the flavour of the orange and anana [2]. In the mango season it is the principal diet of the poor, and supposed to be very nutritious. The Chili pepper [3], and the cardamom, a pleasant spice from the Malabar coast, form a principal ingredient in curries.

The Hindoos are particularly fond of wild honey, which is found in the clefts of the rocks, in caverns, and on the summits of scarped rugged mountains. Of fish likewise, whether fresh or salted, they constantly make use. Whole tribes of men subsist by catching them, and they are conveyed in vast quantities into the interior. Many natives of the Concan are addicted to the chace, and eat the flesh of deer,

[1] Annals of Rajast'han, vol. i. p. 732.

[2] To me the flavour smacks strongly of turpentine, and the liking for the Mango appears quite an acquired taste. The finest I ever met was at Zanzibar.—[R. M. M.]

[3] Forbes, Oriental Memoirs.

hares, quails, partridges, and pigeons. The Chensu, a tribe inhabiting the hilly country above Malabar, destroy and kill all kinds of game. The Telinga Banijigaru, who are worshippers of Vishnu, and are all either merchants, farmers, or porters, eat sheep, goats, hogs, fowls, and fish, and, though prohibited the use of spirituous liquors, may intoxicate themselves with bang (wild hemp). The Madigas, who dress hides, make shoes, or cultivate the ground, eat not only all kinds of animal food, but even carrion; and openly drink spirituous liquors. The Ruddi, a very respectable caste of Sudras, chiefly employed in agriculture, eat hogs, sheep, goats, venison, and fowls, and are permitted the use of bang.

The Palliwanlu, a tribe of Tamul extraction, who are either farmers or gardeners, both eat animal food and drink spirituous liquors. Mutton and fish may lawfully be eaten by the Muchaveru, or shoemakers, who, contrary to the practice of persons of this caste in Europe, are expected to abstain from spirituous liquors. To compensate in some measure for this extraordinary prohibition, they are permitted to marry as many wives as they please.

The Wully Tigulas, another Tamul tribe; the Teliga Devanges, of the sect of Siva; the Baydaru, who are soldiers and hunters, likewise of the sect of Siva; the Curubas, soldiers and cultivators; and the Canara Devangas, all eat animal food, and, in many instances, drink spirituous liquors. The tastes of the Niadis, an outcast tribe of Malabar, are extremely peculiar. They refuse to perform any kind of labour, and consequently are plunged in the deepest poverty.

Unable to catch fish or kill game, they subsist upon wild roots, and whatever they can get by begging; but are occasionally fortunate enough to kill a tortoise, or hook a crocodile, the flesh of which, like the Nubians, they reckon delicious food. The Bacadaru, a tribe of Carnata origin, now sunk into slavery, not only eat animal food, but, to borrow the expressive language of Buchanan, 'may lawfully intoxicate themselves;' an advantage as above observed denied to the cobblers.

According to Buchanan, the other castes of southern India, who are commonly known to make use o animal food, are—the Goalas, or shepherds; the Bestas, farmers and lime-burners; the Mysore farmers; the Curubaru, who eat every thing but beef, even carrion; the Naimars or Nairs, who, although properly Vishnuites, wear the mark of Siva. The Magayer, or fishermen; the Biluaras, who extract the juice from the palm tree; the Corar, (this caste may lawfully eat tigers, but reject dogs and snakes); the Handi Curubas.

The Pariahs, who are supposed to amount to several million of souls, do not abstain even from beef. They possibly form a portion of the aboriginal population, who, refusing, on the rise of Brahminism, to adopt the prejudices of the new sect, were anathematized and excommunicated by those revengeful priests. Forbes tells a story illustrative of the scruples of the lower Hindoos, which is too good to be omitted. 'I knew a gentleman,' he says, 'who having formed a party for a little excursion into the country, provided a round of beef, as a principal dish in the cold collation. As he was going on horseback, he desired the beef might be covered with a cloth, and put into his palanquin to keep it cool: the bearers refused to carry a vehicle which contained such a pollution. The gentleman, on finding that neither remonstrances, entreaties, nor threats, were of any avail, cut off a slice of the meat, and eating it in their presence desired them to carry him to the place of rendezvous. This produced the desired effect; the bearers were the first to laugh at their folly, and exclaimed, 'Master come wise man, with two eyes, while poor black man come very foolish with only one;' and taking up the palanquin with the beef set off towards the tents in great good humour.' Vol. i. p. 2; ii. 139.

Several Europeans have seen a Hindoo eat a whole sheep at a meal. Mr. Caunter thus describes an exhibition of the sort:—'At a village not above eighteen miles from Benares, where we halted for the day, we were visited by a gaunt, grim-looking Hindoo, of some celebrity in the neighbourhood, which he had acquired, as well as the admiration of his caste, by his capability of devouring a sheep at a single meal. He was a tall, bony person, somewhat past the prime of life, with a thin, wiry frame, and a countenance of the most imperturbable equanimity, though as ugly as a sheep-eater might be expected to be. He offered, for a few rupees, to devour an entire sheep, if we would pay for the animal as well as for the different accessories of the meal. There was something so extraordinary in the proposal, that we readily acquiesced. We accordingly prepared to witness this marvellous feat, by purchasing the largest sheep we could find, which weighed, when prepared for cooking, just thirty-two pounds. We purchased it for one rupee, or twenty-two pence. All being now ready the carnivorous Ladra commenced his extraordinary feast. Having cut off the sheep's head with a single blow of his sabre, and jointed the body in due form, he separated all the meat from the bones, the whole quantity to be devoured amounting to about twenty pounds. This meat he minced very fine, forming it into balls about the size of a small fowl's egg, first mixing it with plenty of spice and curry powder. As soon as the whole was prepared, he fried some of the balls over a fire which he had previously kindled at the root of a tree, eating and frying till the whole were consumed. At intervals he washed down the meat with copious potations of ghee, which is sometimes so rancid as to be quite disgusting; and this happened to be the case now. After his prodigious meal, the performer was certainly less active than he had formerly been. His meagre body had acquired a considerable degree of rotundity; and although he declared that he felt not the slightest inconvenience, it was evident that he had taken as much as he could hold, and more than was agreeable. He acknowledged that he could not manage to eat a sheep more than twice in one week, and that this was oftener than he should like to do it.'

Many of the Bengal Brahmins eat fish, and several sorts of animal food; they are not only allowed them, but at some particular ceremonies they are enjoined to do so. But the Mahrattas, though all Hindoos, and the lower classes especially, eat of almost every thing that comes in their way; as mutton, goat, wild hog, game, and fish. Major Moor mentions two places by name where the Mahrattas *eat beef*, and permit cattle to be killed and publicly exposed to sale [1]. He then adds:—'The lower tribes of Hindoos are not so scrupulous as the higher about what they eat, or what they touch; especially if they are not observed by others. When at a distance from their families, and out of sight of their priests, many divest themselves of these nice ideas of purity. Those domesticated with Europeans generally affect to be very scrupulous: an English table covered with a variety of food is necessarily surrounded by a number of servants of different castes to attend the guests. At Baroche, Surat, and Bombay, a Hindoo will not remove a dish that has been defiled with beef, a Mohammedan cannot touch a plate polluted by pork, nor will a Parsee take one away on which is hare or rabbit. I never knew more than one Parsee servant who would snuff a candle, from a fear of extinguishing the symbol of the deity he worships, nor would this man ever do it in the presence of another Parsee [2].'

Bishop Heber observes, 'I had always heard, and fully believed, till I came to India, that it was a grievous crime, in the opinion of the Brahmins, to

[1] I have eaten a very fine beef steak in a Brahmin's house at Calcutta.—[R.M.M.]

[2] Oriental Memoirs, vol. ii. p. 138.

eat the flesh or shed the blood of any living creature whatever[1].' But the Bishop had not sailed up the Ganges to Calcutta before he found himself compelled to abandon this belief. Among the merchant ships and Maldive boats, which crowded the Hooghly, and seemed to reproduce the naval activity of the Thames, he saw the little barks of numerous fishermen, who were employed in catering for the appetites of their wealthy countrymen, Brahmins as well as others. Fish our traveller now found, 'is considered as one of the purest and most lawful kinds of food. Nothing, indeed, seems more generally mistaken than the supposed prohibition of animal food to the Hindoos. Thus many Brahmins eat both fish and kid. The Rajpoots, besides these, eat mutton, venison, or goat's flesh. Some castes may eat any thing but fowls, beef, or pork; while pork is with others a favourite diet, and beef only is prohibited.' He then adds, that though intoxicating liquors are by their religion forbidden to the Hindoos, the prohibition is very generally disregarded by persons of all ranks[2].'

Respecting the Pythagoræan habits of the Brahmins and Hindoos, Heber wrote, 'You may be, perhaps, as much surprised as I was to find that those who can afford it are hardly less carnivorous than ourselves; that even the purest Brahmins are allowed to eat mutton and venison.' And again, in another letter to a friend, he adds, 'I have now myself seen

[1] Narrative of a Journey, &c. vol. iii. p. 347, 8vo. edit.
[2] Ibid. vol. i. p. 9.

Brahmins of the highest caste cut off the heads of goats as a sacrifice to Durga (Bhavani); and I know from the testimony of Brahmins, as well as from other sources, that not only hecatombs of animals are offered in this manner as a meritorious act (a Rajah about 25 years back offered 60,000 in one fortnight), but that any person, Brahmins not excepted, eats readily of the flesh of whatever has been offered up to one of their divinities, while among almost all the other castes, mutton, pork, venison, fish, any thing but beef and fowls, are consumed as readily as in Europe[1].'

Herodotus mentions a rumour that there were cannibals in India, who were said to eat even the bodies of their parents. We find the charge of cannibalism renewed by a modern author of considerable reputation. 'Not only,' says Major Moor, 'do the Hindoos, even the Brahmins, eat flesh, but they eat (one sect at least) human flesh. They do not, I conclude, kill human subjects to eat, but they eat such as they find in or about the Ganges, and perhaps other rivers. The name of this sect is Paramahansa; and I have received authentic information of individuals of this sect being not very unusually seen about Benares, floating down the river on, and *feeding on a corpse.* Nor is this a low despicable tribe; but on the contrary, esteemed by themselves at least as a very high one; and my information stated that the human brain is judged by these epi-

[1] Narrative of a Journey, &c. vol. iii. p. 251, 277, 347.

curean cannibals as the most delicious morsel of their unsocial banquet.'

In some of the districts of Bahar there is a tribe of people called Sheep-eaters, who seize the animal alive, tear open its throat with their teeth, suck the living blood, and actually devour the flesh and entrails, until nothing remains but the skeleton. Lady Anstruther, who made a valuable collection of drawings during her residence in India, has a set of paintings in water colours, done by a native, which contains the whole process of these extraordinary gluttons, from the first seizure of the unfortunate animal, until it is completely devoured. A lithographic sketch, made after a similar set of paintings, of a sheep-eater in the various stages of his disgusting meal, is published in the third volume of the Transactions of the Royal Asiatic Society, accompanied with a brief memoir by General Hardwicke. (See page 336.)

Among all these cannibals and carnivorous people, however, there are undoubtedly many Brahmins and others who rigidly abstain from all kinds of animal food. Nevertheless their aliments are sufficiently varied. The feast of one of these vegetable Brahmins generally consist of seasoned bread, rice, curry, vegetables, pickles, and a dessert. Their ordinary bread is prepared from flour of wheat, juari, or bajera. To this they are fond of adding a thin cake or wafer, 'made from the flour of oord, highly seasoned with assafœtida; a salt called popper-khor; and a very hot massaula, composed of turmeric, black pepper, ginger, garlic, several kinds of warm seeds, and a quantity of the hottest Chili pepper.' All these ingredients are kneaded together with the oord flour and water into a tenacious paste, which is then rolled into cakes thin as a wafer, which, having been first dried a little in the sun, are then baked, like the oaten cakes of the Scotch, until they are quite crisp. The Brahmini curry is generally nothing more than warm buttermilk, thickened with grain-flour, and slightly seasoned with spices. Another of their favourite dishes is composed of a sort of split pea, boiled with salt and tumeric, and eaten with ghee, or clarified butter. When the dinner is prepared the Brahmin first washes his body in warm water, during which operation he wears his dotee, or that cloth which, fastened round his loins, hangs down to his ancles: when washed, he hangs up the dotee to dry, and binds in its place a piece of silk, it not being allowable for a Brahmin to wear any thing else when eating. If a person of another caste, or even a Brahmin who is not washed, touches his dotee while drying, he cannot wear it without washing it again. After going through several forms of prayer and other ceremonies, he sits down to his food, which is spread on fresh gathered leaves, fastened together to the size wanted for the company. The dishes and plates are invariably composed of leaves; a Brahmin may not eat out of any thing else. Tin vessels, or copper tinned, may be used for cooking; but a Brahmin cannot eat out of them. The food, after being prepared in the kitchen, is placed in distinct portions, on dishes of different size, form, and depth, on the large verdant covering in a regular manner. In the centre of the cover is always a large pile of plain boiled rice, and at a feast there are generally two other heaps of white and yellow rice, seasoned with spices and salt, and two of sweet rice, to be eaten with chatna, pickles, and stewed vegetables; the latter are chiefly brenjals, bendre turoy, and different kinds of beans, all savourily dressed and heated with chilies of every description. The chatna is usually made from a vegetable called cotemear, to the eye very much resembling parsley, but to those unused to it of a very disagreeable taste and smell: this is so strongly heated with chilies, as to render the other ingredients less distinguishable. The chatna is sometimes made with cocoa-nut, lime-juice, garlic, and chilies, and, with the pickles, is placed in deep leaves round the large cover, to the number of thirty or forty, the Hindoos being very fond of this stimulus to their rice. These pickles are not prepared with vinegar, but preserved in oil and salt, seasoned with chilie and the acid of tamarinds, which in a salted state is much used in Hindoostan. Brahmins and many other Hindoos reject the onion from their bill of fare. Ghee, which, in deep boats formed of leaves, seems to constitute the essence of the dinner, is plentifully dispensed. The dessert consists of mangoes, preserved with sugar, ginger, limes, and other sweetmeats; syrup of different fruits, and sometimes a little ripe fruit; but the dessert is not common. Such is the entertainment of a rich Brahmin who eats no animal food.

The poor, whose means will not allow them to think of animal food, consume rice, dhall, and other cheap grains, seasoned with salt, spices, and, if possible, a little dried or fresh fish. The Hindoo uses the right hand only in eating. No knives, forks, spoons, or even chopsticks are used. A brass cup, or the hollow of the hand serves as a drinking vessel; but when any utensil is used he is careful not to allow it to touch his lips. On the whole I should say that the Hindoos are an abstemious and very temperate race.

The state of Education in India, progress in the fine Arts—Newspapers, Crime, Government, Commerce, &c. will be found in the ensuing Volume.

APPENDIX.

VILLAGES AND HOUSES OF LOWER BENGAL.

Extract Bengal Judicial Consultation, the 10th Nov. 1825.

(FURNISHED FOR THE "HISTORY OF THE BRITISH COLONIES," BY THE INDIA HOUSE, AND NEVER BEFORE PUBLISHED.)

RETURNS FROM DIFFERENT ZILLAHS.

Thannahs.*	Villages.	Houses.	Thannahs.	Villages.	Houses.
MIDNAPORE.			**DINAGEPORE.**		
Town Midnapore......	556	23373	Rajarampoor	844	36420
Kasheegunge	826	29247	Chintamun	469	16296
Kalmeejale	334	16368	Beergunj	455	23730
Purtabpoor	550	22728	Gungarampoor.........	614	21983
Seebung..................	637	30336	Bunseeharee............	675	22275
Pudumbusan	335	13746	Hemutabad	362	15786
Bamnarah...............	243	10776	Loll Bazar..............	766	26448
Musudpoor	181	14238	Putheram	766	25278
Kanchunnagur.........	257	14091	Puthneetulah	544	19021
Basooleeah	201	8739	Jugdullah	589	19437
Tamal.....................	23	33363	Thakoorgaon	276	26718
Khejooreeah Ghaut...	25	1410	Peergunj	373	14380
Nugwan..................	291	13995	Nabobgunj	348	13020
Mohespoor	195	7371	Hubeah	232	13383
Sagressur	320	11847	Khetlal	344	12003
Putaspoor	453	18174	Raneegunj	544	18186
Chutterpal..............	350	14724	Raneesunkole	208	10959
Phoolhuttah	29	1074	Maldah	269	10329
Kadooryan	268	9612	Poorsah	467	16113
Rymoobundur	355	11832	Budulgotchee	656	23052
Dinamaree	455	19071	Kaleegunj	468	17199
Sildah.....................	595	19748	Bholahat	295	21861
Gurbeetah...............	569	22032	Kaleeachuck............	327	10908
Sursa	222	7860	Gomqureeba............	439	18582
Salpatee	266	7062	Sheebgunj...............	212	11388
			Kotwallee Rajgunj ...	21	3528
Total.........	8536	382812	Total.........	11564	468284

* *Thannah* signifies station; the division usually refers to a police district.

CUTTACK.

Thannahs.	Villages.	Houses.
Bhudruck	870	30465
Jehajpore	870	30480
Urruckpore	748	25971
Cuttack	372	18937
Peeply	511	19233
Gape	661	22281
Torun	678	22491
Hurryhurpore	809	28686
Puhrajpore	552	18918
Assressur	525	18561
Talmal Kunka	373	18087
Zemindary of Kunka	423	14544
Bustah (Joint Mag. Balasore)	392	13170
Balasore	474	18378
Soro Chooramun	690	23706
Khordah Jo. Mag.	757	30123
Ranpoor	256	8982
Pooree	550	33861
Total	10511	396924

TIPPERAH.

Thannahs.	Villages.	Houses.
Jugurnathdiggee	373	12309
Kusbah	332	11775
Burkumptah	260	8931
Toobkeebagrah	632	24330
Lukshaumee	541	17970
Regungunge	373	17016
Kajeegunje	458	15231
Daudcondy	769	25494
Vemeergong	402	16257
Soodaram	206	9702
Chgulyah	159	5832
Thurlah	364	12012
Ramgunge	421	14595
Luckipoor	1030	36258
Bominj	18	3462
Naseernugur	328	13278
Goureepoorah	115	4263
Cutwallee	748	25737
Total	7529	274452

NUDDEA.

Thannahs.	Villages.	Houses.
Hurdee	232	11013
Meherpoor	237	15666
Dumdumma	426	14633
Ugurdeep	146	8424
Kaurah	187	14130
Hauskholly	207	12993
Dowlutgunge	227	12753
Baugdah	305	12120
Drogaon	185	10710
Kakuspookooria	328	15366
Subsah	391	21345
Busseerhaut	371	14832
Sooksagur	320	14268
Santipoor	124	13263
Cotwallee	90	8928
Bally	68	6114
Dewangunge	188	17715
Goverdangah	316	13149
Total	4348	237432

HOOGHLY.

Thannahs.	Villages.	Houses.
Hooghly	174	13905
Bansberreea	89	4455
Benipoor	194	11193
Pandovah	209	22536
Dhuneeakholly	372	20877
Dewangunge	200	16497
Chunderkona	292	16929
Ghattaul	155	14613
Jehanabad	310	18777
Rajbulhat	239	18789
Hurripaul	174	11082
Omtah	129	8016
Baugnaun	359	12900
Rajapoor	210	14676
Bydbatty	230	19803
Coloobureah	248	14679
Kotrah	203	8103
Total	3787	247830

Thannahs.	Villages.	Houses.	Thannahs.	Villages.	Houses.
JESSORE.			**TIRHOOT.**		
Singah	361	17325	Soopool	655	32322
Teermohanee	151	8004	Moozufferpore	1504	54888
Sulkeea	299	14277	Curnaul	365	14616
Mohamedpoor	268	9729	Nugubussee	1110	15018
Khagsal	296	11688	Catrah	630	15723
Pungsah	341	13050	Kajeepore	741	17385
Koostccah	321	14703	Durbhungah	692	29622
Dhurumpoorah	163	10020	Muddehpore	180	5286
Zemighdah	714	29691	Muhooah	552	19686
Kaloopole	177	5841	Rekah	756	23376
Kotechundpoor	233	10863	Buherah	475	21972
Sezially	265	10800	Laulgunje	262	10647
Talah	596	22893	Khezoolee	214	9750
Noabad	616	36777	Dulsing Surae	1214	32337
Lohagurh	334	15666	Jelah	400	18489
Cotwallee	64	4482	Buhoorah	491	18423
Total	5199	236718	Total	10241	339540
BEERBHOOM.			**PATNA.**		
Pachtobee	125	6813	Bankipoor	259	10251
Kaagaon	208	18231	Sooltangunj	11	363
Shahkoolipoor	195	11079	Alumgunj	2	66
Laulipoor	288	15951	Futtooah	181	9510
Kusbah	332	23316	Sheerpoor	57	4734
Kisheunagur	412	22830	Begumgunge	4	366
Ufrulpoor	296	12525	Dhoulpoor	2	666
Shahanah	371	12777	Malsulamee	4	1116
Oopurbundha	518	17094	Sodikutra	2	366
Molessur	528	21951	Mehendegunge	6	849
Nungoolea	202	9603	Mogulpoorah	1	150
Soorey	143	9291	Sadikpoor	9	1116
Deoghur	1071	36645	Colonel Gunj	2	183
Khuroon	94	7056	Peerbuhoree	12	630
Nulhuttee	182	8595	Bikrum	361	14085
Pulsah	165	11004	Noubutpoor	185	6690
Doongong	157	8652	Total	1098	51141
Total	5287	253413			

Thannahs.	Villages.	Houses.	Thannahs.	Villages.	Houses.
BHAUGULPORE.			**PURNEEAH.**		
Kotwallee	167	10650	Deemiah	289	17868
Lokmanpoor	255	18018	Dhumdah	326	22617
Pirjalapoor	391	14490	Mutteearee	257	16650
Chundunpoora	7	231	Bahadoorgunje	394	17931
Foodkeepoor	43	1536	Kulliagunge	284	20376
Shunkerpoor	372	14514	Kishengunge	389	19878
Furakabad	63	2664	Arrareeah	366	19545
Kumurgunj	54	3135	Havelly (Purneah)	391	27405
Poyntee	18	6861	Doolargunge	670	26556
Lukurdwanee	874	29076	Neignagur	539	23052
Joypoor	807	29739	Dundkhorah	489	24189
Kalkapoor	117	4212	Gundwarrah	156	17853
Rajmahal	86	8163	Munneearee	185	8862
Ruttunjung	413	16269	Khurbal	213	9651
Total	3667	159558	Total	4948	272433
SARUN.			**RUNGPORE.**		
Chupra	278	22272	Bogdwar	356	11865
Goldinggunge	137	7593	Foorunbaree	138	10149
Kasmur	190	11946	Fugeergunge	11	9530
Pursaw	336	13077	Benakooree	13	5763
Futtehpore	314	13953	Patgong	24	7776
Musoorah	252	10371	Shadoollapore	310	19239
Dhakha	201	12045	Chilmaree	70	6981
Motteharee	76	8796	Peergunge	425	16914
Kulianpore	282	15648	Burabaree	509	21573
Gorindgunje	187	11247	Barnee	53	13536
Bunjeereea	442	15288	Rungpoor	152	6018
Boggah	284	9957	Deemlah	76	12516
Betteeah	439	2165	Dhaup	586	37863
Koolsapore	786	26823	Kooergunge	69	8766
Sewaun	530	24990	Bhowanygunge	266	9714
Butterdha	374	15852	Durwanee	215	17961
Tajepore	505	23211	Mullung	243	11676
Deroulse	370	18837	Boda	435	27999
Maujee	135	9294	Wullepoor	280	12231
Total	6118	292815	Total	4231	268070

Thannahs.	Villages.	Houses.
JUNGLE MEHALS.		
Oookra	177	10317
Sainpaharee	108	6921
Chooloolea	126	5913
Oondah	537	19791
Bissenpoor	335	19950
Sona Mookee	199	11607
Sitlah	341	14139
Chatna	327	11141
Roypoor	454	15567
Bancoorah	106	4365
Burrabhoom	312	10764
Pachete	1315	55095
Bygunkodur	61	2547
Bangmoondee	87	3573
Mookundpoor	8	264
Kislah	17	912
Amynagore	200	6717
Jheeldah	134	4539
Simlapaul	105	3465
Noagurh	101	3333
Jaypoor	64	2529
Jhureea	226	8169
Maunbhoom	206	6915
Soopoor	205	6999
Katrass	84	3006
Toondee	173	5826
Nugurkeeree	71	2460
Jaynagore	65	2145
Toraung	11	480
Pantcoom	174	5859
Pauran	153	5700
Total	6492	260948
SUBURBS OF CALCUTTA.		
Chitpoor	14	5265
Manicktullah	51	11487
Tazeerant	291	21234
Nahazaree	231	18669
Sulkeeah	123	15417
Total	710	72072
City of Calcutta	53000	265000
Chinsurah	3996	18679
Foreign: Chandernagore	8484	44538
Foreign: Serampore	2973	11445

Thannahs.	Villages.	Houses.
RAMGURH.		
Huruckdeea	2412	81234
Chuttro Chutty	206	7500
Sherghotty	1198	41235
Aurungabad	1208	45321
Nubbingnuggur	605	22317
Mughervun	216	7362
Kana Chutta	124	4092
Catwally Chitra	75	3942
Echaek	318	11478
Itkoree	587	19956
Kuntergunge	199	6567
Puggar	386	13791
Bishun Ghur	306	11502
Chitterpoor	318	12081
Sahpoor	142	4920
Anuntpoor	173	5709
Leslie Gunge	319	10527
Turhussee	320	10560
Gorha	220	7260
Moharazgunge	1175	41883
Bondhoo	427	19317
Burwa	216	7245
Jheeko Chatty	573	20679
Burkagurh	482	16440
Oody Gunge	275	9192
Salidag	160	5697
Kudurma	81	2790
Total	12721	450597
CHITTAGONG.		
Zorawarjung	138	5523
Butteareo	35	8622
Hazaree Haut	40	11907
Phutuckcharee	105	12735
Roojan	123	19584
Puteea	258	27417
Satkonea	192	20997
Chuckerea	32	7524
Ramoo	67	9669
Sundeep	46	5925
Kattya	32	4644
Taknauf	13	2133
Islamabad	27	3480
Total	1108	140160

MOORSHEDABAD.

Thannahs.*	Villages.	Houses.
Hurhurparah	104	8706
Bhurtpoor	203	15348
Julinghee	64	5937
Guwas	201	10875
Sootee	107	6471
Burrovah	104	8289
Doulutabad	218	11301
Mirzapoor	166	11385
Shumsheergunge	170	13449
Bhadwreeath	83	4092
Kulleengunj	110	5451
Gockurn	132	9564
Chyndangah	67	3096
Ranee Talaub	185	9915
Khumrah	122	6531
Dewansurae	131	7278
Nuwadah	29	1674
Govindpoor	134	12546
Burhampoor	12	630
Total	2342	152538

BACKERGUNGE.

Thannahs.	Villages.	Houses.
Bareekura	367	15570
Kalacolly	177	5958
Bokynugur	139	8994
Cheendcea	56	8619
Khalsakollee	45	7191
Tugrah	76	3561
Boapaul	81	12645
Augareeah	158	11073
Kutchooah	134	4656
Gaurmuddea	180	14085
Mendeegunge	538	21447
Mizzagunge	103	7923
Kotwaleeparah	276	11514
Booreehaut	124	4092
Total	2454	137328

RAJSHAYE.

Thannahs.	Villages.	Houses.
Nattore	577	93693
Chowgaon	593	48405
Buggorah	932	42675
Sherepoor	285	22050
Nokeelah	243	16032
Roygunge	454	43911
Hurriaul	540	70695
Shazadpoor	451	53994
Muttoorah	183	18822
Keytooparah	186	29802
Pubnah	520	65061
Belmureeah	482	48318
Bauleeah	393	50907
Godagarry	186	20175
Chapye	195	27936
Rahunpoor	197	14985
Taunore	398	22977
Maundah	463	24750
Doobulhutty	574	29421
Adumdigge	555	24648
Bhouanygunge	763	48174
Total	9170	817431

SYLHET.

Thannahs.	Villages.	Houses.
Parkool	389	19560
Latoo	580	22797
Hingajeeah	262	10650
Russoolgunje	1167	39096
Nubeegunj	404	17874
Sunkerpossah	236	8139
Tanjpoor	591	19620
Rajmughur	445	15738
Noacally	297	12960
Abidabad	243	9486
Bunsikoorah	244	8169
Luskerpoor	622	22815
Laor and Bungung	237	9840
Total	5717	216744

BURDWAN.

Thannahs.	Villages.	Houses.
Burdwan	132	12768
Amboos	318	23676
Cutwa	153	16059
Mungulcote	180	14883
Suleemabad	326	20691
Gangoorea	328	21510
Amoosgaon	204	20565
Raina	247	17256
Pooteenah	205	15711
Muntissur	261	17847
Poobthul	273	17289
Balkishen	141	13602
Indas	434	25656
Total	3202	237516

SHAHABAD.

Thannahs.	Villages.	Houses.
Belountee	195	12060
Dramrown	451	20325
Ekwaree	449	17223
Kurrunjee	468	16212
Burrown	475	16926
Sahseram	865	16464
Telonthoo	178	10278
Sarinja	228	9111
Sanout	249	8802
Ramgurh	289	10356
Mohuneeah	435	16290
Arrah	403	27723
Total	4185	181770

24 PERGUNNAHS. [of Calcutta.]

Thannahs.	Villages.	Houses.
Anreeaduh	111	7302
Putterghottah	144	7324
Etagatchee	356	14088
Govindpoor	203	7818
Bishenpoor	373	13713
Bankeepoor	503	18471
Ramnugur	388	16245
Kudumgatchee	651	24174
Nyhuttee	158	9785
Barrackpoor	4	999
Total	2891	119919

MYMENSING.

Thannahs.	Villages.	Houses.
Ghosgong	598	20436
Nitterkona	958	32499
Niklee	989	36981
Serajgunj	588	26850
Modoopoor	689	23790
Madargunj	843	28353
Futtehpoor	682	24144
Sheerpoor	575	21783
Pakooleea	951	33957
Hajeepoor	582	21312
Nuseerabad	333	16533
Burmee	116	4296
Total	7904	290934

BEHAR.

Thannahs.	Villages.	Houses.
Dureeapore	174	10479
Baur	268	15201
Kilsah	812	33876
Jahanabad	824	30180
Shaikpoorah	613	21447
Koolasgunge	337	15114
Arwul	275	10479
Dawoodnagur	357	16719
Behar	615	34539
Nawabadah	1083	39948
Gya	954	40140
Total	6312	268122

DACCA JELALPORE.

Thannahs.	Villages.	Houses.
Hajegunge	345	16677
Manickgunge	195	9675
Sibchur	296	15831
Talma	197	12000
Furreedpoor	96	4887
Juffergunge	211	9135
Butka	300	12672
Muscoodpoor	420	17517
Nuwaubgunge	223	9231
Boosnah	177	7311
Bailgutchee	83	2739
Total	2543	117675

Thannahs.	Villages.	Houses.
DACCA.		
Jessore	232	8592
Nuranegunge	491	17322
Tezgang	183	6507
Mulfutgunge	255	10872
Rajabarry	355	15750
Salagurh	319	16407
Sabom	312	12399
Ekdallah	422	14628
Total	2569	102477

Note.—From the foregoing official returns, dated Calcutta, 1824 (the latest at the India House), it will be seen that in the Lower Provinces of Bengal there are 157,384 villages, and 7,447,653 houses; the population census has been formed by calculating five inmates to every house (a fair average in India), which gives 37,238,265 mouths. This is the nearest approximation to correctness of the population of a vast section of the empire.

SURAT POPULATION.

Denomination.	Men.	Women.	Boys.	Girls.	Total.
Inhabitants of the city and suburbs of Surat.					
Brahmins	3701	3593	1014	777	9065
Bunnians	7589	7625	2637	1657	19517
Other classes of Hindoos	20299	21122	7665	4730	53816
Moosulmans, all classes	12129	12835	3660	2559	31183
Parsees	3736	4187	1447	1137	10507
Native Portuguese	40	25	9	4	78
Armenians	49	71	14	19	153
Jews	23	20	11	13	67
Total	47572	49481	16457	10896	124406

(*Continued.*)

Denomination.	Men.	Women.	Boys.	Girls.	Total.
Randier, &c.					
Hindoos, comprehending all castes	2600	2500	612	625	6337
Moosulmans	1400	1300	410	318	3428
Parsees	130	125	31	30	316
Total	4130	3925	1053	973	10081
Chowarre, containing 67 Villages, viz.					
Hindoos	3069	3023	1559	1237	8888
Moosulmans	304	310	199	125	938
Parsees	117	118	61	64	360
Total	3490	3451	1819	1426	10186
Cheeklee, 72 Villages.					
Hindoos	8274	8307	6042	5184	27807
Moosulmans	787	809	517	456	2569
Parsees	56	57	37	17	167
Total	9117	9173	6596	5657	30543
Inhabitants of Bulsar, containing one Qusba, 51 Villages, viz.					
Hindoos	8149	8204	5553	3454	25360
Moosulmans	253	290	152	55	750
Parsees	683	711	551	316	2261
Total	9085	9205	6256	3825	28371
Inhabitants of Bhootsur, containing 11 Villages, viz.					
Hindoos	1108	1151	466	415	3140
Moosulmans	1	1	1	...	3
Parsees	8	6	7	1	22
Total	1117	1158	474	416	3165
Inhabitants of Booharee, containing 12 Villages, viz.					
Hindoos	1055	983	491	431	2960
Parsees	19	10	2	2	33
Total	1074	993	493	433	2993
Inhabitants of Bardolee, containing 12 Villages.					
Hindoos	708	690	351	272	2021
Moosulmans	119	131	64	52	366
Parsees	13	17	8	3	41
Total	840	838	423	327	2428

(*Continued.*)

Denomination.	Men.	Women.	Boys.	Girls.	Total.
Inhabitants of Kutargam, Phoolpara, and Koombhurujar, Villages, viz.					
Hindoos	1901	1943	808	516	5168
Moosulmans	82	67	24	22	195
Parsees	4	2	1	1	8
Total	1987	2012	833	539	5371
Inhabitants of Parchol, containing 36 Villages, viz.					
Hindoos	5987	6130	3142	1540	16799
Moosulmans	245	269	142	97	753
Parsees	67	61	32	15	175
Total	6299	6460	3316	1652	17727
Inhabitants of Parnera, containing 23 Villages, viz.					
Hindoos	2458	2521	1547	1314	7840
Moosulmans	47	45	24	20	136
Parsees	10	12	8	5	35
Total	2515	2578	1579	1339	8011
Inhabitants of Soopa, containing 48 Villages, viz.					
Hindoos	3872	3810	2151	1407	11240
Moosulmans	179	179	96	74	528
Parsees	24	7	2	1	34
Total	4075	3996	2249	1482	11802
Inhabitants of Surbhan, containing 33 Villages, viz.					
Hindoos	2646	2660	1660	1125	8091
Moosulmans	157	154	107	82	500
Parsees	65	68	39	11	183
Total	2868	2882	1806	1218	8774
Inhabitants of Wallore, containing 62 Villages, viz.					
Hindoos	3654	3493	1754	1231	10132
Moosulmans	130	148	88	73	439
Parsees	21	9	8	4	42
Total	3805	3650	1850	1308	10613

Note.—The foregoing return is signed "John Romer, magistrate;" I give it, as I do several others of population in this Appendix, for the purpose of stimulating further inquiries into the important subject of the population of British India; I am aware of the difficulties in the way of obtaining correct censuses owing to the cautious jealousy of the natives, but this difficulty may be got over by prudence and kindness.—R. M. M.

Census of the Population of the Zilla Southern Koncan, taken in 1820; distinguishing the males and females of each caste, and separating those of each sex above from those beneath twelve years of age, exhibiting also the number of houses in the occupancy of each caste. (Given to shew the variety of castes in India. R. M. M.)

Caste.	Trade or Business.	Males.			Females.			Grand total of Males and Females.	Number of Houses.
		Under 12 years of age.	Above 12 years of age.	Total.	Under 12 years of age.	Above 12 years of age.	Total.		
Brahmins	Great variety of occupations	11361	22122	33483	5957	22730	28687	62170	10587
Purbhoe	Cultivators of their own property on accounts	736	1348	2084	312	1514	1826	3910	643
Mahrattahs	Mostly cultivators and soldiers	51976	77300	129276	31346	87734	119080	248356	53167
Moosulmans	Of all trades	8353	12191	20544	5289	13075	18364	38908	7404
Souar	Goldsmiths	1937	3279	5216	1016	3577	4593	9809	1822
Kassur	Copper-smiths	627	1019	1646	295	1070	1365	3011	640
Waney	Traders or Shopkeepers	3234	5052	8286	1657	5651	7308	15594	3172
Seempee	Tailors	328	514	842	176	567	743	1585	374
Jeeguur	Sadlers	28	45	73	12	43	55	128	25
Boorood	Basketmakers	160	250	410	102	279	381	791	185
Sallee	Weavers	302	455	757	126	496	622	1379	297
Kostee	Ditto	226	304	530	448	361	809	1339	205

Caste.	Trade or Business.	Males.			Females.			Grand total of Males and Females.	Number of Houses.
		Under 12 years of age.	Above 12 years of age.	Total.	Under 12 years of age.	Above 12 years of age.	Total.		
Sootar	Carpenters	1302	1812	3114	727	1886	2613	5727	1036
Pecreet	Washermen	612	1065	1677	317	1142	1459	3136	670
Dhunghur	Cattle-keepers	459	573	1052	231	582	813	1845	420
Nahavee	Barbers	980	1671	2651	518	1728	2246	4897	978
Tellee Mahrattahs	Oil-makers	1489	2242	3731	875	2399	3274	7005	1272
Tellee Musulmaun	Ditto	131	197	328	83	209	292	620	96
Bhoee	Palanquin-bearers	510	694	1204	380	769	1077	2281	506
Combar	Tile-makers and potters	1299	1890	3189	65	2145	2760	5949	1230
Mumai	Bangle retailers	19	25	44	11	24	35	79	17
Coonbeeu	Husbandmen	9763	14273	24036	6494	16682	23176	47212	9834
Mahrattah goorow	Priests	510	762	1272	333	874	1207	2479	538
Lingay et gorow	Ditto	372	726	1098	238	841	1079	2177	445
Soowlee	Cowkeeper	2620	3509	6129	1450	4076	5526	11655	2589
Bhandarec	Drawers of toddy and distillers	6741	12100	18841	3970	13021	16991	35833	6860
Ghundullee	Mendicants	52	74	126	27	80	107	233	61
Mallee	Gardeners	26	65	91	30	69	99	190	39
Jungum	Priests	579	824	1403	294	859	1153	2556	596
Hulvaee	Confectioners		1	1		1	1	2	1
Chambhar	Shoemakers	1676	2113	3789	1054	2377	3431	7220	1409
Mahar	Degraded caste	11355	14615	25970	6936	10996	23932	49902	10530
Wotaree	Copper casters	9	12	21	9	9	18	39	7

Surraykurree	Spirit sellers	105	122	227	63	139	202	429	90
Senoy	Mostly employed as accountants	371	761	1132	210	757	967	2099	392
Jawul Brahmin	Various calling (only residing in Severndroog Colooka)	235	370	605	117	370	487	1092	189
Bhukoorapee	Cutters of Black stone	8	14	22	11	13	24	46	10
Takeens	Beggars	12	12	24	8	12	20	44	11
Beldaur	Heavers of black-stone	2	3	5	1	3	4	9	3
Dhurgur Cooley	Fishermen	293	544	837	255	544	799	1636	303
Cooley	Ditto	1214	1762	2976	981	1861	2802	5778	1310
Seekeelghur	Steel polishers	4	4	8	3	10	13	21	6
Kurgree Jogee	Beggars using musical instruments	2	1	3		1	1	4	1
Gouroodee	Jugglers	6	10	16	6	14	20	36	8
Koomtee	Foreign beggars	1	1	2		1	1	3	1
Veedur	Heavers of black-stone	6	4	10	3	8	11	21	1
Luigayet Vaney	Shopkeepers	63	118	181	29	122	151	332	87
Kajaree Kamisar	Bangle sellers	6	2	8	1	6	7	15	5
Panturuut	Heavers of black-stone	28	46	74	16	42	58	132	39
Moosulman Golam	Male Slaves	31	63	94	6	27	33	127	16
Mahratta Golam	Ditto	1484	2092	3576	922	2447	3369	6945	1665
Mahratta Butkee	Female ditto	951	786	1737	976	3571	4547	6284	1575
Musulman ditto	Ditto	31	10	41	40	143	183	224	33
Daldee Moosulman	Fishermen	432	626	1058	286	668	954	2012	283
Khawwee	Ditto	405	608	1013	439	692	1131	2144	475
Meetgauday	Salt makers	1047	1731	2778	605	1897	2502	5280	964
Kantkuree	Hardly civilized	68	104	172	63	111	174	346	79
Lawar	Ironsmiths	74	118	192	45	127	172	364	64
Goozer	Shopkeepers from Guezerate	254	1026	1280	174	477	651	1931	506
Surowday	Beggars	98	201	299	68	208	276	575	178
Rawool	Ditto	5	8	13	8	7	15	28	5
Maharin Buttick	Slaves females of Mahar caste					2	2	2	1
Dhuvudd	Iron makers	91	166	259	71	171	242	499	115
Ghudsee Bheekaree	Beggars	20	12	32	12	38	50	82	30

Caste.	Trade or Business.	Males.			Females.			Grand total of Males and Females.	Number of Houses.
		Under 12 years of age.	Above 12 years of age.	Total.	Under 12 years of age.	Above 12 years of age.	Total.		
Bhukeerajee	Ditto	2	2	4		1	1	5	2
Tambutt	Coppersmiths	124	199	323	55	219	274	597	111
Bhawak Gooroou	Priests	374	561	935	233	637	860	1795	301
Dowray Gossavee	Beggars	68	118	186	42	119	161	347	93
Seengur	Hemp preparers	61	87	148	41	72	113	261	60
Bhootay	Beggars and attendants on pagodas	21	35	56	6	39	45	101	23
Rajpoot	Various calling	3	17	20	1	6	7	27	6
Christian Portuguese	All trades, but mostly red-stoneheavers	205	346	551	172	307	479	1030	205
Jogee	Beggars	114	201	315	79	192	271	586	37
Goozooratte Brahmin	As other Brahmins	3	21	24	3	5	8	32	14
Waghay	Beggars	3	1	4	1	1	2	6	7
Heuzday	Eunuchs	5	7	12	2	10	12	24	7
Kusbeenee	Dancing girls				1	2	3	3	2
Kutulkootia	Furriers		1	1		1	1	2	1
Khantuk	Goat butchers	5	13	18	9	14	23	41	9
Goundy	Masons		4	4	1	1	1	5	3
Augree	Cultivators, and salt manufacturers, &c.	1218	1881	3099	682	2079	2761	5860	1415
Purdazsee	Foreigners	7	38	45	4	31	35	80	30
Antaur	Performers	3	7	10	1	6	7	17	4
Khurkhundy	Butchers	5	5	10	1	6	7	17	4
Pautanay Purbhoo	Clerks	19	36	55	7	35	42	97	34

Bhoonsaree	Grinders	32	55	87	38	65	103	190	39
Durwaysee	Beggars Moosulman	3	4	7		6	6	13	5
Kullvantnee	Attendants on dancing girls	31	44	75	34	121	155	230	42
Vehaloo	Musicians	3	4	7	1	3	4	11	3
Bhaut	Poets and beggars	17	22	39	8	26	34	73	18
Phootangur Bhoojary	Grain dealers	8	17	25	3	8	11	36	12
Maunj	Often thieves and hunters	56	58	114	17	62	79	193	59
Bhangsallay	Shopkeepers	16	34	50	12	29	41	91	20
Khutry	Silk manufacturers	19	46	65	12	52	64	129	32
Salvee	Potters	9	17	26	4	21	25	51	6
Punchaul	Goldsmiths	4	15	19	10	14	24	43	10
Wadvul	Gardeners	174	250	424	98	333	431	855	216
Gosavee	Beggars	174	305	479	125	323	448	927	331
Khakoor	Inhabitants of the jungle	251	282	333	217	277	494	1027	196
Gabel	Fishermen	1080	1814	2894	775	1922	2697	5591	1058
Bhowney	Attendants on courtezans.	171	224	395	160	440	600	995	204
Buennay Koodaldavy	Brahmins (as they alledge)	17	43	60	15	35	50	110	16
Vir Raunnany	Beggars	12	25	37	7	30	37	74	21
Seedee	Servants (mostly)	6	6	12	4	12	16	28	7
Gullack	Illegitimate attendants of Brahmins	3	13	16		13	13	29	11
Hethurry	Labourers	11	31	42	11	18	29	71	23
Kaullun	Distillers of spirits	139	242	381	60	300	360	741	188
Kattary	Tanners	2	11	13	6	9	15	28	8
Marwaddy	Shopkeepers	4	96	100	3	2	5	105	38
Vanjary	Bullock drivers and owners	3	9	12	1	9	10	22	6
Pelly Sorail	Jews, who are oil makers	133	211	344	61	238	299	643	147
French	Settlers of French extraction, shopkeepers, &c	3	11	14	10	4	14	28	9
Causar Bungdywably	Bangle makers	39	84	123	31	104	135	258	52
Dakotay	Beggars	6	9	15	6	15	21	36	8
Bhurady	Ditto		3	3		1	1	4	1
Kunojvy	Hindostannee	2	4	6	2	6	8	14	4
Vajeintry	Musicians	20	26	46	13	22	35	81	17

Caste.	Trade or Business.	Males. Under 12 years of age.	Males. Above 12 years of age.	Males. Total.	Females. Under 12 years of age.	Females. Above 12 years of age.	Females. Total.	Grand total of Males and Females.	Number of Houses.
Soukolly	Labourers	60	81	141	37	93	130	271	64
Jair	Various callings		3	3		3	3	6	2
Surojoy Takoor	Beggars	22	50	72	8	54	62	134	35
Kogey	Various callings	14	22	36	10	17	27	63	20
Mooday	Eunuchs	2	5	7	3	4	7	14	5
Fungur Mussulman	Coral makers	4	5	9	4	7	11	20	9
Hallalcore Bhangay	Sweepers, &c.		5	5	1	5	6	12	8
Pulsay	Physicians	20	18	33	1	22	23	61	13
Parsee	Various traders	3	11	14	10	4	14	28	1
Dhorayjal	Leather sellers and makers	1	4	5	1	3	4	9	1
Bhattay	Shopkeepers		12	12		12	12	24	11
	Total	131933	202258	334191	79784	226882	306666	640857	131428

Note.—An Abstract of Mr. Pelley's (the collector) Report for 1820 gives the following details relative to the Southern Koncan: Houses:—of Hindoos, 123,309; Mussulmans, 7,963; Portuguese, 205; Jews, 147; total, 131,624. Population:—Hindoos, 597,150; Mussulmans, 42,034; Portuguese, 1,030; J·ws, 643; total, 640,857; of males, 334,191; females, 306,666. The total number of animals of the cow kind, 392,143; of bullocks employed in agriculture, 120,089; Ditto, otherwise, 97,961. Total ploughs, 58,535. The yearly expense of the whole population is, rupees, 13,012,570. The government assessment, rupees, 1,591,942. The males are to the females as 20 to $18\frac{3}{8}$. The inhabitants to the houses as $4\frac{7}{8}$ to 1; and supposing the Zillah to extend from the Abta river to the Portuguese possessions at Karree, is, 7,000 square miles, the number or mouths to the square mile will be $91\frac{1}{8}$. R. M. M.

Inhabitants of the Collectorship (exclusive of the City) of Poona, and Villages held in Enam and Surinjam.

	Bramins.	Marattah Coonbees.	Mahomedan.	Lungayut Wanees.	Dhungurs.	Mahers.	Mangs.	Chimbars.	Telees.	Gosavee.	Tailors.	Purdeshees.	Ran Coolees.	Panbara Coolees.	Lonars.	Gooroos.	Washermen.	Ramossees.	Carpenters.	Barbers.	Goozerattee.	Weaver Sellers.	Ironsmiths.	Potters.	Other Castes.	Total.
Gentlemen and idlers ...	2176	347	448	6	1	4	...	1	...	3	8	88	13	...	...	1	...	...	...	...	1	3	1	...	43	3144
Traders and merchants	496	186	341	549	131	...	...	...	343	4	596	88	4	...	...	...	...	...	...	...	936	183	...	...	1284	5141
Artisans	750	1488	723	...	161	3132	689	1226	530	1	166	11	392	...	978	427	584	265	886	974	...	163	307	571	900	15323
Agriculturists	1286	44340	258	96	257	621	4	18	61	50	...	111	1905	292	34	59	31	44	21	49	4	...	8	17	220	49786
Day labourers & beggars	153	6325	361	38	3	3686	84	23	55	286	26	78	335	147	15	107	18	410	9	2	2	...	...	...	631	12794
Total.....................	4861	52686	2131	689	553	7443	777	1268	989	344	796	376	2649	439	1027	594	633	719	916	1025	943	348	316	588	3078	86188
Women	5593	59878	2520	828	650	8318	860	1333	1141	201	898	494	2944	600	1107	675	699	728	1068	1083	435	423	362	689	3154	96637
Boys	3360	39611	1569	450	435	6343	622	899	801	142	515	265	2311	411	718	404	458	494	694	738	322	265	262	391	1968	64448
Girls	2127	23337	1031	298	253	3057	299	529	466	59	284	171	1366	222	397	236	289	282	425	441	151	185	145	228	116	37534
Total.....................	15941	175512	7261	2265	1891	25161	2558	4029	3397	746	2493	1296	9270	1672	3249	1909	2079	2223	3103	3287	1851	1219	1085	1896	8313	284817
Bullocks	4278	123046	1784	1299	1068	3992	311	724	2190	196	467	694	3262	643	382	536	399	515	674	810	379	26	240	227	1802	149904
Cows	6244	81558	1206	551	937	3872	322	945	741	248	357	480	4353	845	805	742	475	402	893	953	698	82	298	332	1749	110088
He buffaloes	332	7975	96	14	97	491	86	75	84	20	27	46	624	135	53	78	60	46	91	113	28	5	48	47	163	10834
She ditto	1924	24759	531	145	383	734	78	540	536	80	159	240	1406	228	253	309	272	123	607	455	177	72	152	281	785	35225
Sheep	387	27183	189	16	1971	64	7	14	3	11	213	3	6	...	6	94	3	59	1	...	...	4	1	3	425	30663
Goats	128	8851	593	16	195	998	36	110	101	25	59	27	247	96	50	55	180	366	45	72	3	124	12	92	888	13359
Horses	25	365	7	1	13	4	...	2	...	...	...	...	...	...	4	...	...	...	...	2	3	...	...	...	8	434
Mares	86	1251	8	17	47	15	1	...	...	...	...	8	3	2	9	4	...	...	...	8	4	...	...	...	14	1477
Tattoos	1003	3430	131	106	90	395	60	44	23	26	108	19	25	15	132	69	44	172	86	86	251	2	56	41	253	6677

Government Villages.. 284,000
Alienated ditto, estimated at one-third of Government Villages.................................. } 94,900

379,700

and the City of Poona, about 105,000, will give the whole Population to be about 485,000.

(Signed) H. D ROBERTSON, Provin. Collec.

Abstract Statement of the Population in the Southern Mahratta Country.

STATIONS.	Number of Houses.						Inhabitants.							
							Male.			Female.		Total of each.		
	No. of Families	Ter-raced.	Tiled.	Thatchd	Total of Houses.	Shops.	Men.	Boys.	Total.	Wo-men.	Girls.	Full Grown.	Young.	Boys& Girls.
Darwar	4986	2225	141	2782	5148	133	7497	4016	11513	7529	2743	10272	15026	6769
Mesrecolla . .	7128	1601	598	5291	9490	181	10354	6036	16390	10252	4634	14886	20606	10670
Bellagerre . . .	4753	2155	102	3879	5136	112	7623	4416	12039	7495	3125	10620	15118	7541
Pursugerra . .	5520	4653	63	877	5593	186	8370	4120	12490	8347	3321	11668	16717	7441
Nowlgoond . .	8060	7942	...	205	8147	212	12241	6990	19231	12902	4926	17828	25143	11916
Badamee . . .	11894	11302	...	1216	12518	170	18738	10242	28980	180504	7553	26057	37242	17795
Bagalcatta. . .	11707	10291	...	1971	12262	80	17761	9614	27375	17440	7293	24733	35201	16907
Hoongoond . .	6108	6016	...	346	6362	106	10144	5138	15282	9651	3691	13342	19795	8829
Patchapoor . .	10128	1313	2455	6446	10214	191	16138	10132	26270	16114	6766	22880	32252	16898
Dummull . . .	8198	7785	1	593	8379	206	10363	6922	20285	13148	5340	18288	26511	12062
Bankapoor . .	5941	3227	500	2523	6250	51	9137	5718	14855	9221	4169	13390	18358	9887
Haungal	5954	87	503	5883	6476	55	8550	5322	13872	8508	3612	12120	17058	8934
Andoor	3849	896	220	3178	4289	43	5985	3694	9676	5800	2747	8547	11785	6441
Nar Hoabley .	7565	2950	945	3144	7039	376	12203	7017	19220	12382	4850	17232	24585	11867
Raumbidnorr .	5417	3703	6	2036	5745	38	8225	5187	13412	8022	3650	11672	16247	8837
Goottull	5463	4487	27	1290	5804	89	8105	5539	13644	8187	3759	11946	16292	9298
Kode	5345	549	334	4684	5567	12	8269	4975	13244	7690	3402	11092	15959	8377
Kangenella . .	5066	2392	51	2728	5172	108	7652	5050	12702	7509	3461	10970	15161	8511
	123082	73570	5946	48075	129591	2349	190355	110128	300483	188701	78842	267543	379056	188970
Beyapoor . . .	15700	13384	...	2991	16375	246	23187	13734	36921	23096	10747	33843	46283	24481
Lollapoor . . .	9970	5962	69	3814	9845	407	12897	8003	20900	13907	5596	19503	26804	13599
Total .	25670	19346	69	6805	26220	653	36084	21737	57821	37003	16343	53346	73087	38080
Total of the above 2 cols.	148752	92916	6015	54880	153811	3002	226439	131865	358304	225704	95185	320889	453143	227050

Estimated number of Pindaries in the Dooab, according to their own account, Houses, 800; Population, 5000.

Abstract of Population, &c. &c. in the Deckan.

	Number of Families.	Number of Houses.					Inhabitants.						
							Male.		Female.		Total of each.		
		Terraced.	Tiled.	Thatched.	Total of Houses.	State Shops.	Men.	Boys.	Women.	Girls.	Men & Women.	Boys and Girls.	Total.
Poonah	63398	16608	14190	29341	60139	1158	86188	64448	96637	37534	182825	101982	284807
Ahmednuggur	90217	46254	8821	26243	81318	2248	132016	87362	135020	54326	267036	141688	408724
Kandeish	108374	53442	9207	34560	97209	1146	138295	85408	137920	56398	276161	141815	417976
Dharwar	149152	92916	6015	54880	154611	3002	226439	131865	225704	95185	452143	227050	684193
	406141	209220	38233	14502	393277	7554	582938	369083	595281	24344	1178165	612535	1795700
Sattarah	153978	33424	41849	61182	136453	2411	234912	159094	245517	96761	480429	255855	736284

	Cattle.								
	Bullocks.	Cows.	He Buffaloes.	She Buffaloes.	Sheep.	Goats.	Horses.	Mares.	
	Total.	Total.	Total.	Total.	Total.	Total.	Total.	Total.	
Poonah	149901	110088	10834	35225	30242	13101	434	1477	Exclusive of the city of Poonah, and alienated villages.
Ahmednuggur	212008	198420	17023	46797	114899	26185	637	1863	Exclusive of all foreign territories, and the late cessions from the Nizam, and also of wandering tribes.
Kandeish	180557	228733	11451	62497	60392	83533	318	802	
Dharwar	676632	238949	31084	119057	110036	61112	533	766	Exclusive of the principal Jageers, and of the late cessions from the Nizam.
	810101	776190	70392	263576	315569	183931	1922	4909	
Sattarah	298983	259821	40971	102051	223747	45847	1068	3022	

In the hitherto unpublished Returns from which the foregoing is taken, I find the following detail of Broach Zillah.

	Houses.	Men.	Women.	Boys.	Girls.	Total.	
Hindoos	5337	7198	7495	2982	1808	19483	These statements will, it is to be hoped, stimulate further enquiry.
Moosulmans	2557	3127	3481	1535	1290	9433	
Parsees	547	692	820	346	205	2063	
Christians	26	36	22	18	4	80	
Total..................	8467	11053	11818	4881	3307	31059	

ACCOUNT OF THE POPULATION OF THE CITY OF BENARES *

The total number of Dwelling Houses in the City of Benares, is reckoned at 29,935, which are estimated to contain 582,625 Inhabitants, at the following average for each Class of Building.

		Average number of Inhabitants of each House.	
Houses of Brick and Stone.			
First Class of 1 story high	500	15	7500
Second Class of 2 ditto	5500	20	110000
Third Class of 3 ditto	3600	25	90000
Fourth Class of 4 ditto	1500	40	60000
Fifth Class of 5 ditto	755	100	75500
Sixth Class of 6 ditto	300	150	45000
Houses of mud with tiled roofs.			
First Class of one story high	10200	7 to 10	96900
Second Class of 2 ditto	6076	15	19140
Huts composed of straw and tiles	1325	4	5300
Garden Houses.			
Brick and stone	78	10	780
Tiled roofs	101	5	505
	29935		582625

Included in the above enumeration of houses, are 9088 tenements, which adjoin to, and originally formed part of them, but which are now

* I found this statement among the Marquess Wellesley's papers of 1800—there is no date given when the census was taken. R. M. M.

found to be separately occupied, and may be considered as distinct habitations, as will appear from the following detail of dwelling-houses inhabited by the several descriptions, castes, trades, and professions residing in the City of Benares.

Number of houses occupied by Hindoos and Mahomedans of character, in the service of persons of rank, and of foreign states, vakeels, agents of aumils, and agents in concerns of revenue, and trade, and pensioners, 2500; armed Peons, Rajepoots, Birjbaussee, and Mahomedans, 2000; Hindoos and Mussulmen, gomastahs in the service of merchants and traders, 1500; Hindoos of independent fortunes, who have from religious motives fixed their residence at Benares, 2000; Brahmins* subsisting by charitable contributions, though possessed of property of their own, 7500; Hindoos and Mussulmen following the several occupations of khidmutgars, chobedars, elephant, camel, and hackery drivers, horsebreakers, grooms, sellers of grass, and mussaulchees, 2500; mangees and dandees (Hindoos), 307; physicians (Hindoos and Mussulmen), 110; masons, stone-cutters, carpenters, and porters (both Hindoos and Mussulmen), 2153; bearers (Hindoos), 406; barbers (Hindoos and Mussulmen), 385; washermen, 518; timbrel players, sweepers of places of worship, and washers of dead bodies (Mussulmen), 70; minstrels, prostitutes, mountebanks, and dancing women, 280; Hindoo students, and fuckeers, and Mussulmen who live in almshouses, 250; total, 22,479.

Number of houses occupied by merchants, shopkeepers, tradesmen, dealers, mechanics, handicrafts, and labourers, viz.:—Bankers, shroffs, and money-changers (Hindoos), 820; jewellers (Hindoos), 150; goshayns† (Hindoo merchants), 500; wholesale dealers in cloth (Hindoos), 768; sellers of small wares and toys (Mussulmen), 170; weavers and carpetmakers‡ (Mussulmen), 3030; weavers of gauze and kinkob, lacemen and silkmen (Hindoos of the Rajepoot cast), 580; venders of drugs and spices (Hindoos), 360; brokers, criers, dealers in cloth by retail, hawkers, and pedlars (Hindoos), 1055; dealers in grain (Hindoos, chiefly Rajepoots), 1880; confectioners (Hindoos), 500; tailees, or oil manufacturers (Hindoos), 300; venders of oil by retail (Hindoos, chiefly Rajepoots) 50; sellers of pawn, or tumolees (Hindoos), 800; silversmiths and goldsmiths (Hindoos and Mussulmen), 564; dyers, turners, and makers of hooka snakes (Hindoos and Mussulmen), 157; tobacconists (Hindoos and Mussulmen), 600; tailors and ruffooghurs (Hindoos and Mussulmen), 358;

* Whenever any persons of rank come on pilgrimage to Benares from the Dukkun, they distribute alms to all the Brahmins of this description. On these occasions the Brahmins receiving alms have been reckoned at 70,000.

† These goshayns carry on a very extensive trade. It is calculated that the number residing in 500 dwellings amount to 10,000 persons; and on the arrival of their cheylahs from foreign parts in pilgrimage, 35,000 have been counted at the time of the distribution of the Bundharra.

‡ At the celebration of marriages 30,000 of this class of people have been counted.

platers of silver and platers of tin (Hindoos and Mussulmen), 25; makers of bracelets (Hindoos and Mussulmen), 73; makers of silk twist (Hindoos), 266; brickmakers, limeburners, and potters, or komars (Hindoos and Mussulmen), 835; bakers and victuallers (Mussulmen), 243; butchers, poulterers, fowlers, and fishermen (Hindoos and Mussulmen), 284; labourers of all descriptions (Hindoos, chiefly Rajepoots), 1200; venders of spirituous liquors and intoxicating drugs (Hindoos), 86; sellers of paper and almanacs (Hindoos), 32; sellers of fireworks (Mussulmen), 22; sellers of embroidered leather and cloth, shoes and slippers (Mussulmen), 150; dhomes, chumars, and sweepers (Hindoos), 616; total, 38,943.

In the above detail are not included the following descriptions of persons:—The family and dependants of her Royal Highness the Begum, and of the Prince Mirza Khoorum Bukt, calculated to consist of 1000 persons; the family aud dependants of the Prince Mirza She Goofta Bukt, 300; the dependants of Nawaub Jehaunabadee, 125; the dependants of the son of the late Nawaub, Dil Deleer Khan, 100: the dependants of the Rajah of Nypaul, 1000; the dependants of Rajah Ooditnarain, residing in the city, 400; the dependants of the wife of Gholaum Mahomed Khan, 150; total, 3075.

The following descriptions are also omitted in the above detail, viz.:—Persons supposed to get their livelihood by forgery, 40; persons supported by giving false evidence in courts of justice, &c. 400; receivers of stolen goods, 50; persons supposed to live entirely by theft, 200; notorious gamesters, 40; persons who have been apprehended by courts of justice for theft, punished and released, and still on the town, 150; persons suspected of khauna jungee (or Baunkas*), 400; persons apprehended on charges of khauna jungee by the courts, punished, and released, and now in the city, 100; dissolute and abandoned characters, possessing no ostensible means of subsistence, and supposed to be concerned in frauds, breaches of the peace, &c. 200; total 1580.

Exclusive of the above residents, the number of pilgrims at all times in the city may be taken at 10,000. On certain Hindoo festivals, the number of persons resorting to the city exceed all calculation.

CALCUTTA CENSUS.

An enumeration has been made of the inhabitants of Calcutta Proper, on 1st January, 1837, which states the population to be as follows:—English, 3133; Eurasians (born in India of English and native parents), 4746; Portuguese, 3181; French, 160; Chinamen, 362; Armenians, 636; Jews, 307; W. Mahomedans, 13,167; B. Mahomedans, 45,067; W. Hin-

* The baunkas are bravoes so called from the peculiar curve of their swords.

doos, 17,333; B. Hindoos, 120,318; Moguls, 527; Parsees, 40; Arabs, 351; Mugs, 683; Mudrassies, 55; native Christians, 49; low castes, 19,084. Total, males, 144,911; females, 84,803. Grand total, 229714. Police force, 1358. Puckah (brick or stone) houses, 14,623; tiled huts, 20,304. straw ditto, 30,567; total, 65,495. This does not include Ridderpore, Gardenreach, Seebpore, Hourah, Cossipore, Sulkea, &c. nor the other side of the "Mahratta Ditch." The estimate, therefore, as compared with the adjoining parts of Calcutta, may be compared to London without Westminster, the Borough, &c. Captain Birch, the police magistrate, who made the above census, gives the daily influx of population into Calcutta at 150,000.

THE END.